Guilt, Responsibility, and Denial

The Past at Stake in Post-Milošević Serbia

Eric Gordy

PENN

UNIVERSITY OF PENNSYLVANIA PRESS

PHILADELPHIA

Published by
University of Pennsylvania Press
Philadelphia, Pennsylvania 19104-4112
www.upenn.edu/pennpress

Printed in the United States of America on acid-free paper
10 9 8 7 6 5 4 3 2 1

Library of Congress Cataloging-in-Publication Data
Gordy, Eric D., 1966–
 Guilt, responsibility, and denial : the past at stake in post-Milošević Serbia / Eric Gordy. — 1st ed.
  pages cm — (Pennsylvania studies in human rights)
  Includes bibliographical references and index.
  ISBN 978-0-8122-4535-6 (hardcover : alk. paper)
  1. Yugoslav War, 1991–1995—Serbia—Influence. 2. Serbia—Politics and government—1992–2006. 3. Serbia—Politics and government—2006– 4. Serbia—Social conditions 21st century. 5. Serbia—History—1992– I. Title. II. Series: Pennsylvania studies in human rights.
DR2051.G67 2013
949.7103—dc23   2013011474

For Ivana and Azra

Contents

This book traces the dialogue over the legacy of war crimes, crimes against humanity, and genocide in Serbia as it developed after the Milošević regime was formally removed from power in October 2000. Casting the topic in these terms is already certain to raise controversy, even before the presentation moves into details. Some readers may respond with shock, and ask how dialogue is possible over events that fall below an absolute moral bottom line. Some others may respond with indignity, asking how an accusation that is contested can serve as an initial premise. Some others may contend that the question is incorrectly postulated, and that examining a dialogue about perpetrators in a community that also contains victims is in some way tendentious or disrespectful. What responses of this type would indicate is something that the presentation will explore: twelve years after the process of accounting for the record of that regime has begun, there is very little that is settled or unchallenged in public memory in Serbia. Beginning with factual dispute over basic elements such as the character of the violence that took place and the number of victims, disagreement is very much alive and very passionately engaged over questions of responsibility, over the degree to which the state or public is involved in or obligated by the historical record and over the question of what kinds of responses are sufficient. The debate expands into questions that could be thought of as moral in character, including whether the public can be conceived of as identifying with victims or with perpetrators, and whether the effort to "confront the past" (as the widely used and varyingly understood phrase has it) addresses a genuine social or political need.

It is not surprising that these issues should be surrounded by controversy. It would be more surprising if they were not. Although a strong case can be made that fact finding, prosecution and punishment, official apologies and accounts, and the generation of open public dialogue are necessary as a means of moving Serbian society out of a past characterized by authoritarian rule, confrontation, and isolation, there are two facts that cannot be ignored. First, almost everything that has been done in the field of transitional justice has been undertaken in response to external pressure and conditionality. Second, there exists no real precedent for the expectation that a society recently emerged from violence of the type seen in the wars of Yugoslav succession would produce both institutional and cultural accounts, and do so both willingly and quickly.

Before the UN founded the International Criminal Tribunal for the Former Yugoslavia in 1993, it had founded no international tribunals. The most frequently cited precedent was the International Military Tribunal based in Nuremberg (most observers prefer to forget its counterpart based in Tokyo)—not a voluntary initiative at all but one imposed on Germany by occupying forces that had defeated it in a war. For all the magnification of the Nuremberg legacy, it has become a historical commonplace that public discussion of the kind that was hoped for in Serbia did not begin in Germany until two decades after the Tribunal: at a point when most people who could be directly tied to the Nazi regime were no longer participants in the competition for political power (and when the presence of one who was tied, chancellor Kurt Kiesinger, provided a focal point for debate and confrontation—does anybody remember anything about Kiesinger aside from the fact that Beate Klarsfeld smacked him in the face?). The transitional justice initiatives in Serbia could plausibly be regarded as the first international effort at postconflict justice. In the domestic context it could also be considered precedent-setting, as the second half of the twentieth century saw a number of post-regime change and post-civil war initiatives in the world, but no corresponding effort to address large-scale violence against civilians occurring in an international conflict. It might be fair to say that at the moment of regime change in Serbia in 2000, the project of accounting for the past carried high hopes, but that these hopes were only weakly supported by precedent and scantly accompanied by conceptual clarity with regard to what was involved.

The range of initiatives advocating a settling of accounts entered into a political environment where more than the recent past is unsettled. The controversy that developed reflected a background fact that has been observed in many other contexts: Serbian society is deeply divided, both in terms of social and political goals and in terms of understanding the ways in which the society has developed and the direction it is headed in the future. This severe social division has been used to explain a number of factors, from the question of how the Milošević regime was able to survive in power to why the crimes happened in the first place. Wide differences in understanding the present were recapitulated in interpretations of the past, both during the period of violence and after it. Much of the time material interests were at stake, as figures associated with the regime that had left power sought to protect their reputations and influence, and figures associated with the incoming governing groups sought to discredit them. The competition between the incoming and outgoing elites was made more complex by the fact that these two groups had considerable overlap and were often only barely distinguishable from one another.

There are two widely diffused conventional accounts of the record of transitional justice in Serbia, each of which is true but incomplete in its own way. The first concentrates on achievements and breakthroughs: the first trials of high military commanders and heads of state, the first region-wide system of special prosecutors, the first exchanges of declarations and apologies, the first legal judgments on genocide and on sexual violence as a war crime. The second concentrates on disappointments: a long record of obstruction, relativization, and denial; retrenchment of forces complicit in the operation of a criminal regime; repeated instances of impunity. It would be difficult to say that either account is wholly right or wrong; both the achievements and failures of the process are best understood in the social and political context of contemporary Serbia, which is the context that this study tries to take into account.

In the decade after 2000, Serbia provided a unique opportunity to observe a process of transitional justice in real time, with many expectations and institutions already in place. From a methodological view this has both advantages and disadvantages. The principal advantage is of course access to ongoing events, in their intensity and complexity and carrying their emotional weight. Much of the material used here is derived from sources like the daily news, read at the same time as the rest of the reading public, and from events I was able to attend, sometimes directly and sometimes vicariously. The principal disadvantage derives from a lack of distance from the events under discussion—not only temporal and analytic distance but also emotional distance. As a researcher I was not immune to the controversy and complexity of the environment I was examining, nor to the feelings of elation and disappointment that inevitably accompany a process laden with expectations related to categories that, however uncertain, have to be regarded as fundamental, like truth and justice. Added to this is the fact that a situation that is ongoing can change unexpectedly. Some events that took place while the research was ongoing compelled me to revise the entire manuscript and research plan. They changed again between the time the manuscript was submitted and production of the book began, and will have changed again by the time the book reaches the reader's hands.

While I cannot say that researching a controversy as it was ongoing made my work any easier, I can say that it helped me to generate a feeling for something that formal and conventional approaches to this sort of issue, whether they come from political science or law, might very often miss: a process developing in a real society populated by real people experiencing real conflicts, and governed by an elite that is limited, compromised, and self-seeking. It was not easily amenable to mechanistic formulations or graphic representation. Rather, it was dirty, complicated, contradictory. As much as this may have presented a personal disadvantage, I think it provided an epistemological advantage. After all, we do not live in Hegel's ideal universe but in a real world not of our choosing. We are not mystified by the confusions and contradictions we encounter day to day; in the best case we try to understand them and function around them. Why would outside observers expect people in another country, or people approaching a political problem that is prominent in the media, to go through their lives differently? I have tried to understand the people whose written and spoken words make up most of the material in this study (whether I like their words or not—that is a matter of opinion and orientation) not as historical subjects or as abstractions, but as human beings.

The story told in this account is what those human beings encountered and what they made of it. We can say that given the record of civic engagement and information that preceded the change of regime in 2000, they encountered a process almost ready to begin. Observers of various kinds had been tracking and compiling information about criminal abuses from the moment the wars began in 1991. They were prepared for a project to engage the public and institutions with the knowledge that they had, and to demand an accounting. This project got off the ground with resistance, which in many instances proved to be strong. The encounter between the efforts to move knowledge and dialogue forward and the impulses to hold it back are described in this book as three "moments": these were incidents where a dramatic event or the emergence of new information appeared to have the potential to move public understanding dramatically forward. In each of those "moments" the effect was considerably less than could have been anticipated at first. The principal reason effects were limited was the engagement of various actors—media, political, and intellectual actors, but also forces in public opinion—to deny, recontextualize, or trivialize the dramatic events and information.

Resistance limited the potential of "moments," but did not defuse their force completely. In a sense the forces of resistance proved to be creative: unanticipated issues were raised, boundaries of discourse were shifted, and the discourse of rejection was compelled to undergo refinement rather than remaining crude. Consequently although there does exist a discourse of denial that has persisted since the Milošević period, it is not the same discourse of denial. There are not many people left who will, as they may have done in 2000, deny facts that have been demonstrated. Instead it is possible to observe a migration of discourse from denial of facts to dispute over their meaning, and contention over the authority of people who present them. Whether this constitutes meaningful movement or not is at least partly a matter of standards and interpretation. I propose in the concluding chapter that accounting for the past is a project partly failed and partly achieved, and that the incompleteness of the effort leaves visible traces in Serbian society.

And then there were, in addition to the "moments," some "nonmoments." These were incidents where the lines dividing the participants in the discussion became clear but did not move. Although the presentation discusses four "nonmoments," there were undoubtedly many more of these, some of them small in scope. What the "nonmoments" may show is the limits on how far public memory is capable of moving, at least for a time.

Taken together, the "moments" and "nonmoments" might be thought of as telling a more complex and possibly more troubling moral story than the one with which the period of research began. It is a story that may have implications for similar situations in the future. We are compelled to ask why the discussion got as far as it did, why it did not go farther, and what this means for Serbian society in the present and similar transitional justice initiatives in the future. To the degree that the particular set of social and historical circumstances discussed here is unique, it is unique for the reason that we have been offered the ability to trace the progress of a transitional justice initiative, not only procedurally and formally but also discursively and substantively. We can talk not only about what happened, but also about what people who participated in the moment said it meant to them.

The lesson from this experience may be the same one that I try to teach whenever I am asked about events in the region: if you want to understand the politics, look at the culture. The principle applies particularly well in an instance where a number of political actors imagined that it would be possible to achieve social and cultural goals using instruments of law. While it is not wholly implausible that a legal cause could lead to a social or cultural effect, a deeper understanding of the environment is required. Toward the beginning of the study some public opinion research from 2001 is examined: it suggests that people who were asked did not feel that they knew all they wanted to know, and that they did not trust all the sources that were regularly available to them. Additional material from literary and media ethnography seemed to suggest that the whole process of learning about the past was burdened with fear and distrust, and slowed by the silence (or negative engagement) of institutions people did tend to trust. What all this suggests is that processes could have gone farther, not just with greater engagement on the part of institutions but also with a more sustained effort on the part of tribunals, courts, investigators, and activists to communicate with the public. One factor that probably limited the entire process was the fact that both the advocates and opponents of transitional justice carried out their activity in a way that was confined to small groups. This could be a reason that there was a small number of "moments" to consider: it was only big news that allowed the discussion to break out of closed circles. This is a lesson that may have been partly learned, as post-ICTY transitional justice efforts have sought to separate the production of historical accounts from the production of verdicts, and to cultivate the involvement of educational, religious, and cultural institutions. The magisterial distance of law from the Serbian public did not encourage popular engagement.

Finally, a brief note about the structure of the book. The narrative shifts as it progresses from a narrower scope to a broader one, and from what might be considered technical and legal questions to some wider philosophical and moral issues. I think that this is faithful to the direction of the story as it developed over time. The chapters are arranged to alternate between detailed empirical elaboration of the "moments" that are examined and thematic exploration of questions and themes that are provoked by the "moments." Two of these thematic chapters are mostly informative in character, reporting in one instance on early post-2000 public opinion research in Serbia and offering an overview of the major international and domestic transitional justice initiatives. The third is a bit more ambitious (and longer!), tracing varieties and refinements of discourses of denial and responsibility. While the empirical and thematic chapters could be read separately, the ordering of the chapters is meant to lead readers through the logic that brought the study from apparently clear and relatively simple moral questions to greater complexity and uncertainty, and to an insistence on the importance of the cultural and social context.

Chapter 1

Guilt and Responsibility: Problems, History, and Law

The International Criminal Tribunal for the former Yugoslavia (ICTY) issued its final indictments in 2004, and these were confirmed in 2005.[1] The remainder of the Tribunal's activity consists in completing cases that have already begun and preparing for cases that have yet to begin. Prosecution is still being prepared against Ratko Mladić and Goran Hadžić, who were apprehended in 2011. In November 2008 the president and prosecutor of the Tribunal anticipated, provisionally, that trials should be completed in 2010 and appeals completed in 2011.[2] Clearly this did not happen, and the ICTY completion strategy is likely to be revised to 2015 or possibly later.

By some accounts the success or failure of ICTY will be measured in legal terms: did it adhere to fair procedure, generate evidence of unassailable quality, and establish precedents that offer a foundation for the future application of international humanitarian law? By some accounts its success or failure will be evaluated numerically: were enough people charged with crimes, did a sufficient proportion of crimes result in charges, and were indictments fairly distributed among members all the groups that participated in the wars? By some accounts its success or failure will be assessed politically: did it encourage the promotion of peace, the development of democratic states, and the elimination of conditions that could lead to large-scale violation of international humanitarian law in the future?

It will be far more difficult to evaluate ICTY in social or (to use a pretentious word) moral terms. Such an evaluation would certainly require multiple levels of analysis. Nonetheless no assessment of the effort would be complete without at least attempting such an analysis. The Security Council resolution that established the Tribunal suggests such a standard:

Expressing once again its grave alarm at continuing reports of widespread and flagrant violations of international humanitarian law occurring within the territory of the former Yugoslavia, and especially in the Republic of Bosnia and Herzegovina, including reports of mass killings, massive, organized and systematic detention and rape of women, and the continuance of the practice of "ethnic cleansing," including for the acquisition and the holding of territory,

Determining that this situation continues to constitute a threat to international peace and security,

Determined to put an end to such crimes and to take effective measures to bring to justice the persons who are responsible for them,

Convinced that in the particular circumstances of the former Yugoslavia the establishment as an ad hoc measure by the Council of an international tribunal and the prosecution of persons responsible for serious violations of international humanitarian law would enable this aim to be achieved and would contribute to the restoration and maintenance of peace,

Believing that the establishment of an international tribunal and the prosecution of persons responsible for the above-mentioned violations of international humanitarian law will contribute to ensuring that such violations are halted and effectively redressed.[3]

By its declared goals, then, ICTY ought to restore and maintain peace and security while also halting crimes and effectively redressing them. The standards for evaluation therefore have to be broader than technically legal or strategically political criteria. They have to take into account what would constitute maintaining peace and security and redressing crimes, while also considering how the recurrence of crimes can be prevented. To assess this *legal* institution we have to ask *social* questions.

The principal social question I ask is how the conflicts and the crimes committed in the course of them came to be understood by people in Serbia. This study examines the legacy that confronted the country when Slobodan Milošević was compelled to leave power in October 2000, the institutional and informal efforts to create an account of this legacy, and asks how ICTY and related institutions interacted with other forces in the process of building a set of public memories (some of which were widely shared, while some were confined to relatively well-defined groups).

The field of public memory is diverse and broad. Considerable variation exists in just how "public" elements of public memory are. No study of public memory can hope to be either final or exhaustive: as people's perceptions and conditions change, public memory changes with them. This study traces the development of public memory: how it changes over time, how far change reaches, and what might account for change.

I am particularly interested in answers to questions of guilt and responsibility, emphasizing how people answered two questions in particular: (1) Who should be blamed for all the misery that took place? (2) Who is obliged to find ways of repairing damage where necessary, rebuilding relationships where demanded, and assuring a peaceful future where possible?

Framing the Question

The issue of guilt and responsibility in contemporary Serbia involves generating persuasive historical accounts, which are likely to be generally accepted, that establish what happened in the recent past and which individuals, institutions, or forces are responsible. The wars of succession that followed the dissolution of Yugoslavia in 1991 were a source of trauma for residents of the region and also a topic of global political controversy.[4] Both the trauma and the controversy derive from the same source: the commission of war crimes,[5] crimes against humanity,[6] and genocide,[7] in the course of the wars. Consequently the challenge of generating historical accounts carries a political burden. Historical accounts are expected to help in determining who is guilty, how social responsibility is to be distributed, and how peace and reconciliation can be developed. Neighboring countries and international institutions take an interest in this process—they will measure the progress of the country according to how far public opinion in Serbia is willing to accommodate the grievances of its recent enemies and break with its recent past.[8]

This challenge would already be difficult enough were it not for some unique problems: a historical problem, a problem of balance, and a problem of precedence of jurisdiction.

When Does the Past Begin?

If it is necessary to break with the past, when does the past that needs to be rejected begin? This question is particularly sensitive in the former

Yugoslavia, since the instrumentalization of historical memory played an important role in the mobilization of nationalist sentiment and, eventually, nationalist violence. Four answers are most commonly offered.

1. Resolution of guilt from World War II (1941–1945). The war saw on the territory of Yugoslavia an international war between Allied and Axis powers, a guerrilla war between Partisan and occupation forces, and a civil war between Partisan communists, Croatian Ustaše, and Serbian Četnici (including a number of subordinate, smaller, and some forgotten forces).[9] In addition to severe war-related damage, this period saw genocide committed by the Ustaša regime in Croatia,[10] massacres of Croatian prisoners of war by the Partisans,[11] and numerous crimes against civilians by all forces. The postwar Yugoslavian government never seriously investigated or confronted these crimes, and debating them was treated as taboo throughout the Communist period.[12] A strong case can be made that among the factors that made nationalist mobilization possible in the last years of SFRJ was the continually unresolved problem of guilt, and hence unsettled grievances, from World War II.[13]

2. Grievances from the Communist period (1945–1990). Although the Yugoslav Communist regime was less repressive than other European Communist regimes, especially after 1965, there nevertheless remain serious grievances against it. These include grievances involving expropriation of property, forced resettlement (including expulsion of ethnic Germans and Italians), arrest and imprisonment of political opponents, and abrogation of political and civil rights. The largest-scale act of repression was the imprisonment of pro-Soviet Communists after the break with the Soviet Union in 1948.[14] Though not as dramatic or violent, a case can be made that the potential of Yugoslavia to become a democratic state was severely hampered by the marginalization of the "liberals" from the Communist hierarchy after 1972.[15] The wars that followed the breakup of SFRJ in 1991 directed attention away from these events, meaning that issues arising from the Communist period have never been comprehensively addressed. Other former Communist countries have approached these questions through a variety of means, including "rehabilitation" of former political opponents, restoration of expropriated property, and restrictions on political rights of former domestic intelligence and security officers ("lustration").

3. Determination of responsibility for the breakup of SFRJ (1980–1992). Over the past decade there has been considerable debate on this theme,[16] and when Vojislav Koštunica named his ill-fated Commission for Truth and

Reconciliation,[17] in 2001, it was posed as one of the themes for the commission to address. Legal and political issues are at stake in this debate. Namely, if one accepts the position that SFRJ was a state broken apart by secession, then the wars would have to be regarded as civil wars over minority rights and the distribution of territory. If one accepts the position that SFRJ dissolved into its federal elements and ceased to exist, then the wars would have to be regarded as international conflicts assisted by Serbia. This issue is, of course, while possibly relevant to questions of the criminal accountability of states and the applicability of international agreements,[18] not relevant to questions of individual accountability for crimes.

4. Addressing crimes of the wars of succession (1991–present). The conduct of the wars of succession shocked many, as the wars produced the greatest numbers of deaths, refugees, and incidents of violent abuse seen in Europe since 1945. In most cases, justification for atrocities was offered by nationalist programs seeking control of territory, and in many cases establishing control of territory involved killing, intimidating, and forcibly moving local residents. At the same time, rigid control of public information led to a situation in which even now many people say they are not well informed about the wars. Feelings of guilt, victimization, and resentment are widespread, and are very likely intensified by the failure to produce reliable accounts. Establishing facts and taking appropriate legal action are widely viewed as necessary to put a symbolic end to the atmosphere of war.

The wars of succession take priority for most international observers. The other three variants, while important in their own right, can be read in this context as distractions or signs of ideological obsession. Nonetheless, all the levels of concern enumerated here are very much alive in public debate throughout the former Yugoslavia. Sometimes the themes are raised in a transparently instrumental way, as with efforts in Serbia to document the collaboration of other ethnic groups in World War II, or efforts in Croatia to demonstrate that the Yugoslav federation always operated to Croatia's disadvantage. But the interrelation of these issues is clear, as one set of unresolved grievances feeds into subsequent conflicts.

The Question of Balance

War crimes, crimes against humanity, and acts of genocide were committed by ethnic Serbs, in the name of Serbian interests or the Serbian state, with the involvement of Serbian institutions, and with some degree of support (how much is an object of controversy) from Serbian people. These crimes are generally regarded as constituting the majority of crimes committed in the wars of Yugoslavian succession.[19] The accounts and responses provoked by these crimes constitute the bulk of material of this study.

However, these crimes were not the only crimes committed during the wars. Corresponding with feelings of guilt and responsibility in Serbia are senses of grievance and victimization. At least 200,000 Serbs were forced to emigrate from Croatia after the reconquest of the self-declared RSK in 1995. Almost as many were forced to leave Kosovo in the period after the signing of the Kumanovo agreement in 1999, and violence against the Serb population remains a concern.[20] Serbs were victims of massacres, inmates of prison camps (for example, Čelebići),[21] and objects of forced migration during the wars. When Serbian politicians complain that these instances are investigated and prosecuted less intensively than crimes committed by Serbian forces, their complaints resonate in domestic public opinion. ICTY declined to pursue charges against NATO for bomb strikes against civilian targets in 1999, while charges against the Bosnian Muslim authorities for abuses and killings perpetrated against the Serb population in Sarajevo during the war remain uninvestigated. Weak prosecutions against Bosnian militia commander Naser Orić (convicted of minor charges and sentenced to time served, then acquitted on appeal), or the Kosovo politician Ramush Haradinaj (acquitted after a series of incidents of witness intimidation),[22] also contributed to a sense of imbalance.

An emphasis on crimes committed "in the other direction" might be thought of as an exercise in comparative victimization, functioning as a type of avoidance or denial. This study is concerned with internal discourses rather than comparative victimization. While at some point it will be essential for citizens of all the countries of the former Yugoslavia to generate, through discussion, debate, and research, an account that recognizes all the crimes committed in the name of various "national" interests and identities, a necessary condition for this to occur is that people in each of those countries reach something like a consensus about their own responsibility. For accounts to be compared externally, internal accounts have to have already been developed.

The Problem of Precedence

In all the former Yugoslav states involved in armed conflict, concurrent struggles were taking place. One involved armed forces and paramilitaries fighting one another while simultaneously, often, committing crimes against the civilian population. Another involved the nationalist-authoritarian regimes of these states abusing their power through corruption, repression, and some crimes against domestic political opponents—broadly put, wars of states against the societies they claimed to represent. These struggles were sometimes violent, but usually carried out by administrative and cultural means.[23] Now that the regimes that carried out these struggles are for the most part out of power,[24] the question whether international or domestic crimes should receive priority is a matter of recurrent controversy. Crucially relating to the question of trials and extraditions, there is a sense that given constraints of time, domestic trials might preclude international ones, and vice versa.

Violations of International Law

Most international interest concentrates on the commission of war crimes and crimes against humanity in the wars of succession from 1991 onward. This is reflected in the founding of ICTY, the one international institution most involved in investigating and prosecuting these crimes. It is also reflected in the subsequent founding of special courts and prosecutors for war crimes in the countries of the former Yugoslavia.[25]

ICTY is obligated by its statute to investigate and prosecute three types of offenses: war crimes, crimes against humanity,[26] and genocide. The UN resolution that established the Tribunal sets forth as its principal goals "to put an end to such crimes and to take effective measures to bring to justice the persons who are responsible for them," and also to "contribute to the restoration and maintenance of peace."[27]

When Slobodan Milošević was arrested in April 2001, there existed an international charge for war crimes and crimes against humanity against him and four other political and military leaders of Serbia in connection with one incident—a massacre of civilians in the Kosovo town of Račak (Reçak) in January 1999. After his arrest the indictment against him was revised to include charges of genocide. Charges of genocide were filed against a number of wartime political and military leaders of the Serb entity in Bosnia-Herzegovina,[28] but have not been applied to the leadership of the Serbian regime with the exception of Milošević.[29]

Political leaders from the war period may have believed that they could escape prosecution and persuade the public that their crimes were, if not themselves legitimate, committed in a context that made them retrospectively legitimate. Such a conclusion is suggested by the behavior of Milošević on his arrest in 2001. At that moment both international and domestic prosecutors discussed the possibility of wide-ranging charges being laid against him. But the only charges that had actually been filed were ICTY's charges for the Račak massacre and a set of domestic charges for abuse of an official position for political power and personal gain. Milošević himself opened the door to new domestic and international war crimes charges in an appeal filed shortly after his arrest The appeal denies diverting money from the state budget for personal gain, claiming instead that any diverted money was secretly used to finance paramilitaries in Bosnia-Herzegovina and Croatia and to supply SRJ state security services.[30] This constituted an invitation for questions about direct connections between his regime and the organizations that had proximate responsibility for international crimes to be brought into the legal procedures against Milošević. Milošević's appeal claimed a level of state involvement that he had always denied while he was in power, with implications both for the character of the "joint criminal enterprise" to violate international humanitarian law and for the civil suits brought by Croatia and Bosnia-Herzegovina against SRJ.

In terms of criminal liability under international law, the incidents of greatest interest are the following:

1. Massacres of the civilian population. The largest massacre occurred in Srebrenica in 1995, when forces under the command of Bosnian Serb general Ratko Mladić, after conquering the town, rounded up and murdered at least 7,000 residents. Three military officers have also been charged with the massacre of about 300 civilians who took refuge in a hospital outside Vukovar in Croatia in 1991. They were tried and retried several times in domestic courts before a verdict was reached by ICTY, while a local politician accused of complicity in the massacre committed suicide in prison in 1998.

2. War against civilian populations. Several cities were besieged during the wars, the best-known cases being Vukovar, which was almost completely demolished by bombing in 1991, and Sarajevo, which was the object of constant sniper and missile attacks between 1992 and 1995. Attacks not demonstrably related to any military objective were made against other cities, including Tuzla and Dubrovnik, as well. Charges of this nature can

also be applied for less concentrated and smaller-scale incidents, such as destruction of property after taking a territory or with the goal of intimidating residents of an area.

3. Measures designed to forcibly change the ethnic structure of a local population. These include forced resettlement, intimidation, imprisonment, and also murder. All these means were used to force members of different ethnic groups to relocate, creating monoethnic territories, especially in Bosnia-Herzegovina in 1992–1993, in Croatia in 1995, and in Kosovo by one side in 1999, and by another side afterward. These are the actions for which the distasteful, imprecise, and distressingly widespread term "ethnic cleansing" was invented.[31]

4. Murder, rape, and torture of prisoners. Several prison and relocation camps in Bosnia-Herzegovina became known for the abuse of prisoners, and some of these have already become the subject of prosecutions. The ICTY's earliest, largest, and most complex cases included prosecutions against people suspected of abuses at the KP Dom Foča, Omarska, Trnopolje, and Keraterm camps. In one of the first cases to be prosecuted against Bosnian Muslim forces, three people were convicted of murder and war crimes (but not crimes against humanity) in connection with atrocities at the Čelebići camp in 1992.

Violations of Domestic Law

Especially in the months just following the removal of Milošević from power in 2000, considerable attention was paid to revelations regarding abuses of power for personal and financial gain. These included the distribution of state property in the form of luxurious houses and apartments, manipulation of the banking and currency exchange systems, and corruption in connection with the sale and privatization of state-owned corporations. Charges concentrated heavily on a few figures who are widely considered to have been the main exponents of regime corruption: former premier Mirko Marjanović,[32] former deputy premier Nikola Šainović,[33] former customs director Mihalj Kertesz,[34] and others.[35] A few cases went to trial: Kertesz was tried for diverting public funds through offshore banks, and the Karić brothers, who built a business, banking, and media empire through regime patronage, were eventually compelled to leave the country. Milošević's wife Mirjana Marković was charged, together with her daughter

Marija, with minor real estate offenses (as she has been in hiding she has not formally answered the charges).[36] Like other charges not directly related to acts of violence, it is entirely possible that behind the prosecutions and threats of prosecutions may lie other motives: either to assure compliance or to persuade the accused profiteers to give evidence against more important figures, perhaps for more serious crimes. Over time, the impressive corruption of succeeding regimes has come cumulatively to present a barrier to prosecution of cases of this type.

Members of the regime also conspired to falsify election results, the most controversial being the local elections of November 1996 and the presidential and parliamentary elections of September 2000. Both elections were followed by massive protests. After the 1996 elections, the regime was forced to pass a "special law" recognizing the results, which it had earlier declared invalid when it discovered the opposition had won. In 2000, the regime tried first to declare victory, then to force a second round, and finally to nullify the election results. This effort was stopped by massive protests in October 2000, which forced Milošević to resign.

Among the most widely publicized acts of domestic political violence in the Milošević regime are the murder of newspaper editor Slavko Ćuruvija in 1999,[37] the attempted murder of politician Vuk Drašković (four people were killed in the attempt) in 1999,[38] the murder of organized crime figure Željko Ražnatovic-Arkan in 2000,[39] and the kidnapping and murder of former president Ivan Stambolić[40] in 2000. In addition to these, attention is occasionally drawn to several acts of ethnic violence committed or organized within the borders of Serbia: the kidnapping and murder of nineteen ethnic Muslim passengers from the Belgrade-Bar railway at Štrpci in 1993,[41] the intimidation and expulsion of ethnic Croatian residents of the village of Hrtkovci in 1992,[42] and the kidnapping and murder of seventeen ethnic Muslim passengers from a bus in the village of Sjeverin in 1992.[43]

All the crimes ICTY can prosecute are also crimes under the Criminal Code of Serbia. The domestic Criminal Code also includes some charges ICTY does not have the authority to level, such as promoting ethnic and religious hatred, aggression, and crimes against peace.[44] Charges of "provoking public danger" were applied against Dragoljub Milanović, former director of Radio-Television Serbia, for failing to remove his employees from RTS headquarters when it was bombed in 1999.[45]

The various elements of corruption, fraud, theft, and violence could possibly to be tied together into a wide-ranging charge of conspiracy—

defining the parties in power during the Milošević regime and their associates as constituting a criminal organization responsible for corruption, fraud, political violence, and war crimes. While accountability for war crimes in Kosovo that were committed by police and military forces falls under direct chain of command, accountability for similar crimes in Croatia and Bosnia-Herzegovina might be limited to financing the organizations that committed them,[46] unless evidence of more direct connections is revealed.[47]

There may indeed exist a temptation to consider conspiracy prosecutions of this sort, not least because it seems obvious that the regime's domestic and international abuses were linked. However, the (limited) previous experience of using conspiracy theories in international trials has been mixed. The International Military Tribunal at Nuremberg rejected conspiracy as a basis of prosecution. But conspiracy was the principal basis of prosecution at the Tokyo Tribunal. This led to some convictions that could easily be considered miscarriages of justice. For example, Hirota Koki was sentenced to death for conspiracy to wage aggressive war on the basis of his membership in Japan's Cabinet (foreign minister between 1933 and 1936, prime minister in 1936 and 1937, and foreign minister again in 1937 and 1938), and despite the fact that as a politician he opposed the actions for which he was prosecuted. Similarly, General Yamashita Tomoyuki was sentenced to death for atrocities committed by troops under his command in the Philippines in 1944, despite convincing evidence that he neither knew about the atrocities nor was able to communicate with his troops at the time. The same standard was applied against Generals Kimura Heitaro and Muto Akira, who were also sentenced to death.[48] The Tokyo Tribunal's use of conspiracy as a basis of prosecution undoubtedly led to great efficiency in the prosecution and conviction of suspects. But this efficiency came at the cost of the Tribunal's credibility, and probably did much to *prevent* serious public engagement with issues of responsibility in Japan.

A further obstacle to wide-ranging prosecution of figures from the Milošević regime in Serbia is that the regime never entirely left power. In June 2008, following parliamentary elections that produced a protracted coalition crisis, the party formerly chaired by Milošević joined the governing coalition led by the Democratic Party. A number of figures from the Milošević period found themselves occupying high public office again. The leaders of the parties sought for a time to portray the coalition as a sign of reconciliation between the opposed forces of the previous decade.[49]

Why Establish Anyone's Guilt?

> The smell of corpses from the freezer truck found at Tekija, buried long ago in the capital city, is spreading through Serbian public space and offers a shocking reminder of what everybody who had a grain of conscience in this country already knew: war crimes were committed (also) in Kosovo. They were not incidents, but official policy, the realization of which included the leading figures of the military-police establishment. Their Rashomon over the last week demonstrates that (yet) another horrifying neologism— "reclamation of the terrain" [*asanacija terena*]—was the work of the state, like the killing.[50]

The investigations and arrests of leading figures from the Milošević regime, including Milošević himself, marked a turning point brought about by a combination of forces, including public opinion, international pressure, and the early actions of the post-2000 Serbian government. Another turning point came about through a combination of chance and orchestration, in the interaction between silenced local knowledge, a minor local media outlet, and a window of opportunity. Information became public about an incident in 1999, when a local resident witnessed a freezer truck being pushed into the Danube River near the eastern Serbian town of Tekija. A diver engaged to investigate found the truck; police opened it to find it full of human corpses. The interior ministry instructed the police not to investigate, warned prosecutors that a "state secret" was in question, and ordered the bodies to be removed and destroyed or hidden in another place.[51] The truck itself was destroyed by police at Petrovo Selo.[52] While many local people certainly knew about the freezer truck,[53] police did not investigate and media did not report the incident until two years later, when an article in the local *Timočka krimi revija* (Timok Crime Review) was picked up by national, and eventually international, media. Not long after, police began to release information about a program to destroy evidence of massacres in Kosovo, under the code name "Depths 2,"[54] and to declare that evidence traced the program directly to the commanders of the police and military and to Slobodan Milošević personally. Over the next month, more burial sites of massacre victims were "discovered."

If the case were only a question of establishing that massacres took place and that evidence was destroyed, its main significance would be legal.

Probably its principal legal effect in Serbia was to force prosecutors to begin reconsidering the decision not to charge Milošević and his associates with war-related crimes (otherwise there was a distinct political preference for less controversial corruption charges). It may well have compelled the government to consider the domestic capacity to try such cases and opt for ICTY's capacity instead.

The main significance of the case, though, probably lay in the way it brought war crimes into public discussion. As the investigation began, interior minister Dušan Mihajlović declared, "I think that this case will give a completely different picture of our so-called patriots."[55] The popular commentator Stojan Cerović, who had been arguing in his weekly column against cooperation with ICTY in the preceding months, dramatically revised his assessment:

> If we want to avoid the Hague Tribunal, the reason can absolutely not be that we do not believe that crimes were committed—because we can see the evidence swimming to the surface—nor that we think we have some justification—like that other people did the same thing—because we do not believe those justifications ourselves. What I mean is that, to the extent that we have any kind of moral sensibility at all, it is not possible to paper this sort of thing over, even if no earthly judge were ever to find out about it. . . .
>
> If in this case we do not find the guilty parties and do not think about their punishment, then no court in the world, not even The Hague, can help us. It would mean we as a society have already been punished by being sent back to Edenic moral idiocy [*beslovesnost*]. Or if you prefer local mythology, it would mean that we have lost both of the kingdoms mentioned in relation to Kosovo.[56]

It appeared briefly that the "freezer truck case" might be the incident that would finally make denial of crimes impossible, finally make the connection between the Milošević regime and the crimes obvious, and force public examination of responsibility to begin. This would have meant that the first half of 2001 would have seen the arrest of Milošević, marking the break with the period in which his authority was feared, and the "freezer truck case," marking the break with the period of reflexive denial. Instead this case became simply the first of several that seemed to signal a major turning point, in which initial publicity offered the possibility that new recognitions would spur a new type of public discussion, but in which shock turned into relativization, and relativization to a space between silence and denial. A similar pattern would recur after the extradition of Milošević, the murder of prime minister Zoran Djindjić, and the release of the "Scorpions" film showing paramilitary units participating in the Srebrenica killings. Once the freezer truck was out of the river, more information could flow, but the currents remained complex.

A debate ensued about who should be prosecuted in the "freezer truck case." A rhetorical war began to be fought between the police and the military, mostly in the form of alternating statements to the press, about whether spokespeople for any one force had accused the other force of involvement. Government spokespeople mentioned the case when arguing in favor of cooperation with ICTY, especially in June 2001 when the issue of a law regulating cooperation began to divide the parties that made up the federal government. Whether because of the revelations from Tekija or other factors (such as the conditional character of financial assistance), talk of both domestic and international prosecution began to sound more normal after the revelations. In fact no domestic prosecutions arose from the case, and it featured only briefly during the presentation of evidence against Milošević during his inconclusive trial before ICTY.

But prosecution and the willingness to prosecute do not tell not the whole story. Both the people who advocated legal action and the people who resisted it might be described as acting from the same motivation: a belief that regardless of what person or people might be charged, the result of any trial would reflect somehow on other members of the social collective, and have repercussions on senses of self and feelings of identity. At stake then is no longer just the guilt of war criminals, but the feelings of responsibility held by the people around them. By imposing the question of guilt, the "freezer truck case" raised, for many people for the first time, the question of responsibility.

The Difference Between Guilt and Responsibility

One of the frequently stated goals of confronting the recent past is to assure that the events that marked it will not be repeated. This effort requires asking questions that go deeper than the investigations required for criminal prosecution. The principal questions deal with causes: how was an environment maintained that made the commission of crimes possible?

Generating answers to these questions requires research into social and political history, but also demands uncomfortable self-interrogation. Was the ideological justification that legitimated criminal activity widely shared? To what extent did people acquiesce to the regime that was responsible for these crimes? How widespread was knowledge about crimes and their perpetrators? Did citizens have the capacity to change the regime or its policy?

The questions engage acts and positions for which people might feel responsible but not guilty—they are not criminal acts. These generally relate less to public or widely consequential interventions by people or institutions, and more to questions individuals might pose to themselves about how they experienced the period of dictatorship and war, and about whether their approach to this experience allowed them to maintain an understanding of themselves as uncompromised and morally responsible.

Approaching responsibility in these terms involves constructing an understanding of the recent past. Arguing why Milošević should be tried domestically, Prime Minister Djindjić remarked, "We have to reconstruct our own past through this legal process, because not only is Milošević a part of our past, but so are we, and because Milošević would not have become what he is without us."[57] Understanding the recent past implies not only rendering causes and conditions narratively, but also interrogating the role of social groups and individuals in the experience of traumatic events. Politicians have borrowed the word "catharsis" from the psychological literature to describe this social process.[58]

Almost all domestic and international discourse has revolved around questions of guilt and how or whether guilty people will be punished. It is also necessary to broaden the discussion beyond this certainly moral but mostly practical theme. Guilt needs to be addressed but so does responsibility. The remainder of this chapter offers brief definitions and discussions of these two concepts, various dimensions of which are explored in detail in the rest of the book.

Guilt: A Legal Category

Legal trials are concerned with the guilt of perpetrators of crimes, seeking to document and punish it. In these institutional settings guilt is a legal concept,[59] whereby a person can be defined as guilty if he or she can be shown have done something illegal.[60] The definition is accomplished on the basis of evidence tying the person to the act, and findings of guilt are factual findings; they have nothing to do with how the person might feel about having committed the act. The *Oxford Companion to Law* offers the following definition: "Guilt. The concept of having committed some failure of duty, usually a crime or offence, and consequently being liable to some penalty. A person accused may admit guilt, or be found guilty on the evidence. In the case of common law crimes guilt normally coincides with having committed moral fault, but in the case of some statutory offences guilt may arise by merely having done something or allowed it to happen without moral fault at all."[61] The scope of guilt is conceptually limited. Only a person who has committed a violation can be regarded as being guilty.[62] This also extends to considering potential guilt: only individuals can be tried and eventually convicted. The idea that a society or a political collective might be guilty, appears in political rhetoric but makes no sense as a legal idea. The political notion of collective guilt also has several obvious theoretical shortcomings. Probably not the least of these is the inclination to impose a false collectivity that erases social and political differences. At a minimum this approach is offensive to diverse people within collectives, while at worst it can constitute a sort of self-fulfilling prophecy that encourages people to identify with criminals because they share an ethnic background.

Responsibility: Individual, Collective, Political

If problems posed by guilt are legal and technical, problems posed by responsibility are social and moral. Conceptions of collective guilt function, if they function at all, as invitations to reflection on responsibility. Here it is important to maintain the conceptual distinction, rather than treating responsibility, as popular rhetoric often does, as a sort of "guilt lite."

Karl Jaspers offers some of the most useful guidance on this question, and most of the discussion here relies on his discussion of guilt and responsibility. His post-World War II reflection *The Question of Guilt* begins by confronting the widespread sense that Germany as a whole shared guilt for the crimes of the Nazi regime, which were only beginning to be widely publicized when he wrote the book.[63] Jaspers distinguished between the stigma placed on Germany from outside and the task that confronted it from inside: "the fact that the victors declare us to be guilty is a political fact with the widest possible consequences for our lives, but it does not help us in the most important task, with our internal transformation."[64] Jaspers echoes the distinction noted by H. D. Lewis, who in his entry on "Guilt" in *The Encyclopedia of Philosophy* notes, "We may in any case be morally guilty and legally innocent—and vice versa."[65] Here I draw on that insight to separate legal culpability from moral responsibility, so that both can be observed without confusing the two.

Jaspers distinguishes legal guilt from three other forms:

1. Political guilt. The concept of political responsibility represents a factual state, in which all citizens of a state collectively bear the consequences of political decisions made by the state. This relationship of cause and effect operates regardless of whether these citizens supported the political decisions made by the state: my views on tax policy may not be the same as those of the majority of legislators, but this does not change my tax obligations. The concept of political responsibility also postulates a (varying) degree of moral participation. Jaspers asks rhetorically: "Do we Germans have to be held responsible for offenses which other Germans committed against us or which we managed somehow to miraculously escape? Yes—to the extent that we permitted that sort of regime to exist in our country. No—to the extent that many of us with the deepest conviction opposed that evil and did nothing which would cause us to recognize moral complicity with it. *Demonstrating somebody's responsibility does not mean demonstrating that person's moral guilt.*" Political responsibility applies to all people whose "lives are carried out within the framework of the state." Jaspers recognizes that some "completely apolitical" people might be excluded from this category, but construes the privilege of being apolitical to apply only to narrowly defined groups whose existence takes place outside the political sphere, such as monks.[66]

2. Moral guilt. This category refines the legal concept of command responsibility, which dictates that a greater degree of guilt applies to an officer or politician who issues an illegal order than to a soldier or official who complies. By contrast, Jaspers argues: "I carry moral responsibility for all of my actions as an individual, as for all of my other actions, including the carrying out of political and military orders. The simple principle that 'an order is an order' never applies. A crime is still a crime even when it is committed on orders." Jaspers casts moral responsibility not as a legal issue but as an issue of the conscience of the individual, specifying that "everybody has to decide how to judge himself, but since communication exists,

we can discuss these things among ourselves and help each other to achieve a clear moral self-recognition." He identifies the environments in which to draw conclusions about moral responsibility as "my own conscience and communication with friends and people close to me who out of love are concerned for my soul."[67] Individualization of moral guilt, for Jaspers, does not diminish the obligation all people have to interrogate their own false declarations of loyalty, beliefs in the legitimacy of the regime that committed offenses, and personal compromises.

3. Metaphysical guilt. Jaspers begins his discussion of this category by postulating, "Solidarity exists between people as members of the human race, which makes everybody co-responsible for all injustice and unfairness in the world, and especially for crimes committed with their knowledge or in their presence." This form of responsibility, while diffuse and not easily expressed in terms of law, politics, or morality, is fundamental, since "if people did not have any kind of metaphysical guilt, they would be angels, and the other concepts of guilt would have no content." The feeling of metaphysical guilt produced by knowledge of crime "destroys the absolute solidarity of people with one another."[68] It can be understood as a universal feeling that interferes with a person's conception of self as fully human.

To avoid confusion, it may be appropriate to consider the latter three forms proposed by Jaspers not as variations of *guilt* but as varieties of *responsibility*. Jaspers uses a different terminology, but implies the distinction in specifying instances for each form: for criminal liability a court, for political guilt force and the will of the victor, for moral guilt the individual conscience, and for metaphysical guilt God.[69] Herein the term "guilt" refers to a specific status defined by a judicial institution. The term "responsibility" refers to states of feeling or judgment operating on the level of relationships, perceptions, and individual self-assessment.

Concepts of collective guilt make little sense from any point of view. As Lewis points out, "If guilt, in the proper sense, turns on deliberate wrongdoing, it seems that no one can be guilty for the act of another person—there can be no shared or collective or universal guilt."[70] At its worst, collective guilt recapitulates the nationalist collectivism that produced an environment conducive to crime. But the question of collective *responsibility* may not be so clear cut. Following Jaspers, at least one form of collective responsibility, "metaphysical guilt," is common to every person. We do not have to share his mysticism to understand feelings of responsibility as functioning partly on the level of the individual, and partly in the context of *identities* and *relationships*. In this sense responsibility has to do with our sense of who we are, our sense of one another, and people's sense of us. Collective perceptions and feelings are involved at all these levels.

Some wordplay might help to illustrate how responsibility is distinct from guilt. The first part of the word is "response." In his essay on "responsibility" in the *Hastings Encyclopaedia of Religion and Ethics*, David Fyffe invents the synonym "answerableness."[71] The rhetorical figure works in Serbo-Croatian as well: the root of *odgovornost* (responsibility) is *odgovor* (answer). Here responsibility is taken to mean the ability to respond—in the sense that there is a need for answers and an effort to produce answers.

This study approaches various aspects of the effort to establish guilt and address responsibility. It moves from an examination of initial states of public opinion in Serbia to an exploration of some of the first "moments" when it appeared that a wide-ranging dialogue might begin. The discussion is structured to move from detailed examination of "moments" to theoretical and contextual analysis that tries to answer the question of why some incidents turned out the way they did. Then several "nonmoments" are examined, in which positions and understandings remained in place despite events. The picture that emerges is one of a social process begun but not completed, with divisions and contested understandings remaining. The conclusion suggests some explanations for this mixed state of events and proposes some possible means of moving forward.

Chapter 2

The Formation of Public Opinion: Serbia in 2001

There are obvious difficulties in describing the state of readiness in Serbian society to engage with questions of the recent past and responsibility for it just after the change of regime on 5 October 2000. Processes were not only ongoing, but might also be perceived as having been just at their beginning, at least as far as large-scale public opinion is concerned. But any kind of explanation of the development of public opinion needs a starting point. This study takes as its starting point the moment at which it was possible to engage in discussion free of overwhelming constraint.

It is of course not the case that all discussion began in 2001. Public opinion had been in some ways prepared before the change of regime. On the one hand, it had been prepared to resist the topic. Part of this consequence derives from the cumulative effects of propaganda campaigns and campaigns for the control of information directed by the previous regime—if they can be said to have had any effect, then that effect probably remained in place in the period immediately following the end of that regime. These effects were likely enhanced by several factors. First, there was an extended period during which substantive positions people held about concrete issues of responsibility were mixed with generalized if momentary feelings of resentment or revenge, contributing to a lack of clarity regarding what was at stake. Second, the entire issue of responsibility in Serbia remained and remains clouded by the fact that even if forces controlled and financed by the Serbian government committed the largest share of crimes, they were not the only forces to commit crimes. Third, while most people in Serbia had at best secondhand experience of the wars in Croatia, Bosnia-Herzegovina, and Kosovo, nearly everybody had direct experience of the NATO bombing campaign in 1999. The perception was and still remains quite popular in Serbia that any admission of responsibility in the wars of succession could amount to a justification of the NATO campaign, which was almost universally opposed in the country for reasons that would not surprise anybody.

It might be reasonable to expect that the effects of regime-era public opinion would diminish as the regime receded into the past. In this chapter it is argued that a set of conditions needed to be present for such a shift in public opinion to occur. For a variety of reasons, not all of these conditions had been achieved a decade later.

The discourse of responsibility did not emerge suddenly in Serbia. At least on a small scale, public discussions of the question began at the same time the war began. Most of these initiatives came either as private initiatives or as efforts on the part of independent (and generally small) groups of intellectuals. Among these have to be counted the ongoing "Druga Srbija" campaign of the Belgrade Circle of Independent Intellectuals (Beogradski krug nezavisnih intelektualaca), the ongoing documentation efforts of the Belgrade Center for Human Rights (Beogradski centar za ljudska prava) and the Fund for Humanitarian Law (Fond za humanitarno pravo), and perhaps most visibly, the conference "Istina, odgovornost, pomirenje" (Truth, Responsibility, Reconciliation) held in Ulcinj in the spring of 2000. Some other contributions were made in publications such as *Republika*, which was broadly associated with civic and antiwar movements, and *Helsinška povelja*, associated with the Yugoslav Helsinki Committee. The independent radio station B92 also maintained efforts to inform the debate, translating and publishing books of analysis and documentation about the wars,[1] featuring discussions of the issue in its broadcast programs,[2] and dedicating special issues of the journal *Reč* associated with the station to the theme. However, the debate could not reach a wide audience, partly because most major media were controlled by a regime that had a concrete interest in suppressing the question, and partly because the fresh experience of war (combined with mostly one-sided information about the war) did not prepare many members of the public for an open discussion.

Inevitably, early takes on the state of public opinion are likely to be distorted. It will quickly become apparent in this chapter that the most commonly used means for exploring public opinion, opinion surveys, are of only limited use in this case. It will be necessary as the narrative develops to put together some richer, if less numerical, sources in order to indicate more fully the dilemmas in public opinion at the time and to suggest some of the directions that might have been available.

Contradictory Survey Findings

Before the arrest and detention of Slobodan Milošević over the weekend of 31 March–1 April 2001, a series of public opinion surveys were conducted, generally around the question of arrest and prosecution of war crimes suspects, but with a particular focus on the figure of Milošević and the question whether he ought to be tried in Serbia, extradited to ICTY, or both.

The results of these surveys are contradictory, and consequently it is not a simple matter to get a picture of the state of public opinion from them. From the point of view of survey research methodology, this is not surprising: surveys are least reliable in unstable political environments, particularly when the questions deal with matters of great sensitivity. There has also been extensive discussion about the weakness of survey research in the states of the former Yugoslavia in particular, especially because in the period since 2000 surveys generally failed to predict the results of elections.[3] It is worth pointing out, too, that many of these surveys dealt with matters on which there was rapid change both in the surrounding situation and in the way media publicity was carried out. These are also sensitive and complex matters for which surveys might not be the most appropriate instrument.

One possible explanation for the lack of clarity in survey results might simply be that opinion was still in formation, or was in transition, with regard to several of the questions asked. It may be possible to make a more ambitious suggestion that after decades of varying types of authoritarian rule, public opinion itself was still in a formative stage in Serbia in 2001. This suggestion was offered by sociologist Stjepan Gredelj in presenting the results of a general survey, when he presented among his conclusions that "at last something is changing in Serbian public opinion, and at last critical thought is appearing."[4]

In relation to known or suspected perpetrators, particularly people who held positions of power in the Milošević regime (as well as Milošević himself), there seemed to have been a general consensus that they ought to be charged and tried. There was somewhat less of a consensus on the question of what they ought to be charged with and tried for, with some people emphasizing offenses against the domestic criminal code, and others emphasizing offenses against international law. Opinion became sharply divided over the question of whether they should be tried in domestic courts or extradited to ICTY, although over the first half of 2001 a majority seemed to be developing, arguing that the former rulers ought to be tried both by domestic courts and ICTY. Some discussion was promoted in 2001 (among others by Serbian premier Zoran Djindjić) of an arrangement whereby charges for war crimes and crimes against humanity could be heard in Belgrade, with some level of official participation by ICTY prosecutors and judges.[5] In general, however, while there continued to be strong resistance to ICTY, the position of complete rejection seemed to become a less popular one, held mostly by nationalists and supporters of the former regime, during the course of 2001.[6]

An informal online survey by the daily newspaper *Večernje novosti* asked the question, "Do you think that the arrest of the former president of SRJ Slobodan Milošević was justified?" and found 66 percent answering yes and 34 percent no.[7] While these results are as reliable as the results of any nonscientific online survey with a nonrandom sample, the readership of *Novosti* is nonrandom in an interesting way: the paper was not only the most prominent pro-regime paper in the 1990s (together with *Politika*), its readership was also demographically closest to Milošević's base of support (older, less educated, rural).[8]

However, other surveys produced contradictory results. A survey released in May 2001 by the Strategic Marketing agency, *Seeing the Truth in Serbia* (*Vidjenje istine u Srbiji*), found that more people blamed the United States than Milošević for the bombing campaign of 1999, and more people blamed former Croatian president Franjo Tudjman than Milošević for the fall of Yugoslavia. The same survey also found that respondents identified the indicted war criminals Ratko Mladić, Radovan Karadžić, Željko Ražnatović, and Slobodan Milošević as the "greatest defenders of Serbhood."[9] These results suggest methodological rather than political problems: respondents were asked about immediate "responsibility" for particular events rather than situations, and responded consistently. Similarly, the list of "defenders of Serbhood" gives the appearance of demonstrating more support for the indictees named than probably existed, since only people (and we do not know how large a group this is, although election results tell us it is a minority) who accept the nationalist ideas of the regime represented by the names on the list would be likely to offer any answer at all to a phrase like "defenders of Serbhood."[10] It is probably unnecessary to point out that respondents who were not ethnically Serbian (35 percent of the population of Serbia in the 1990 census) may not have automatically regarded the category in a positive light.

The Strategic Marketing Survey of May 2001 is primarily interesting for the contradictory nature of several of its results. It gave pessimistic findings in relation to the possibility of reconciliation, with 21 percent of respondents aged between eighteen and twenty-nine, and 34.6 percent of those over sixty, declaring they were completely unprepared for reconciliation. Similarly, 29.4 percent of respondents between eighteen and twenty-nine and 44.2 percent of those over sixty expressed extreme distrust toward members of other national groups.[11]

On questions related to responsibility, respondents in the survey showed a marked tendency to project responsibility onto factors far from themselves. For example, asked to name the most important reason for NATO intervention against SRJ in 1999, 29.8 percent named "the policy of the Milošević regime," while 55.2 percent identified either the political or economic "interest of the West."[12] The factor of distance applies on comparative scales as well. Asked to choose between two options for "guilt for misfortune," respondents named Slovenes (45.3 percent) more than Serbs (10.8 percent), the United States (27.3 percent) more than NATO (25.2 percent), the "international community" (44.8 percent) more than "all the peoples of the former Yugoslavia" (20.5 percent), Milošević (42 percent) more than "the people who elected him" (17.6 percent), and the interests of international business (53.7 percent) more than the interests of domestic business (11.2 percent).[13]

This form of projection did not necessarily arise from ignorance about the behavior of Serb military and paramilitary forces in the wars. Asked to name three events "which first come to mind" in relation to the war in Bosnia-Herzegovina, the three most frequent responses were atrocities committed by Serb forces: the mortar attack on the Markale market in Sarajevo (48.1 percent), the siege of Sarajevo (28.8 percent), and the massacre in Srebrenica (21.3 percent). Respondents named atrocities committed by other forces far less frequently: the bombing and destruction of the bridge in Mostar (12.7 percent), the sniper attack on the Serb wedding party in Sarajevo in 1991 (12.6 percent), and general "crimes against Serb civilians" (7.2 percent).[14] However, this pattern did not apply when the same question was asked about the war in Croatia. Although the siege of Vukovar was the second most frequently offered response (53.1 percent), actions on the part of Croat forces were dominant, such as the reconquest of the Knin region (55.3 percent) and the arrival of refugees from Croatia (30.5 percent). Only 5.3 percent of respondents named the bombardment of Dubrovnik.[15] Asked to identify three war crimes committed by Serbs in the preceding ten years, a large majority named the massacre in Srebrenica (69.4 percent), while large numbers named the destruction of Vukovar (31.4 percent) and the massacre in Račak (18.6 percent).[16] Results were more spread out when respondents were asked to name war crimes committed against Serbs: the three most frequent responses were the exodus of Serbs from Croatia (49.1 percent), the NATO bombing (35.4 percent), and the "suffering of civilians in Kosovo" (16.2 percent).[17]

A curious contradiction emerged with regard to the question of knowledge. The preceding results suggest that knowledge of at least some events was widespread in Serbia. At the same time, when asked directly, respondents did not indicate that they believed they were well informed: 22.3 percent of respondents considered themselves well informed about the wars in Croatia, while 19.4 percent considered themselves well informed about the wars in Bosnia-Herzegovina.[18] Nor did respondents indicate that they believed their fellow citizens were well informed.[19]

However, when asked the long and possibly confusing question, "Has it ever happened that a new fact which you have learned from any source about any event related to the conflicts (wars in Croatia, Bosnia-Herzegovina, Kosovo) caused you to change your thinking or position about the role (responsibility) of the warring sides?" an overwhelming 85.5 percent answered in the negative.[20] Despite this somewhat discouraging result from the point of view of efforts to promote information, the survey results suggested some potential ways in which efforts to disseminate information might have a more meaningful effect. The results indicate a wide gap between the sources of information people trusted and the sources they actually used. Asked to name their primary sources of information during the war, responses broke down as shown in the first table. When people were asked what sources of information they trusted, the structure of responses was different, as in the second table.

RTS-TV/state media	80.4%
Independent papers (*Blic, Glas, Danas*)	67.9%
Stories of witnesses	62.3%
Stories of relatives	45.5%
State-controlled papers (*Politika, Ekspres, Novosti*)	43.1%
Independent radio/TV (ANEM, B92)	42.4%
Personal experience	17.4%[21]

Source	Trusted	Did not trust
RTS-TV/state media	23.2%	42.5%
State-controlled papers	28.8%	36.5%
Independent papers	44.7%	17.9%
Independent radio/TV	62.4%	16.2%
Relatives	68.6%	16.2%
Witnesses	62.2%	15.4%[22]

The results suggest that efforts to shape opinion by using media already inclined to participate in a campaign of reshaping opinion would suffer from some important limitations. First, the question of availability of information arises—why did people tend to use most the sources of information they trusted least? The answer would most likely have to do with the structure of distribution and availability, and immediately suggests that one source of disjunction between events and perceptions has to do with the quality of information people receive. Second, aside from the broadcast programs offered by ANEM and B92, respondents expressed the most faith in interpersonal sources, particularly relatives and witnesses. The personally close category of "relatives" attracts more trust than the potentially unlimited category of "witnesses." Here, as in the attribution of responsibility, distance is a factor. International media, especially the programs sponsored by governments with an eye toward influencing public opinion in Serbia (such as the VOA and BBC language services) are not mentioned, but the distance of these sources might interfere with the level of trust they enjoy. The same might be said of international nonmedia sources, such as statements from international governments, the United Nations, or ICTY.

The clear implication here is that if minds were likely to be changed, the way that would happen would have to be through the stories people tell one another, rather than the stories people are told by institutional sources. To offer a concrete example, Serbian prosecutors did not declare an intention to investigate Slobodan Milošević for war crimes after the ICTY indictment, or after demands for prosecution by European and American politicians, but after domestic media revealed a case in which there was clear indication of efforts to remove evidence of massacres on the part of high state authorities.[23]

An earlier survey by the same agency raised related questions. Here respondents were asked about the possible guilt of specific individuals and about the prospect of cooperation with ICTY. While a great majority believed that Milošević was probably guilty of corruption, treason, and electoral fraud, only 10 percent believed he was guilty of war crimes. Most respondents expressed some degree of opposition to cooperation with ICTY, especially to extradition. About half responded that Serbia should cooperate with ICTY only in exchange for international aid.[24]

The findings of surveys asking directly about the question of responsibility and the role of ICTY may only get us so far, however. We have seen from the review of results presented above that some findings are contradictory, that there are problems with regard to how widely information is believed, and that public opinion on concrete questions is more likely than not in a state of transition. Given the not entirely clear findings of survey research on questions directly related to guilt for violations of international law, it might be instructive to explore some indirect avenues toward the question.

In the first place, institutions that might deal with questions of guilt had weak credibility at the end of the Communist period and continued to be largely discredited afterward. In 1999 a survey indicated that just 23 percent of citizens expressed faith in the judiciary as opposed to 45 percent who did not.[25] This put the judiciary well behind institutions with traditional authority (65 percent trusted the military and 14 percent did not; 56 percent trusted the Church and 18 percent did not), and behind some other institutions remarkable for their corruption and lack of credibility (the Serbian Academy of Sciences and Arts was trusted by 45 percent and distrusted by 18 percent, police were trusted by 39 percent and distrusted by 35 percent).[26] Yet the judiciary "scored" higher than political institutions, whose authority was rejected in the survey by majorities ranging from 51 percent (opposition parties) to 62 percent (ruling parties).

In relation to institutions that could approach questions of responsibility more informally, traditional institutions like the military and the Church enjoyed relatively high levels of public trust. The military was, however, poorly positioned to engage in an exploration of the recent past because of its extensive complicity in the worst events of the period. The same could be said for the Church.[27] Media were similarly distrusted, privately run media (trusted by 19 percent, distrusted by 37 percent) somewhat less than state-run media (16 percent, 61 percent).[28] Perhaps in searching for institutions that could be helpful in addressing psychic and emotional needs related to responsibility, a residual high level of trust was still enjoyed only by cultural and educational institutions.

These general points regarding perceptions of institutions, though, are at best signpoints along the way to the fundamental question, which is how people perceived themselves in the light of the experience all of them shared to some degree. Some interesting research has linked the power of nationalist mobilization to the various dimensions of personal powerlessness people felt during the declining years of SFRJ.[29] This current of research continues a trend of general lack of hope for the future already noted in the 1960s, but which became overwhelming in Serbia in the 1990s.[30] A meaningful change in feelings of hope and self-efficacy would not be likely to occur without major changes in social and material conditions, but also without a fundamental transformation of values and self-perceptions. Such processes are neither impossible nor unknown, but they occur slowly and subtly, and are unlikely to be massive. In this regard, public opinion surveys are unlikely to be of much help at all. The indicators we are after are mostly cultural in character.

What this early snapshot of public opinion probably does show is that Serbian society in 2001 was neither wholly prepared for the confrontation with the past that was being demanded of it nor did it entirely reject the idea. There were institutional weaknesses that made a quick engagement less probable (if quick engagement was indeed ever probable): these included a political and legal establishment with severely degraded credibility, a media system largely discredited for a variety of reasons, and institutions of traditional authority with severe restrictions on their capacity for active engagement.

The data also suggest that any efforts or initiatives to promote campaigns for public engagement would have had to meet several conditions in order to succeed. They would have to be perceived as having their origins in the society rather than being imposed from without. Within the society, they would have to be perceived as originating from or involving institutions with meaningful public credibility. They would have to be perceived as taking into account not only calls for regret but also sources of grievance. And they would have to involve, not only authoritative sources directing discourse toward the public, but active exchange of discourse among the public.

Further on in the text, analysis of the work of ICTY and related initiatives will show that these efforts did not meet the conditions described above and so did not make the expected contribution to the process of developing a discourse around guilt and responsibility. In this regard, they were not helped by a political and institutional structure that was either unprepared for the challenge or declined to take it up. This meant that much of the work of developing an understanding of the recent past took place not in the field of politics and law, but in that of culture.

If the surveys cited so far have offered representations of latent or existing public opinion around 2001, the explorations in the following chapter draw on cultural expression to get at what might have been emergent public opinion.

Chapter 3

Moment I: The Leader Is Not Invincible

The previous chapter indicated that public opinion surveys offer at best a mixed view of the state of public opinion just after the end of the Milošević regime. Part of the reason for this may be that opinion was in fact mixed, as could be expected in a period when a strongly ideologized form of control of information was coming to an end, and when uncertainty remained regarding what might follow. Another part of the reason may be that opinion was still in formation, just as political institutions and the parties and movements that would influence them were also in formation. Many of the perceptions and understandings that would become important in the years to follow were in negotiation in this period. While it may be uncertain what perspectives were dominant in 2001, contention between residual and emergent perspectives was clearly visible.[1]

This chapter explores some of the negotiation that took place around these perspectives by examining two cultural-political moments: (1) the discussion of the arrest of Slobodan Milošević at the end of March 2001, the moment at which it became clear that the former absolute ruler was neither untouchable nor invincible;[2] and (2) the emergence of the literary genre of "regime memoirs," in which writers would, using diary, fiction, and polemic, generate an account of the meaning of the period that had just ended.[3] It was in cultural sites like these that positions and themes were elaborated that would come to define the discussion over the following decade.

Initial Responses to the Arrest of Milošević

As criminal investigations commenced following the inauguration of Serbia's government in January 2001, major political actors frequently insisted, sometimes instrumentally, on the independence of prosecutorial and investigatory agencies. This was clear when Vojislav Koštunica refused (before, several days later, relenting) to meet with Carla Del Ponte, chief ICTY prosecutor, claiming that cooperation with the Tribunal was not a responsibility of the federal president. The ministers who met with Del Ponte echoed the arguments about separation of powers. When the U.S. government imposed a deadline of 31 March 2001, by which time Milošević had to be arrested or economic aid would be blocked, several Serbian government representatives argued that they could not order police to make an arrest or complete an investigation without compromising the independence of law enforcement.

Milošević was arrested nevertheless, just in time to meet the deadline—an event that marks a symbolic break, consolidating the power of the incoming regime. It is one thing to defeat an opponent politically, and quite another to hold this opponent politically responsible, to puncture the perception, built up over years, that he is above the law. Nobody who saw Milošević driven off to the Belgrade central prison believed afterward in the myth of his invincibility.

The government that carried out the arrest spoke about it very little while it was taking place and immediately afterward. Many government figures either would not give information or, in Koštunica's case, did not seem to know themselves what was happening.[4] One vice-president, Žarko Korać, was shown around the world claiming, inaccurately, that Milošević had already been arrested half a day before he was. Federal premier Zoran Žižić declared that the arrest "is not under the jurisdiction of the federal government."[5] Prime minister Zoran Djindjić told reporters that he had not been following events on the night of 31 March, but had been watching the popular film *Gladiator* with his son.[6]

The strange silence of the people in charge probably derived from complicating factors. First, there was the danger, which turned out to be exaggerated, that the arrest might lead to confrontations or violence between supporters and opponents of Milošević.[7] Second, any declaration that Milošević was being arrested would inevitably lead to the question of what he was being arrested for, a question people in power preferred to avoid as it raised subsidiary questions of whether international oversight should be accepted and whether people in Serbia or elsewhere had the most legitimate claim to being Milošević's victims. Third, the U.S.-imposed deadline for financial assistance was controversial. Every official statement declared that arresting Milošević right on the deadline day was a coincidence, but these declarations were not generally regarded as persuasive. So government representatives had good reason to avoid the question of whether they were more interested in establishing the rule of law or acting out of a more practical financial logic that looked like blackmail.

People outside the government showed none of the reticence of their political representatives. I followed just one popular channel for public comment: the postings in the "comments on the news" section of the web site of Belgrade's B92 radio. This section invites people to send responses to news items, which are then published on a separate page. What follows is a categorization of several of those comments (in my translation) as a broad picture of the responses people shared about the arrest.[8]

The Process of Arrest as a Reflection of the Nature of the New Regime

The arrest itself was a process full of confrontations and confusions lasting from 7:00 P.M. on Friday, 30 March, until Milošević was finally taken into custody around 4:35 A.M. on Sunday, 1 April. During those thirty-four hours, there were small clashes between the police and Milošević's personal military guard and private security, there were contradictory statements from media and government spokespeople, and there were some brief gestures of heroism on the part of Milošević's supporters and relatives.[9] Although the arrest was eventually carried off without major violence, it looked like an organizational and tactical fiasco.

The first comments responded to the inability of the police to make the arrest swiftly, and interpreted this as a sign that the new government was either incompetent or continued to fear Milošević:

> (Aleksandar, 31 March): Milošević is not God above all people and law that he can resist arrest.
> (Beogradjanin u Washington DC-u, 31 March): [he came to power in] 1986, and now 15 years later he is still laughing in all our faces.[10]
> (Mirjana Grkavac Maksimović, 31 March): Is our police really so incompetent that it needs so much time to arrest one person? How can Milošević reject an arrest warrant? Who is in charge here?

Other writers focused on what appeared to be the insubordination of Milošević's military guard. Prime Minister Djindjić had stated in January that the military unit at Milošević's residence was "guarding the house, not the person,"[11] but the guards refused entry to the police on the grounds that they were not invited visitors. The police had to remove the military guard from the gate by force. Some writers interpreted this as a sign of that the army remained loyal to Milošević, especially since it continued to be commanded by his last appointee:

> (Mile, 31 March): So it's all clear. President Koštunica, who is so proud of his "legalism," uses General Pavković—once Milošević's favorite—to interfere with the police doing their legal duty. And all that from populist motives, so the federation will fall apart and in the next election he can win votes for his own, until recently minority DSS party, which has been known only for giving statements to the press.

A (tragi?)comical element emerged at the moment of the actual arrest, when Milošević's daughter Marija fired a gun (a gift from General Pavković, engraved with his signature and portrait) in the direction of the car that was taking Milošević away. One couple (Mira and Predrag, 1 April) composed a comical poem about the shooting. Another writer (Milan Palinić, 1 April) quoted a canonical movie joke: "Did you hit the air, Marija?"[12] Perhaps the sadistic pleasure these writers took in Marija Milosević's desperate gesture could be understood as a sign of relief at the arrest?

The Question of What Milošević Was to Be Charged With

One of the questions raised by the arrest was whether Milošević ought to be arrested at all, and if so what for. Some people continued to support him, declaring that he defended national goals and could not be considered a criminal:[13]

> (Nenad, 31 March): I don't regard him as guilty, he defended the homeland from a satanizing that was prepared in advance. He is a hero, not a traitor.

However, most people seemed to agree that he ought to be arrested and charged with something. The government's indictment charged him with embezzlement, theft, and abuse of power—attempting to assure that he be arrested and tried in Serbia for violations of domestic law.[14] Several commenters expressed outrage at the absence of war crimes from the indictment:

> (Maja, 31 March): For abuse of power? Shouldn't he be tried for genocide against the Bosnian, Albanian and Croatian people, or maybe for the destruction of SFRJ, or for the decline of the Serbian people? I think that Milošević did many things that were worse than ABUSE OF POWER!!!
>
> (Branislav Zekić Zeka, 31 March): The fact that He has been arrested is very good news. But that he will be charged for embezzlement, building without a permit, and unpaid electric, sewer and heating bills. . . . Garbage! That is throwing crumbs to us, because every honest citizen of Serbia has at least a few, more or less bloody, reasons to bring charges against our former president. I hope that he will be tried in Belgrade for all of the crimes he committed against his own people, for all the killings he ordered, for treason and theft and especially for all the things he is charged with by the Hague Tribunal.

It is difficult to distinguish to what degree such comments represented legal interpretations and to what degree they could be considered as expressions of hatred or revenge toward Milošević personally. One of the principal arguments that Koštunica offered in favor of moving slowly against the previous holders of power was the need to avoid what he called "revolutionary justice."[15]

Belgrade or The Hague?

Closely tied to the question of what Milošević was to be charged with was the question of where he should be tried, or more specifically whether he should be extradited to ICTY. People who rejected this possibility raised issues ranging from the fear that an international trial of a former president would amount to an imposition of collective guilt to doubts about the fairness and objectivity of the Tribunal:

> (Vuk Vujović, 31 March): Now, anybody who thinks about it even a little bit knows that he will be tried in The Hague as a former

president, which automatically and immediately means that if he is found guilty, everything that the Serbian people did during the period when Milošević was president will be declared a crime. That means every commander or soldier who was on the battlefield will be a war criminal, every dead soldier will be a war criminal, and every mother who cried for her child will be a war criminal.

(siniša, 31 March): Our country is in the condition it is in and one more betrayal or surrender of our citizen to The Hague, even if it is the former president, brings a bad image to all members of the Serbian nation. Our citizens should only be tried in our country for their actions. Any other decision is shameful and stamps us with recognition as a genocidal horde which only understands force and blackmail. I wonder who would defend our exhausted country if it ever really needed it. Many patriots have already been arrested and sent to The Hague for no reason, hiding out and believing that if they need to show their innocence, they would be able to do it in their own country. But they have been deceived by the current regime who sends them as scapegoats to the executioners in The Hague, who instead of honest and fair trials have sentences prepared in advance by their American mentors.

(Boris, 31 March): Do the people who are doing the arresting know what is waiting for them tomorrow if they are not co-operative?

Other writers argued that since Milošević had committed both domestic and international crimes, he should be tried for both. Sometimes this was expressed jokingly—for example by the Vojvodina politician Nenad Čanak, who suggested that Milošević should be tried in The Hague and then serve his sentence in a Serbian prison (where conditions are worse than in the resortlike Scheveningen prison used by ICTY):[16]

(aca, 31 March): It would be best for us to offer some compromises to the West . . . first, that WE (the Serbian people) try and convict him, then after his fiftieth year of prison we send him to The Hague. Or better, we should CLONE him . . . we're satisfied, they're satisfied. . . .

Some writers who advocated extradition expressed this as a desire for revenge, although several writers advanced the thesis that by trying and convicting the person responsible for organizing and financing war crimes, guilt could be transferred from the social collective to an individual:

> (Vlada, 31 March): I don't know how people can still support and feel sorry for him after all the evil he has brought us. Did he regret any of the lives that he gambled away? Let him go to The Hague if he has to!! He doesn't deserve any better.
>
> (marko, 31 March): Arrest that murderer, traitor and WAR criminal Milošević. Send him immediately to The Hague so we can remove the guilt from the whole Serbian people . . . just do that and show that you are for change, for a better future, for equality between people without regard to religion, nationality or political belief, don't forget we are in the 21st century.

Clearly more was at stake in the question of extradition than an assessment of the charges or of the legitimacy of ICTY.[17] People who wrote in to give an opinion also expressed general orientations about sovereignty, the nature of individual and collective responsibility, and the use of ICTY as an instrument in domestic and international politics.

Is Milošević Serbia?

Also at stake in the controversy over the arrest was the extent to which people recognized a personal stake in the fate of Milošević. Through this dispute the question was raised of whether people continued to identify Milošević as a symbolic (if no longer official) representative of the Serbian people. Here the clearest signs of willingness to break with the recent past could be observed, as many writers not only rejected any identification with Milošević, but criticized the people who did:

> (Petar, 31 March): I really enjoy the comments from people who see the arrest of Milošević as their own shame, and the people who think it is a shame "for the whole Serbian people." I am ashamed too, but only because this bloodsucker was arrested only after almost fifteen years of robbing and pillaging a country that was once beautiful and that once had a future. I can only hope this is the beginning of sobering up and real denazification, although I think the job will never be finished, because I have the impression that what people

hold most against Milošević is that he didn't succeed in creating Greater Serbia.

People who made a connection with Milošević on the level of identity were accused by these writers of a sort of false consciousness—here the question of authenticity of experience was raised, with Milošević supporters being identified with a nationalist diaspora that is pictured as both more extreme than the domestic population and also as uncaring and alien, not sharing the fate of people living in the country:

> (Dejan, 31 March): I like all the messages coming from "patriots" and "great sons and daughters of Serbia" from the diaspora. I personally know a ton of heroes who, as soon as our "humanitarian aid packages" started arriving from the Western countries on 24 March 1999 [the date bombing began], ran off with their tails between their legs to THOSE SAME COUNTRIES. Pretty patriotic, isn't it? The new millennium, it seems, brings us a lot of surprises. One of them is the "remote-control patriot."
> (Olja Bročić, 31 March): If by Saturday morning that man is not on a helicopter to Scheveningen or in a Yugoslavian jail, I will ask for political exile in any foreign country, tear up my Yugoslav passport, and forget I ever lived here. I authorize RTV B92 to publish this statement as they choose and forward it to the president of Yugoslavia and to the Ministries of Internal and Foreign Affairs.
> (ZoranP, 31 March): All the people who have gone to stand by Slobodan should do just that, they should be with him. I hope there is space for all those people.

Here the proposition was offered that in order for Serbia to move into the future, it needed to separate the character of the recent past, personified by Milošević, from the self-perception of identity on the part of people in Serbia:

> (Raina von Kraemer, 31 March): HE has to disappear, first of all from the HEADS of his "admirers." There is no need to talk about HIM anymore. Let's start a new life—. WITHOUT HIM

This perspective might simply illustrate the level of resentment directed toward the former dictator. But it could mark a perceptual step toward generating an account of the recent past: to objectify it in some way, initially probably in a negative way. Here the argument seemed to be that if people were able to imagine Serbia as Serbia-without-Milošević, then new possibilities could be opened.

The brief overview of readers' comments here suggests that the arrest of Milošević sparked a debate over questions of responsibility and a search for a usable understanding of the preceding ten years. Concerns over factors like threats to sovereignty, imposition of collective guilt, and resistance to moral posturing on the part of powerful countries did begin to emerge as justifications, and have constituted obstacles to the further development of this debate.

Both subsequent events and an intervention by Milošević himself would play a role in the development of the discussion that began in late March 2001. The day after his arrest, Milošević filed an appeal in which he declared that he had not stolen money but rather had diverted it from the state budget to finance paramilitaries in Croatia and Bosnia-Herzegovina, thus introducing a point domestic prosecutors had wanted to avoid and international prosecutors had been trying to prove. Not long after Milošević's arrest the news story broke in Serbia about the "freezer truck case" discussed in Chapter 1. The importance of these events might be understood as showing first that people accused of crimes no longer themselves denied things that other people denied for them, and second that violations could be traced through a chain of command to the highest sources and so could not be dismissed as incidental.[18] The claim that the state was defending itself against the freezer truck victims could only seem plausible in an environment where open discussion is made inaccessible, and that at least seemed to be no longer the case in Serbia.

War and Identity in War Diaries

Questions of national identity were already complex before the collapse of SFRJ. At various moments, a series of Yugoslav states promoted or backed away from the promotion of a synthetic "Yugoslav" identity, encouraged or discouraged the public expression of ethnic, national, and local identities, and made efforts of varying intensity to subsume particular identities to a concept of "brotherhood and unity." In the post-1945 period identity issues invoked the fear that expressions of ethnic or national pride could grow into nationalist displays, which risked raising the unresolved question of guilt for the behavior of nationalist movements during World War II.[19] The complete rejection of "brotherhood and unity" by nationalist regimes after 1990 also involved an effort to dismiss the association of nationalities with the crimes of the World War II period Serbian and Croatian quisling states—a concern that is especially apparent in the polemical historical works of Franjo Tudjman.[20]

The wars of succession that followed the dissolution of SFRJ did not have the effect of freeing national identity from constraints imposed by a guilty past. Instead they burdened these identities further with a consciousness of a guilty present. This is clearly visible in an examination of diaries and autobiographical works produced in Serbia during the war period. A number of writers produced "war diaries" examining events they had experienced or witnessed, and exploring their own responses to them. There is no way of knowing how many people shared the impressions offered in these works, most of which were consciously presented as an alternative to official "patriotic" propaganda, but enough of them were produced that they might be considered a meaningful subgenre of contemporary Balkan literature.[21]

First, writers displayed a keen consciousness of the way that Serbs were perceived in the world as the primary perpetrators of atrocities. Mileta Prodanović tells of meeting an old and prominent East European writer at a conference. "I shook hands with the old man (who was the only Nobel laureate I had ever met personally), told him where I was from, and at once noticed a change in his blue Slavic eyes."[22] Discomfited by the writer's gaze:

> I understood. The old man was disappointed. The questions which he really, undoubtedly, wanted to ask me could be, for example: "And how many unfortunate Bosnian children did you slaughter with your own hands? Did you participate in mass rapes? Are you a relative of one of the leaders of the paramilitary formations, or maybe just one of the 'weekend warriors'?" I ran to my hotel room, ripped off the top of the plastic container of red ink for my "Rotring" pen with my teeth, spread the ink over my shirt, and rubbed it on my hands. When I returned to the lecture room, I could see the relief on the face of the old poet. It seemed to me that he even nodded his head a little bit.[23]

Other writers tried responding directly to the negative global reputation of Serbs, rather than taking refuge in bitter humor. Vladimir Arsenijević quotes an e-mail message he wrote to an Albanian friend:

My compassion really and naturally belongs only to people, regard-less of their nationality and/or religion. I know that everything we have been going through in this country for the past decade or so is simply a long chain of consequences of our President's irresponsible and highly destructive behavior. You say that people are suffering here just for the fact that "they are Albanians" and I totally agree with you—they do—but you should also know that what you are concerned with is just one part of the big problem. Because many more people than just those of Albanian nationality have been going through enormous problems here, for a very long time now. It is a kind of inverted nationalism to think that only those citizens who are of non-Serbian nationality suffer here. There is no favouritism in this society, you can be sure of that. Everybody is Albanian here, and this is not just an apt, if shabby, analogy. . . .
And as for us, Bashkim, people like you and me, Serbs as well as Albanians, those who suffered a lot although they never caused any of this to happen, well—we are just flesh, valueless bodies for both parties to play with. That seems to be our most common ground. I'm sorry to say that. Because this is what Our region has given us, such a hideous legacy. We are Nothings. We can easily be killed, and hardly anyone would blink, but many would cheer, because—we are Those Who Are Easily Killed. And, even if we manage to escape the borders of our misguided, stupid, sad countries, we are still not in a position to shake off that negative identity. Our countries, small and miserable as they are, nevertheless remain stronger than us.[24]

Regardless how they approached the problem, all these writers needed some reply to what they recognized as the international perception of collective guilt about Serbs. Sometimes this took the form of satirizing the imposition of an unwelcome identity, sometimes it took the form of attempting to find a specific social location for blame, and sometimes it took the form of skepticism toward Serbian identity itself.

However, other people's stereotypes about Serbs were not the only bur-den that faced Serbian writers. They also had to develop an approach toward inflated patriotic models of identity that were offered up constantly in state-sponsored media. At the same time that media in other parts of the world generated the image of Serbs-as-war-criminals, another mythology was developing in state-sponsored nationalist media of Serbs-as-Ubermenschen, the oldest,[25] most virtuous, and altogether finest people. Goran Marković offers an account of one Dr. Jovan I. Deretić,[26] a self-declared "historian" promoted on television:

> He was speaking about some Serbon Makeridov, a conqueror who lived long before Alexander the Great and conquered much more territory than him. . . . That Serbon, the father of all nations, was a Serb. That is to say, all his descendants, or rather all known peoples, have a Serbian origin. Contemporary Serbs, in fact, are just some of the many Serbs who, over time, became Greeks and Celts and so on. Serbs, according to this lively old fellow, are not a nation but a race. In fact, why hide it, all Indo-European peoples have Serbian origins.
>
> Even that lesser conqueror than Serbon, Alexander, was named Aleksandar Karanović and he was of Serbian origin too. He conquered the world with an army that was recruited from areas settled by Serbs, our ancestors were so brave. And the most beautiful girls, who can be seen on ancient Greek vases, were also Serbs, there is indisputable evidence for that. . . .
>
> About this doctor. Of course, Deretić has the right to assert whatever he likes, just like the audience has the right to believe it or, like me, simply to ignore it. But something else is in question: the context of the story. It was disgusting, and at the same time typical. The host of the program, a Serb primitive who is delighted by every Serbian heraldic symbol, even completely nebulous ones, in archaeological digs, and who triumphally grins over every bit of "evidence," even the most suspicious, of the Serbian origin of everyone and everything, and his interlocutor . . . were perfect partners in this pig's race of nationalism. It was a real orgy of stupidity in the service of deceiving exhausted people, a last effort to inject hungry and scared people with the feeling that they still have a reason to live. I am not against nationalism a priori. I do not think that love for one's people is negative by definition. What makes me angry is not even the falsehood or artificiality of what those two people were claiming. I am ashamed because my feeling of belonging to a nation

has been made into something crude, used for dirty purposes, because my personal feelings are being sold publicly by TV Palma, like prostitutes in Gavrilo Princip street.[27]

Similar themes are apparent in other diaries of the period, in which a falsified collective pride, widely publicized, is perceived by the writers as an attack on individual pride, and massively promoted nationalist feeling makes national identity impossible.

A similar response is offered to the discourse of victimization. Arsenijević responds to the efforts of state television to promote a feeling of victimization with what seems to be insensitive rationality. Describing a television clip from a bomb shelter, he tries to place the rhetoric and its motivation in perspective:

"He is completely hysterical!" a young mother said in a shaky voice into the microphones of the state television news, squinting from the bright lights which were pointed right into her eyes as if she were at a police interrogation. In her arms she was holding a baby who did not seem the least bit hysterical.

"How does he behave?" asked the invisible interviewer, with pathos.

"Sometimes he laughs. Sometimes he cries," the young mother answered.

But isn't that what babies generally do? Sometimes they laugh. Sometimes they cry. All the time, even in the shelters when you are bombing them.

But I don't think the problem is with the baby.

What is worse, it's not with the mother either.[28]

Here the writers face an unusual rhetorical challenge. Faced with genuine danger associated with the bombing campaign, they simultaneously feel compelled to resist official media messages telling them that they are victims, and should feel angry and helpless. This requires dismissing some real troubles, or explaining away some real situations.

On the other hand, there is a distinct consciousness that, while inflated claims were promoted regarding "maintaining threatened identity" or "resisting the New World Order," the countries making these were in fact small, remote, and politically marginal. Prodanović offers an ironic self-location which begins with an interrupted story:

> organizations for the protection of animals began a campaign for the permanent protection of the striped-neck swan. These recently little-known birds have their habitat in. . . . Well, after all, it is not important where their habitat is—the average resident of the civilized world cannot pronounce the name of that country. The most important things are principles and the determination to sacrifice oneself completely for the sake of an idea.

These are just a few additional reasons why we, East Europeans, even after the fall of the Berlin Wall and the arrival of perfect democracy to our small and lost-in-East-European-space homelands, even when it is now possible to buy at our kiosks condoms in thousands of shapes, colors, flavors, and fragrances, and not just the Czechoslovakian "Tigar" brand like in the time of the single-party dictatorship, still try to emigrate to one of those states where so much attention is paid not just to the rights of people but also various types of animals, to one of those countries where order, peace, and mutual respect reign, where even in times of senseless racial violence one can sense an unusually high degree of political correctness.

The governments of the great democracies of the West, of course, would be faced with insurmountable problems if they tried to cram masses of morally, materially, and mentally neglected people from Eastern Europe into their clean cities, into cities with well-maintained facades and rows of well watered flowers, if they let these lazybugs into the hives where every worker bee knows its place. To prevent this undesirable migration, invisible barriers have been placed in the form of visas. People of the East, it is known, fear two things—drafts and bureaucratic procedures. About the East European fear of drafts, those murderous currents of air in rooms, about the awful diseases one can get by exposure to drafts, entire tracts have been written—the fear of bureaucratic procedure is less well researched, but no smaller. This fear is well known to great and small strategists in the West, and so in order to receive a visa, aside from the rigid conditions, barriers have been established in the form of numerous questionnaires, which people who wish to feel the

enchantment of orderly countries, or even to settle in these countries, must fill out in the unpleasant waiting rooms of embassies and
consulates, after long waits in line[29]

The passage suggests that the antipatriotism of these writers did not function as substitution. The transparent lies and overwrought nationalist rhetoric of the regime did not force many people to believe that the regime's
external opponents (whether these were regional competitors, the NATO
alliance, or an abstractly conceived "West"),[30] or even internal opponents
(epitomized by the opposition political party leaders) were necessarily any
better.

Instead, there seems to develop an ambivalent attitude among these
Serbian writers toward their own identity as Serbs. This is bolstered not by
some other nationally structured alternative, but by taking refuge in various
aspects of individuality. Arsenijević explains his friendly relationship with
the ethnic Albanian writer Xhevdet Bajraj partly by the fact that neither was
nationalistically inclined, and both liked the same kind of music. Marković
talks about his inspiration by (and eventual disillusion with) organizers of
protests around Serbia after the end of the bombing campaign, but by the
end the most probable vision of the future he can generate is:

> When the moment of liberation comes, the most important assis-
> tance we can get will be—psychiatric. We will need a whole lot of
> good doctors who will have the will and the knowledge to wrestle
> with the effects that the last decade or more has left us.
>
> And in that awakening of mental health it will be most necessary
> to establish a basic criterion: what is normal and what is not. I know
> that is not easy and that these things change, depending on the soci-
> ety and culture in question, but this will really be a special case,
> worthy of the deepest observation. This country will be an Eldorado
> for future scientists, something like a laboratory with live people
> instead of white mice.[31]

Under conditions where a small group felt prepared, like the writers discussed here, to offer some kind of more or less moral stories to their readers, but many more were certain that they have gone through a period of
madness that may not have ended, it is easy to understand why "public
opinion" may not be so apparently solid.

The discourse of responsibility came out of the confines of antiwar groups and people engaged with it as a vocation, and began its public life with events like the ones presented in this chapter. At all points it was a complex and uncertain process, and by no means was there any certainty that "confrontation" or "catharsis"—psychological terms used by politicians—would take place. The examples here indicate an interplay involving several unstable elements. On the one hand people began openly discussing their experience of historical events and of themselves and their social environment. On the other hand the discussion was subject to balances of political forces and unpredictable events that would see the feelings articulated mobilized in varying directions. The evolution of the discussion was not predictable from the way it began.

In hindsight we know several things the observers cited here did not know in 2001: the Milošević trial dragged on for years and ended without resolution; institutions failed, emerged, and changed; and things that once appeared to be clear became confused. In short, the story continued.

Chapter 4

Approaches to Guilt

As long as the Milošević regime controlled most media in Serbia, denial and claims of victimization were the most generally available perspectives on guilt. In other countries of the former Yugoslavia, rejection of the possibility that crimes were committed constituted, at least for some people, an essential part of national identity and national pride.[1] Two weeks after Slobodan Milošević was sent to face trial in The Hague, ICTY presented the government of neighboring Croatia with indictments against two army generals, Rahim Ademi and Ante Gotovina. After a bitter political debate, the government accepted the indictments and agreed that the accused would be delivered for trial. However, just as large displays of public sympathy in Croatia in February 2001 interfered with the arrest and trial of General Mirko Norac, accused of the massacre of Serb civilians around Gospić in 1991,[2] in July there were also indications of a current of denial in public opinion.[3] A group of ten prominent Croatian athletes, led by the tennis champion Goran Ivanišević, published an open letter against the indictments, declaring: "This is an effort to alter the fact of who is the victim and who is the aggressor. The only truth is that Croatia was the victim, and its generals and soldiers were heroes."[4]

The position advocated by the athletes had considerable resonance in public opinion,[5] though it was not the position of a series of Croatian governments. President Ivo Josipović and his predecessor Stjepan Mesić have been outspoken in advocating for the need to acknowledge and try crimes committed by Croatian forces. However, for states whose legitimacy derives in part from the celebration of their wars for independence, the argument over responsibility represents an ongoing source of controversy. Recognition of the guilt of people who committed crimes risks calling into question the wars that were fought and the independence that was gained through them.

The legitimacy of Serbia's statehood depends far less on perception of the aims of the wars as legitimate (though the legitimacy of the Bosnian Serb entity depends on this very much indeed). Serbia neither gained nor fought for independence, but was an entity from which other states declared independence—a condition that strengthened security in the continuity of Serbia's statehood while undermining its prestige as a state. There is less motivation to advance positions like those advocated by the group of Croatian athletes discussed above. This perversely fortuitous circumstance, combined with the passage of time and the widespread diffusion of evidence of violations, has meant that the position that there is no guilt to be assigned is held by a vocal but diminishing minority.

An early challenge to the consensus of denial came with the broadcast of the BBC-produced documentary *A Cry from the Grave*, about the 1995 massacre in Srebrenica. The film had been shown a few times in private showings to small audiences in Belgrade, and in 2001 was broadcast on the independent B92 television station (launched to supplement the radio station in October 2000), to controversial reception.[6] In July 2001, three months after Milošević was delivered to The Hague, the documentary was broadcast on the state RTS television network, to a considerably larger audience. An exchange in the Serbian parliament followed the broadcast, with Branislav Ivković, a leader of Milošević's Socialist Party of Serbia (SPS), accusing B92 and RTS of selectively ignoring crimes, and of broadcasting exclusively "propaganda" aimed at "establishing a feeling of shame and embarrassment among the Serbian people." But after watching the film even Ivković backtracked from this position. When asked by a reporter whether he thought the massacre in Srebrenica did not in fact take place, he replied that he "allowed that there were crimes."[7] While this was not much of an admission, it came from the chief representative of the political party from whose ranks ICTY's most prominent indictee came, and suggested that even Milošević's supporters could be receptive to new information.

Similar conclusions could be suggested on the basis of a (nonrandom sample telephone) survey conducted in July 2001 by the weekly magazine *NIN*. Although only 36.5 percent of respondents supported the decision to send Milošević to The Hague, 57.5 percent agreed that he was responsible for war crimes. Among the main objections to Milošević's extradition were the hurried manner in which it was carried out,[8] the compromising timing of the act,[9] and the belief that an international trial would make it impossible to bring Milošević to account for domestic crimes.[10]

While the change of regime and the increased availability of information may have encouraged a higher level of readiness to address questions of guilt, the question remained as to how. This chapter discusses the main mechanisms that have been used for establishing guilt and affirming responsibility in the wars of Yugoslav succession: national courts in the countries involved, international courts and tribunals, and "truth commissions."

The Role of National Courts

Clearly the domestic judicial institutions of the countries where violations of international law were committed play an important role in addressing guilt for those crimes. There are no crimes in the statute of ICTY or ICC that are not also crimes under the criminal codes of all the successor states to Yugoslavia (as they are in the criminal codes of every UN member state). The Hague and Geneva Conventions on the conduct of war are also binding on all combatants. Toward the beginning of the wars in October 1991, the Yugoslav army issued a declaration detailing its recognition of the obligations imposed by the Hague and Geneva Conventions.[11] A joint declaration of the warring parties in the Croatian conflict and the International Committee of the Red Cross in 1991 detailed obligations under the two conventions, and the three warring parties in Bosnia-Herzegovina signed a similar joint declaration in 1992.[12] Combatants demonstrated their recognition of the authority of international law in indirect ways as well: Vasiljević tells of a discharged paramilitary fighter in the Bosnian War who was issued a document declaring that he "participated in the struggles for the liberation of the Serbian territory of Zvornik and did not participate in any criminal activities."[13]

Obviously these agreements and declarations did not achieve much in terms of actually preventing violations.[14] On the contrary, a tremendous abyss between the public rhetoric of political leaders and the actual behavior of their administrative and military forces was apparent throughout the wars. The declarations do show, however, that at no time during the wars could the leaders of any state or entity claim that they were unaware of or did not recognize their obligations under international law. These obligations were not imposed, but derived from domestic law, from agreements voluntarily signed by the combatants, and from declarations made openly by the combatants. Among the obligations are the duties to prevent violations and to record and punish violations.

If one factor contributed more than others to the involvement of international organizations and the United Nations in the wars of Yugoslav succession, it was the failure of the warring parties to meet the obligations they had recognized under international law. Not only were violations not prevented, they were committed at a level that both aroused international concern and appeared to represent state policy.[15]

The story of information gathering, prosecution, and punishment is somewhat more complicated. Trials were conducted in Serbia, Croatia, and Bosnia-Herzegovina, principally against members of minority groups charged with committing offenses against members of the majority population.[16] For the most part these trials were of a piece with the war itself. In Serbia, a few trials for war crimes committed by Serb paramilitary forces did take place—for example, the prosecution of the Vučković brothers that began in Šabac in 1994. Vojin Vučković was convicted of illegal possession of weapons and Dušan Vučković for firing on a group of Bosnian civilians, murdering twenty of them and injuring sixteen.[17] This was, however, a "substitute" prosecution—members of a paramilitary formation were charged, but there was no inquiry into the state sources of their command and supply. In many such cases prosecutions were filed but the trials were not carried to conclusion. In the Vučković brothers case, the principal suspect, Dušan Vučković, had been dismissed from the army in 1982 with a diagnosis of alcoholism and severe psychological illness, meaning that (1) a rhetorical wall was constructed between the military and the crimes, and (2) a ground was established not only to contest a prison sentence, but for any observer to trace the crimes to an individual condition rather than a political setting. Vučković was in fact charged with only a small portion of the offenses to which he had confessed, and the role of the Serbian Radical Party (Srpska Radikalna Stranka, SRS), which organized his paramilitary formation, was never raised.[18]

Acting on evidence of both violations of international law and failure of legal bodies, the UN Security Council adopted a series of resolutions (721, 752, and 764) in 1991 and 1992, declaring the conduct of the wars to be a matter of international concern. In Resolution 771 (1992) the Security

Council enumerated violations of international humanitarian law and demanded that all sides cease committing them. The 1992 London conference on Yugoslavia adopted an instruction to governments and international organizations to inform the UN about the observance of Resolution 771, and this instruction was formalized in Resolution 780 (1992), which established a commission of experts to report on violations. On the basis of the commission's report of February 1993, the Security Council adopted Resolution 808 (1993), which called for the establishment of an international court and called on the secretary general to prepare the court's statute. The secretary general's response was adopted in Resolution 827 (1993) as the ICTY statute.

This series of events indicates that at least one major factor that led to the establishment of ICTY, the first international criminal tribunal to be set up by the UN, and hence the first concrete assertion of the right of international governance in humanitarian matters, was the failure of domestic courts in the former SFRJ to do their job. Mark Ellis argues:

Although the Tribunal has primacy over national courts, which defer to its competence, it still has recognized the right of national courts to conduct war-crimes trials. In creating the Tribunal, the United Nations made clear that its intention was to encourage states to prosecute war criminals. It was not interested in depriving national courts of their jurisdiction over these types of crimes. However, so long as national judicial systems are viewed as partial, ineffective, and incapable of diligently undertaking prosecutions, the Tribunal will rightfully retain its primacy over those selected criminal proceedings that are taking place in the national courts.[19]

More simply, a prominent ICTY defense attorney, Michail Wladimiroff, who defended Dušan Tadić in the first ICTY trial,[20] remarked that "if the states of the former Yugoslavia would properly prosecute their own perpetrators of war crimes and crimes against humanity and do so with the same quality of fair trial, there would be no need for the International Tribunal for the Former Yugoslavia."[21]

However much the inactivity of domestic courts may have provoked the formation of ICTY, it was not designed simply to substitute for domestic courts. ICTY began to define its unique role beginning in 1998. At that time, after a series of trials of low-ranking figures like Dušan Tadić and

Dražen Erdemović, ICTY adopted a policy of restricting its focus to major perpetrators. In 2000 and 2001 this became apparent (and possible) with the arraignments of some formerly senior political actors: Momčilo Krajišnik,[22] Biljana Plavšić,[23] and of course Slobodan Milošević. In relation to Croatia, it filed its major indictments against generals (the two politicians most likely to be charged, Franjo Tudjman and Gojko Šušak, died in the meantime, as did Bosnian HDZ leader Mate Boban). Here the model adopted was not to substitute for domestic jurisprudence, but rather to engineer widely publicized demonstration trials, along the lines of the International Military Tribunal in Nuremberg. At the same time, although the ICTY statute foresaw "primacy" over national courts, ICTY rarely exercised this primacy in individual cases. This led to considerable leeway, as well as considerable potential for abuse, on the part of courts in Croatia and Kosovo.[24] In some instances referral of cases took on a political character, as it seemed that Croatia was rewarded for cooperation with the promise that cases like the Gospić case, involving violations committed by Croatian forces, would be referred to domestic jurisdiction.[25]

In the period since the regimes whose behavior sparked the establishment of ICTY left power, the states of the former Yugoslavia have been the site of several innovations and experiments in transitional justice. Aside from the founding of the first UN tribunal, the region has seen the first regional system of special prosecutors and special courts for violations of international humanitarian law, the first invocation of "confronting the past" as a principle of conditionality, and the first efforts in the civil sector to develop cooperative approaches to reconciliation.

Since the successor states to the former Yugoslavia are nonrevolutionary states, some expectations placed on transitional justice conflicted with one another. States were expected to transform institutions that had been complicit in deeds that were now to be punished, but not to destroy them to the degree that they could not function or integrate with international organizations.[26] Taking the difficulties faced by the states into account, the fact that transitional justice initiatives have produced a mixed record might be less noteworthy than that they have occurred on a meaningful scale at all.

There were always compelling reasons for preferring domestic over international trials. Controversies around issues of sovereignty and perceptions of bias have led to the development of a political current that rejects ICTY, while the distance of the court's seat in The Hague from the publics in the region has contributed to difficulties in communication. At the same time, the challenge of prosecuting such cases successfully has been understood by many in the domestic legal profession as an opportunity for prosecutors and courts to demonstrate their capacity to operate independently and contribute to a resolution of humanitarian law issues from within the country rather than without. In addition to their importance in developing local institutional capacity, several recent domestic cases have also contributed to the development of cooperative relationships between judicial and law enforcement institutions across borders, particularly between Serbia and Croatia.

When ICTY completes the trials currently before it the issue of international versus domestic prosecution will be moot: all prosecutions will be domestic.[27] In terms of political efficacy, local courts enjoy greater grounds for legitimacy than ad hoc tribunals, and their work is less likely to be perceived as an imposition from outside. In terms of gathering evidence and receiving accusations, too, there may be advantages of geographic proximity to victims, perpetrators, and crime scenes (these could be disadvantages in cases where witnesses might be intimidated). Since many of the most important suspects are people who played roles in domestic politics, too, domestic courts offer the possibility of trying them for both domestic and international offenses. Finally, if there is to be anything like a comprehensive approach to war crimes, a major role for national courts is inescapable simply because ICTY never had the intent or capacity to investigate and try anywhere near the number of people who could potentially be charged, nor did it ever have authority to try people for crimes not delineated in its statute.

Serbian courts entered the post-2000 period burdened with considerable difficulties. First among these was their poor reputation. The independence of the courts from political agencies was questionable in the Communist period, and worsened rather than improved during the period of nationalist authoritarianism. Both judicial personnel and judicial processes were subject to political instrumentalization. The Milošević regime frequently produced judicial decisions as political weapons: the independent newspaper *Borba* was shut down, the results of the 1996 and 2000 elections were overturned, and political opponents were harassed and intimidated through the courts. Judges who declined to allow their courts to be used for such purposes were fired.[28]

Consequently judicial institutions in Serbia received consistently low measures of public confidence in surveys. A 1996 survey found 57 percent of respondents declaring lack of trust in judicial institutions, with 37 percent expressing trust.[29] This was less than the level of distrust displayed toward representative institutions such as the federal parliament (62 percent), the federal government (61 percent), the Serbian parliament (62 percent), the Serbian government (60 percent), and political parties (71 percent). However, among law enforcement, administrative and civic institutions, only the Serbian police (57 percent) and state-owned media (65 percent) received equal or higher ratings of distrust.[30] This put the judicial system on a level of public esteem comparable to that of some of the most despised and reviled institutions in Serbia.

There would have been good reason to expect levels of trust to be lower still with regard to the ability of courts to try humanitarian law cases, considering the record the Serbian judiciary compiled from 1991 onward. Particularly controversial would have been the large number of dubious convictions on terrorism charges, principally against Kosovo Albanians.[31] The most widely publicized of these was the conviction of 143 ethnic Albanians from Djakovica, despite a lack of evidence connecting any single one of them to any terrorist acts or attempts. The presiding judge in the case, Goran Petronijević,[32] admitted that there was no evidence of guilt, but justified the verdict with an interesting innovation in legal theory: "It was not possible to demonstrate individual guilt, but for the essence of the crime of terrorism that is not necessary."[33] The precedent established by this case degraded the reputation of Serbian courts for competence to try crimes of this type, as well as presenting an inconvenience for political authorities who argued for a principled rejection of concepts of collective guilt.

The task of enabling judicial organs to function independently and capably got to a slow start after the change of regime in 2000. A record of pressure from the executive on the judicial authorities, from ordering verdicts to altering personnel, left a deep effect. The material situation of the courts was also difficult, as their budgets for office and trial space, investigation, and salaries of judges and other officials remained below levels in other parts of government. For capable attorneys, the financial compensation for judicial work could not compete with the potential rewards of private practice.[34] Shortly after being named to preside over the Supreme Court of Serbia, Leposava Karamarković described the situation in an address to judges:

For decades in this country the principle of utilitarianism (*svrsishodnost*) dominated instead of the principle of legality, and it reached its shameful height during the previous regime. Legal pragmatism occupied the place of the legal system. In pursuing its goals, the oligarchy did not want its hands to be tied by formal or abstract rules or norms. So it expressed contempt for the law and for legal form, and recognized it only to the extent that it was useful.

That led to the worst possible consequence for the legal system of any country—the legal system collapsed, fell apart, and life went on in spite of it and outside it. And so a schizophrenic reality developed in which everybody was (declaratively) in favor of legality, while everybody knew that real life was in another category, in which interests are realized, and while the existing legal system simply postulated some idealistic and unattainable relationships.

The masters of manipulation brought fear into the courtroom, ordering up not only trials but sentences as well. Judges were reduced to minimal pay and a humiliating position, probably because it was believed that it is easier to direct and rule poor people without interference.

Few judges in the legal system managed to remain upright and oppose such methods, and when somebody did, and suffered because of it, and eventually lost their job, most other judges remained silent and acted as if it was not their problem. That indicates that some of the responsibility for their current state is borne by the judges themselves, who did not react when in the dissolution of Yugoslavia cities were destroyed, people were killed and shocking ethnic cleansing was carried out.

If more judges had resisted the influence and demands of the executive branch, the results might have been different.[35]

Even given the best of wills there existed considerable obstacles—tasks of extensive reform, replacement of personnel, and internal accounts of responsibility—before courts could take on the obligations of a credible and independent judiciary. Branislav Tapušković, president of the Society of Lawyers of Serbia, offered a pessimistic prognosis in 2001: "I am very familiar with the situation in the judiciary, I know how many people there are who have already violated many principles, and who do not deserve to be in the judiciary, but who is going to replace them? It takes at least a decade to make a good judge, and I simply cannot see how it is possible to get out of this vicious circle."[36] The challenge was further complicated by the uncertain political situation: reconstructing the judiciary depended not only on the extent of the damage done by the old regime, but also on the uncertain intentions of the new one.

An early illustration of institutional competition and confusion is provided by the law federal president Vojislav Koštunica proposed in 2001 to regulate the cooperation of the Yugoslav government with ICTY. The law was intended as an alternative to direct adoption of the ICTY statute, the course eventually taken; it would have guaranteed the involvement of domestic courts in actions against people indicted by ICTY, and provided greater guarantees of the rights of indicted suspects.[37] Facing an unsuccessful vote, the government withdrew the law from parliament and adopted it instead as a decree. Milošević's lawyers appealed to the Federal Constitutional Court for a ruling finding the decree unconstitutional, and on 28 June received a suspension of the decree pending a ruling. The republican government of Serbia acted quickly to circumvent judicial delay by adopting the ICTY statute, which requires suspects to be delivered to the tribunal, as domestic law.[38] Milošević was immediately afterward transferred to ICTY, leading to a debate (which divided the governing parties) over the legality of the act. But the legality of the constitutional court's action was also unclear.

Shortly after the protracted legal conflict, Omer Karabeg's radio program *Most* featured an exchange on the topic between Dragor Hiber, chair of the judiciary committee of the Serbian parliament, and Slobodan Samardžić, a political scientist and advisor to Koštunica. Hiber contested the court's action:

The session of the Federal Constitutional Court held on 28 June was called by the presiding judge of that court, or a person who represented himself as such, a judge of the court, Dr. Milutin Srdić, whose term on the court ended by law two weeks earlier. When that fact became public, Srdić said, well, because the court was in need he would stay in office a bit longer, but would go into retirement anyway to maintain legality. That day he established that his term of office had ended, and so the session was called, the quicker the better, by the oldest, that is the most senior, member of the court. So two things are possible.

The first is that the Federal Constitutional Court did not know who was or was not a member of the court, which means that it was not in a condition to apply the constitution to the question of its own composition. If it cannot do that, how can it apply the constitution to any other question. The other possibility is that the court knew, but nonetheless permitted its session to be called by a self-declared presiding judge. If that is the case, then it is no longer a constitutional court, but a group of citizens with suspicious intentions.[39]

Samardžić disagreed with Hiber's dismissal of the court's intervention, but nonetheless agreed that the credibility and legitimacy of judicial institutions were not clear. He argued:

To begin with, the fact is that from 5 October until now the constitutional court has not been reformed. That means that the political forces which govern this country have made a very sensitive omission. That has to be done as soon as possible, if we want to create a new legal system. The constitution is another matter. Serbia is stuck there, because in order to change its own constitution it has to wait for a new federal constitution, and that is not being created for reasons which are familiar to everybody.[40]

The issue whether the Federal Constitutional Court or the Serbian government acted legally is bound to remain controversial. Regardless of this specific issue, the incident demonstrates that the new authorities in Serbia faced a situation in which the legitimacy of legal institutions and even basic legal documents remained open to debate. This offered at best an unstable framework for extensive engagement on the part of judicial institutions.

The capacity for domestic prosecution was enhanced after 2000, when the last of the wartime regimes left power. Vladimir Vukčević became the first special prosecutor for war crimes in Serbia in 2003. Bosnia-Herzegovina's War Crimes Chamber was established in December 2004 and began work in March 2005. While the Croatian parliament had made a declaration on the legitimacy of the state's military efforts in 2000,[41] in response to pressure from the European Union special war crimes chambers were designated and the first cases began to be referred to them in 2005.

Throughout the region credible domestic prosecution started slowly. Early prosecutions in Croatia had been widely perceived as being selective.[42]

With the establishment of special chambers major cases began to be tried on a larger scale by domestic legal institutions, with a shift away from a balance that favored prosecutions of Croatian Serbs for violations committed as members of rebellious paramilitary forces, and an increasing number of cases involving violations by Croat forces against civilians. The periodic OSCE report raised concern about systematic bias as late as 2006.[43] But dramatic instances of impunity in Croatia, including the longstanding untouchable status of such former paramilitary commanders as Tomislav Merčep and Branimir Glavaš, began to be aggressively addressed following the accession of Ivo Josipović to the presidency in 2010.[44] Nonetheless, concern remains that many cases that could be referred to the specialized war crimes chamber remain instead in the regular courts.

The special chamber for war crimes was established in Bosnia-Herzegovina in 2005, and 122 cases had begun to be heard by 2009.[45] The number of cases hardly corresponds, and probably never can do so, to the number of people who could potentially be charged with offences. Some barriers to prosecution were imposed by basic political structures like the Dayton Peace Agreement, while there are also persistent issues of jurisdiction arising from the simultaneous operation of three different judicial systems, as well as from ongoing confusion as to whether the applicable law derives from the Criminal Code of Yugoslavia, which was in force at the time of the conflict, or from the Criminal Code of Bosnia-Herzegovina, which addresses issues of war crimes in greater detail but did not come into force until 2003.[46]

Serbia faces both a large number of cases and large challenges to prosecuting them. Some of the most prominent war crimes prosecutions since 2000 have involved the members of the "Scorpions" paramilitary group, members of which were convicted and sentenced in 2005 for a massacre of ethnic Albanian civilians in Podujevo, and in 2007 for participation in the Srebrenica genocide.[47] The Scorpions cases crucially involve the role of military and state security services in the supply, organization and command of paramilitary forces—an issue highlighted by nongovernmental advocacy groups that participated in the cases. Efforts to try the perpetrators of the Ovčara massacre near Vukovar in 1991 failed. A conviction with harsh sentences was rendered in 2005, though this was subsequently overturned. The last word in the case was thereby forfeited by Serbian courts and fell to ICTY, which convicted two of the main suspects in the massacre and released a third.[48]

The regime that left power in Serbia in 2000 also left behind a number of cases of domestic political violence. Here too the record is mixed. During the investigation of the murder of prime minister Zoran Djindjić in 2003, the 2000 murder of former president Ivan Stambolić was also solved and convictions were rendered in both cases. However, other cases remain unresolved: the attempted murder in 2000 of politician Vuk Drašković has resulted in several convictions all of which have been reversed on appeal, while nobody has been charged in the 1999 murder of newspaper editor Slavko Ćuruvija. Suspicion remains that other unsolved killings, like that of journalist Radoslava (Dada) Vujasinović in 1994, can also be traced to regime-related forces, but these cases remain unprosecuted.

The close association between crimes committed in the course of the conduct of war and nearly all other types of major crime in the region has highlighted the persistent need for cross-border cooperation in prosecution and law enforcement. In 2009 two cases from Croatia made this need apparent and indicated some of the ways in which progress has been made. Serbian police arrested Sreten Jocić ("Joca Amsterdam"), the chief suspect in the murder of Croatian journalist Ivo Pukanić and his employee Niko Franjić, acting on information shared by Croatian police. The trial of Jocić was conducted jointly by Serbian and Croatian courts.[49] Around the same time the Croatian politician and former paramilitary commander Branimir Glavaš was convicted of war-related murders and attempted to escape sentencing by fleeing to neighboring Bosnia-Herzegovina. At Croatia's request he was quickly arrested by Bosnian police and prosecutors began to request his extradition.[50] The prospect of cross-border trials could help resolve issues of witness protection by allowing for testimony to be given remotely, but it is faced with legal obstacles, among them high barriers to extradition.[51]

That the record of domestic prosecution should be mixed is hardly surprising. Domestic institutions—some new and untested and some old and burdened by legacies of subordination and complicity—took on a set of extraordinarily complex and politically sensitive issues, and did so in an atmosphere of diminished trust in institutions, political instability, uncertain access to evidence, lack of clear jurisdiction, and frequently hostile public sentiment. They confronted this set of problems while simultaneously building institutional capacity and the capacity to coordinate with their colleagues in states that were until recently unfriendly. Despite some disappointments and reversals along the way, the most important precedent being set by domestic legal institutions may be the fact that precedents are being set at all.

The problems faced by domestic legal institutions are not insurmountable, and indeed they will have to be overcome—any comprehensive approach to war crimes and crimes against humanity requires that domestic courts be extensively involved. There is no shortage of statements from government spokespeople that they regard the competence of domestic courts, not only as a matter of national pride, but also as a sign of the extent to which they have succeeded in enabling judicial institutions and rehabilitating the reputation of the state. Considering that a large segment of public opinion not only regards ICTY as a biased and imperially imposed institution, but also suspects the post-Milošević government of being beholden to this imposition, there exists ample political motivation for much more intensive involvement on the part of the Serbian judiciary. The experience so far, however, also suggests that skepticism about the ability of the Serbian judiciary to meet the challenge is well founded.

Critical Observations About ICTY

As Max Weber observed,[52] bureaucracies once founded tend to take on a life and logic of their own. This may be the case with ICTY, particularly considering some of the early euphoria among human rights activists for the principle of international jurisdiction it has come to represent, and some of the subsequent disappointment at less than triumphal outcomes. One of the reasons for the establishment of ICTY was the clearly visible failure of domestic courts to try offenders in more than a symbolic manner. But if we are looking for reasons to explain why ICTY survived, and managed to shift from a long period of relative inactivity and failure to success in receiving custody of the world's best known indictee—then in some interpretations back to failure in some lengthy, unresolved cases—these reasons should probably be sought outside the former Yugoslavia. Founded through compromise, hampered by faults of design, and unevenly supported by the states that influence it most, ICTY has made meaningful history both through its successes and failures while remaining a touchstone for dispute in the region.

Among the dramatic advances attributable to ICTY has to be counted its contribution toward demolishing the doctrine of sovereign immunity whereby high-ranking political and military officials have traditionally enjoyed exemption from prosecution. In addition to Milošević, the Tribunal has tried top-level government leaders such as former Serbian president Milan Milutinović, who was acquitted on the ground that he did not exercise command, and former Kosovo prime minister Ramush Haradinaj, who was acquitted amid suspicions of extensive tampering (the case was subsequently reopened). Milošević, of course, died in custody before his trial was completed. Some high-ranking military commanders have been convicted, including Rasim Delić,[53] Dragoljub Ojdanić,[54] and Nebojša Pavković[55] (Sefer Halilović was acquitted,[56] and Janko Bobetko never faced trial).[57]

Regardless how the prosecutions themselves might be evaluated—this will remain a topic of dispute—the greatest significance of some ICTY cases may derive from the fact that they reached trial at all. Although the Milošević case remained unresolved, it set a precedent for the reach of legal responsibility. More uncertainty remains in the cases of both former Bosnia-Herzegovina president Alija Izetbegović and former Croatian president Franjo Tudjman, where there were only general statements after their deaths that they would have been charged had they survived. Other heads of state brought before ICTY were either not real heads of state (like Milan Milutinović) or not heads of real states (like Milan Babić, Goran Hadžić, and Radovan Karadžić). Nonetheless the fact that some heads of state were tried at all represents a major defeat for the doctrine of sovereign immunity.[58]

The euphoria that greeted some of ICTY's major precedents stands in stark contrast to low expectations nearer the time of the Tribunal's founding. It is not clear whether ICTY was ever intended to function as an institution. The legislative history of the founding of the Tribunal suggests that it was a compromise response to evidence that violations were being committed—more than doing nothing, but far short of aggressive intervention. There is also some anecdotal evidence suggesting that international policy makers deliberately ignored and blocked the work of ICTY, considering it a distraction from the work of making agreements with the very people most likely to be charged.[59] Richard Goldstone, the South African jurist who was the first prosecutor of ICTY, describes the atmosphere at the time of his arrival:

When I arrived in The Hague on August 15, 1994, to take up office as chief prosecutor of the International Criminal Tribunal for the Former Yugoslavia, it had effectively been written off as a lost cause.

The tribunal had been established by the UN Security Council 15 months earlier, yet investigations into war crimes had not begun. The judges, who had been appointed almost a year before, were frustrated and openly talked of resigning. The United Nations was facing its worst-ever financial crisis and staffing a new sub-organ of the Security Council was a big problem. The whole idea that Balkan leaders then pursuing genocidal wars would actually end up in the dock was, in many quarters, dismissed as fantasy.[60]

Gary Bass describes Resolution 827 as "an act of tokenism by the world community, which was largely unwilling to intervene in the ex-Yugoslavia but did not mind creating an institution that would give the *appearance* of moral concern."[61] In its first years, ICTY issued a series of indictments against very low level figures, some of them evidentially thin. On succeeding Goldstone as chief prosecutor, Louise Arbour dropped seventeen of these indictments.[62]

The character and the international reputation of ICTY changed, not least because of the constant efforts on the part of a series of prosecutors to force governments to recognize the authority of the Tribunal, and to appeal to public opinion with news of arrests and indictments (although the introduction of "sealed indictments" by Arbour remains controversial). The decision to concentrate on high-ranking officials helped to overcome some of the credibility problems derived from early prosecutions against people who neither gave commands nor made policy. Perhaps the most dramatic sign of this shift was the issuance of an indictment against Milošević in 1999, making him the highest-ranking official to have been charged in an international court at the time.[63] This is despite the fact that both the timing (during a bombing campaign against Serbia by NATO) and the content (which dealt with a massacre in Kosovo about which there is factual dispute, while ignoring any violations from the wars in Croatia and Bosnia-Herzegovina) of the initial indictment were the subject of intense critique. During the course of 2001, the voluntary surrender of Biljana Plavšić and the delivery of Milošević to ICTY resulted in a much higher profile for the institution, although doubts remained about its ability to achieve its goals.

While most of the praise directed toward ICTY has derived from its dramatic setting of precedents, it has also attracted criticism for some per-ceived shortcomings. Broadly speaking criticisms of ICTY fall into three categories: (1) uneasy relationships between the Tribunal and the publics in the region, (2) difficulties in the conduct of trials and the treatment of evidence, and (3) political consequences of the Tribunal's activity and the effects of ICTY-related conditionality in the region.

Among the domestic publics of the former Yugoslavia, there is some resentment that the institution is externally imposed and operates outside the countries whose citizens it tries. The distant location of the Tribunal is compounded by the fact that no natives of the region act as judges, prosecutors, or registry officials. The only capacities in which a citizen of a state of the former Yugoslavia can appear before the Tribunal are as a defense attorney, a witness, or an indictee. Nor has communication been a priority of ICTY: its "Outreach" office was founded only six years after the founding of the Tribunal, in 1999. Its activity has been largely confined to providing information to journalists and members of the legal profession rather than communicating with the public in a more unmediated fashion. Both knowledge about ICTY and measures of trust in it have been consistently low throughout the region.[64]

The disputed legitimacy of the Tribunal has led to situations in which established courtroom procedure has been followed with only the greatest difficulty. An important precedent was set by Milošević at the beginning of his trial, when he rejected counsel and instead led his own defense. On the one hand, this probably had the consequence of strengthening the case against him, as he would inadvertently introduce evidence to which the prosecutors had not had access before.[65] However, it also enabled the defendant to use the proceedings to give speeches to the television cameras, to engage in long, irrelevant exchanges with witnesses, and to provoke extended delays. Vojislav Šešelj filled much of the Tribunal's time with similar but more antic behavior, most of it directed toward the media.

A more fundamental problem has involved ICTY's inability to protect witnesses. The first prosecution of Ramush Haradinaj failed largely due to intimidation of witnesses.[66] Partly because of ICTY's limited capacity to protect witnesses and control the activity in its trial chambers, it has been the site of very long trials conducted with frequent delay. Milošević waited nearly a year for his trial to commence after his arrest in 2001, and it was still incomplete at the time of his death in 2006; Šešelj was taken into Tribunal custody in February 2003 and his trial began in November 2007.

A more general source of criticism of ICTY has been its effect on politics in the region. In some ways the conditionality of "cooperation with ICTY" for issues such as EU accession and access to financial assistance empties the justice processes of meaning. Rather than confronting the past, states are expected to meet the far more minimal requirement of delivering individuals to the Netherlands for trial. Sometimes this has led to cynical observations that accused criminals have less difficulty traveling to EU countries like the Netherlands than ordinary visa applicants. In some instances verdicts or sentences have led to controversy, raising the suggestion that though trials may establish a documentary record they do not necessarily lead to reconciliation—but by replaying conflicts encourage their revival.

The question whether ICTY is a biased institution has been raised repeatedly since its founding. Unfortunately, the point has been made from so many sides and at so many times for wholly propagandistic purposes that the genuine questions at stake are often obscured. Milošević referred to ICTY as a "concentration camp for Serbs" before he was arrested and sent there, and at his arraignment in July 2001 he rejected the legitimacy of the Tribunal, arguing that it has "the task of fabricating a false justification for war crimes committed by the NATO pact in Yugoslavia."[67] Others in Serbia have argued that ICTY is an institution established to defame Serbs (in Croatia, to defame Croats), that it is beholden to members of the NATO alliance, that its primary function is to exert pressure on former Yugoslav states while absolving other countries of responsibility, and so on.

As long as it remains the case—and it always will—that not every crime committed during the wars of succession in Yugoslavia is prosecuted, the charge of selectivity will have some resonance. While more individuals associated with Serb-commanded militaries and paramilitaries have been charged by ICTY, prosecutors appear comfortable with justifying this imbalance with reference to the larger number of crimes committed by these forces, a point on which there is not serious dispute. In the context of discussions over the indictment against Milošević, the then justice minister of Serbia, Vladan Batić, gave ICTY prosecutor Carla Del Ponte a letter requesting that she charge political leaders of other states that committed crimes in which Serbs were victims.[68] No such charges followed. The fact that Izetbegović and Tudjman were never charged, despite the prosecutor's declaration that the intention to charge them existed, remains a sticking point among critics of the Tribunal's objectivity. So does the fact that the Tribunal declined to pursue charges against NATO countries for attacks against civilian targets in 1999, and declared itself unable to investigate and prosecute charges related to accusations of organ harvesting involving officials of Kosovo and Albania.[69] Residual resentment at failures of this type interfere with the capacity of ICTY to be perceived as an honest arbiter of fact in the region.

Yet some of the strongest arguments regarding bias relate to prosecutions carried out not by ICTY, but by other authorities in the region. Earlier in the chapter some concern was discussed related to domestic prosecutions in Serbia and Croatia. A further set of complications arose from trials for violations of international humanitarian law in Kosovo, which were carried out by international courts under the supervision of the United Nations Mission in Kosovo (UNMIK). These courts performed considerably below the standard of ICTY in protecting the rights of the accused. For example, in June 2001 two people, Čedomir Jovanović and Andjelko Kolašinac,[70] were convicted for war crimes committed in Orahovac in 1999. The Fund for Humanitarian Law issued a protest, detailing that

> The accused were not given the right to use their native language. Their trial was conducted in English and Albanian, so that they did not have the opportunity to follow the progress of the investigation, contest evidence or to use evidence. The accused were not able to follow the statements and questioning of witnesses, because translation was not made available. Only the portions of the proceedings which were entered into the record were translated into Serbian, so that the accused could not find out what the judge did not enter into the record, or use it in their defense. . . . Jovanović and Kolašinac did not attend the discovery session which was held in Belgrade on 8 June. The evidence given in Belgrade was not presented in Prizren, so that the accused did not know what the evidence accused them of, and what parts of the evidence could be used in their defense.[71]

The statement added that evidence was improperly handled (the suspects' statements were read to witnesses), and also questioned the conduct of the presiding judge. Leaving aside the critique of this particular trial, it seems clear that when different judicial institutions are used to enforce international law, this may undermine legal requirements of equal treatment. Concerns of this type figured among the motivations for the establishment of the International Criminal Court (ICC), a permanent body with global jurisdiction that would replace the establishment of ad hoc tribunals with limited oversight. In practice, however, ICC cases have only been brought against participants in civil wars in Africa,[72] while ad hoc tribunals continued to be established.[73]

"Truth" Commissions

Consistent with a broad perception that judicial processes are bound to be unsatisfying and incomplete, and that a systematic approach to justice requires some nonlegal processes such as discussion of causes of conflict, sharing of testimony, and investigation of forms of responsibility that do not fall under categories of legal guilt (such as promotion of violence and intolerance in media), there have been several initiatives to promote the role of "truth commissions" in the region.[74] Of all the initiatives to create commissions in the region since 2000, only one—the Republika Srpska (RS) commission on Srebrenica—has resulted in an active body that produced a report. In Bosnia-Herzegovina three attempts to create a commission failed, while in Serbia an early initiative resulted in the appointment of a commission with a vague mandate that was immediately hit by resignations and carried on in a state of inactivity for two years before being disbanded. A regional initiative by nongovernmental organizations to found a joint commission has been active since 2008, but the outcome of this effort remains uncertain.

One of the critical points that has presented a constant obstacle to truth commissions has been the perception that they offer an unpalatable exchange of "truth" for "justice"—that is, they can tell more complete stories than judicial bodies, but at the expense of the opportunity to punish wrongdoing.[75] As a consequence many local initiatives have been dismissed as attempts to substitute low-cost symbolic activity for criminal prosecution. As Jasna Dragović-Soso summarizes the various initiatives in the region:

Why have these attempts to create truth commissions failed until now? There have been three principal stumbling blocks: a lack of genuine political will among power-holders in the region to engage constructively with processes of confronting the recent past; a complicated relationship with international actors, including the ICTY, which have shaped domestic processes in ways that have not always been conducive to quests for "truth and reconciliation"; and a deep and still enduring problem of divisive and fragmented visions of the recent past throughout the former Yugoslavia, encountered not only on an inter-ethnic level but even within civil societies of the same national group.[76]

The regional REKOM initiative to mobilize popular support for a nonstate commission may yet change the equation,[77] but for the time being most initiatives have failed due to a combination of institutional obstacles, bad faith, and popular skepticism.

Discussion about the creation of truth commissions already began during the war in Bosnia-Herzegovina, and was concurrent with debates over the founding of ICTY. A "side-letter" to the 1995 Dayton Peace Agreement obligates the parties to establish "an international commission of inquiry into the recent conflict in the former Yugoslavia. This will include participation by the governments of the states involved, as well as distinguished international experts to be named by agreement among the Republics of former Yugoslavia. The Commission's mandate will be to conduct fact-finding and other necessary studies into the causes, conduct, and consequences of the recent conflict on as broad and objective a basis as possible, and to issue a report thereon, to be made available to all interested countries and organizations."[78] But no such commission was ever established.

Repeated initiatives to establish a commission in Bosnia-Herzegovina, some of them originating with civil society, some with international actors and some with political parties, proved unsuccessful, as victims' associations objected and the extensive involvement of nondomestic organizations like the United States Institute for Peace (USIP) tended to discredit the enterprise.[79] Locally initiated efforts in Bosnia-Herzegovina were further restricted by the Dayton Peace Agreement, which provides a limited amnesty covering many offenses related to the conflict (but excluding offences falling under the mandate of ICTY).[80]

The only commission to have produced a report—hence plausibly the only successful commission—was the Srebrenica commission appointed by the parliament of Republika Srpska in 2003. This initiative did not come about voluntarily, however. Its founding was ordered by the Bosnia-Herzegovina Human Rights Chamber—RS appealed but backed down when high representative Jeremy Ashdown intervened. Despite repeated attempts at obstruction the commission produced a report in June 2004. It was a meaningful report: it detailed the locations of burial sites, provided information about people missing since 1995, and documented the planning of the killings and collusion of RS civilian and military institutions.[81] In October the report was followed by a parliamentary resolution recognizing the crimes and in November the RS government issued an apology to the families of the victims.[82] In succeeding years, as Srebrenica continued to be a point of contention in regional politics, RS politicians occasionally backed away from the commission report. A later initiative by the RS government to compel the founding of a corresponding commission to investigate abuses against Serbs in Sarajevo was abandoned after a long stalemate. Given the failure of initiatives for a broadly based commission and the collapse of the Sarajevo commission, the Srebrenica commission may remain the only completed initiative in the region unless the REKOM campaign succeeds.

Similarly, in Serbia an early postregime effort at establishing a commission ended in failure. Federal president Koštunica ordered the creation of the Truth and Reconciliation Commission in March 2001,[83] meeting an unenthusiastic response both from international governments and from Serbian prime minister Zoran Djindjić, who saw the initiative as an obstacle to his efforts to reconstruct relations with Western governments. With weak domestic and international support, the commission faced an uphill and ultimately unsuccessful struggle in acquiring even such necessities as a budget adequate for its operations or office space.[84] The initiative met criticism from the outset, due to both the manner of its founding without consultation and the makeup of its membership. There was also suspicion regarding Koštunica's motivation in forming the commission—was it meant to make a contribution to public memory or to displace the work of ICTY? Suspicions toward the commission appeared to be confirmed almost immediately following its creation, when law professor Vojin Dimitrijević and historian Latinka Perović, two prominent antinationalist intellectuals, resigned from it, publicly expressing their deep skepticism toward the whole endeavor.[85] Uncertainly conceived and lacking support from all sides, the Serbian commission faded away leaving no transcripts and producing no report.

Is it possible to draw any conclusions on the basis of the experience of judicial and extrajudicial mechanisms for addressing questions of guilt so far? Certainly the record has been mixed. The mixed character of the record may tend to draw attention away from some successes of judicial institutions in apprehending and trying perpetrators, raising awareness and setting standards for human rights, creating a documentary record of crimes committed, and enhancing the capacity of domestic institutions. It does seem clear, however, that some of the more ambitious social and moral goals associated with legal initiatives have proved elusive. The repeated false starts of "truth-seeking" initiatives underscore the point that it is easier to approach the past procedurally than substantively. Memories of the past remain disputed, and transitional justice initiatives have not bridged those cognitive divisions. In this regard it could be said that legal "truth" has not contributed to social "reconciliation."

Several factors have interfered with the goals of reconciliation. In the first place, political elites in the region have for the most part participated in transitional justice unwillingly, seeking to do the minimum necessary to satisfy internationally imposed conditions without doing so much that they alienate more nationalistic segments of public opinion. Second, the institutions of civil society have not been united, either in terms of their goals or in terms of the means for achieving them. Similarly, judicial institutions have been inconsistent. Domestic ones have not emerged completely from the legacy of subordination to political institutions, while international ones operate with a degree of distance and opacity that affords them little genuine authority in the region. Generally, domestic elites and institutions do not appear to be entirely prepared to embark upon the major work required to "confront the past," while international actors often appear to have only a superficial interest in the question, reducing the sociocultural work of reconciliation to a series of concrete targets, like the delivery of suspects, without considering the multiple meanings of their initiatives in the public arena.

It is possible that the contribution of criminal trials is limited to a narrowly defined field. The demand to "confront" the past takes the shape of law and politics but involves far broader social and cultural processes. The role of the state is essential, but the state is better at generating compliance than at producing contributions of substance. It is in the cultural process of understanding that versions of the past will be elaborated and compete with one another. These versions are being produced, both in public discussion and in creative cultural activity. But they receive little official or international attention because they do not result in reports or convictions. While a new understanding of the recent past might emerge from cultural discourses, it is probably not surprising that a few years after the end of the last armed conflict it has not yet emerged. The legal and political initiatives of the last several years have helped offer a necessary if incomplete contribution to the development of new discourses. But to see those discourses taking shape, it is necessary to shift attention away from the courtroom, and toward ongoing events and perceptions.

Chapter 5

Moment II: The Djindjić Murder, from Outrage to Confusion

Never popular among the public and despised by the nationalist right and the remnants of the Milošević regime, Serbian prime minister Zoran Djindjić became the object of a sustained smear campaign after he ordered the transfer of Slobodan Milošević to ICTY. It became common to find him described in the press as a traitor, together with accusations that he collaborated with international intelligence services and criminal organizations. For his part Djindjić ignored his detractors, claiming, "I did not take this position in order to be popular. I came here to complete a historical task, to bring order to Serbia, and the first one to bring order is never popular."[1]

He also ignored threats on his own life. On 21 February 2003 an assassination attempt failed.[2] The conspirators planned to block the highway where Djindjić's car and its security escort were traveling to the Belgrade airport, then attack the automobiles with hand-held rocket launchers before completing the job using machine guns. The attack fell apart in its first stage: the truck driver Dejan Milenković succeeded in blocking the highway, but Djindjić's driver and the driver of the first security car reacted quickly, steering onto the embankment then hurrying onward to the airport. The guards in the second security car blocked Milenković's escape and apprehended him. The armed attackers saw that Milenković had failed and escaped. Following a series of failures by police and security services, through which Milenković was able to spirit away evidence of the attempted assassination (including three mobile telephones used for coordination), Milenković was charged with minor traffic offenses and released three days later: he then disappeared and was not heard of again until his arrest in July 2004.[3]

For his part, Djindjić was satisfied with the police fiction that Milen-ković was a bad driver, and downplayed the incident with a joke. He told reporters, "I think it was a careless driver who was learning to drive on the highway, and since we are an impulsive people, people will often create problems for themselves, so this person, instead of practicing driving in his own yard, did it on the highway. I think it would be an exaggeration to say he was threatening my security. These are normal situations in life, we are a Mediterranean country where people are a little more relaxed, and that has its good and bad sides."[4] The dismissal began to appear improbable when information about Milenković began to reach the public. Nicknamed "Bugsy," he had passed from the service of organized crime figure Ljubiša Buha (Čume) into the competing criminal group led by Milorad Ulemek (Legija) and Dušan Spasojević (Duća).[5] These names were all well known to the public because of the association of Ulemek and Spasojević with the State Security-commanded Unit for Special Operations (Jedinica za speci-jalne operacije—JSO, also the "Red Berets")[6] and because a major action against organized crime groups was underway. Already on 22 February, journalist Jovan Dulović was pointing out the low probability that a person with just those associations would happen to block the road.[7] Djindjić responded by dismissing the importance of the event even if it were an attack: "If somebody thinks they can prevent the law from being carried out by removing me, then they are deceiving themselves, because I am not the system. The system will continue to function and nobody will get amnesty by getting rid of one or two state officials."[8]

In fact there was a group that thought precisely that. Operation "Wit-ness" was meant to commence a full-scale assault on organized crime, strengthened by the introduction of a protected witnesses regime. The lead-ing protected witness was to be Ljubiša Buha-Čume, who was already offer-ing dramatic statements to the press to raise expectations about what he might reveal. Djindjić's political opponents sought to discredit the action in advance, claiming that the targets were mistaken and that Djindjić, rather than sincerely intending to confront organized crime, had simply chosen sides in a conflict between two criminal groups. The more powerful of the groups, the "Zemun clan," had two arguments that its members thought might be appealing to the public: some of their members took credit for helping to bring about a peaceful transfer of power in 2000 by abandoning Miloševic,[9] and others were identified with an attitude of resistance toward ICTY. And they had one status that seemed to offer them political prestige:

a leader of the "Zemun clan" was Milorad Ulemek-Legija, who had recently been removed as commander of JSO, and JSO was promoting itself around Serbia as a line of defense against terrorism and other threats.[10]

January and February 2003 saw an exchange of statements to the press between Čume and Legija. Čume offered a statement promising to reveal the involvement of JSO in several unsolved crimes, including the attempted murder of politician Vuk Drašković in 2000, the kidnapping (then not yet known to be a murder) of politician Ivan Stambolić in 2000, and the kidnapping of businessman Miroslav Mišković in 2001.[11] Legija responded in an open letter, tying the accusations against him and his associates to ICTY and the influence of Western countries over Djindjić's government. The letter draws a connection between Čume's charges regarding his (ordinary) criminal activities, the failure of the government to shield him, and accusations (which had not then been made) of crimes that could be prosecuted by ICTY:

> Instead of calculating and telling everybody clearly on 8 October 2000 [the first full workday of the post-Milošević government] what the price, counted out in human heads to be delivered to the Hague Tribunal, of our joining into the integrations of the modern world would be, they turned to their narrow political interests and frictions, revealing in the worst possible way their true nature. . . . And it immediately became clear to their global mentors that instead of equal political partners they had before them political servants who constantly retreat to new levels of humiliation. . . .
>
> It is a pathetic country and the police in it if their cases have to be resolved by the testimony of Ljubiša Buha Čume. Even sadder is the fact that such people are used to shame and discredit others, people who care very deeply indeed for this country and its people and have demonstrated it countless times.
>
> I cannot but imagine that all this is the work of the same people, to whom nothing is sacred and who do not care a bit for anything that is Serbian! Not even for those who bled and whose dead bodies were spread across the battlefields and of whom all that remains is a modest memorial on a faded photograph in the room dedicated to our heroes in Kula [the JSO base]. If you cannot and will not respect the former or the current commanders, at least respect the dead ones! Nobody, not even history, will forgive you. Even less so

the people you are trying to win over, completely unnecessarily, in this way. You should know, every nation respects its soldiers.[12]

The effort by Legija to associate his group with patriotic feelings and to accuse the government of lacking them was not coincidental. Between 9 and 17 November 2001, JSO, with operational assistance from the Zemun clan, staged a rebellion at their base in Kula during which they blocked a highway leading to Belgrade. The immediate pretext for the protest was the arrest of Predrag and Nenad Banović on an ICTY arrest warrant.[13] The Banović brothers had been members of a paramilitary group under the control of JSO, and cases such as these contributed to fear among JSO members that they could be charged and prosecuted as well.[14] The JSO members demanded passage of a law regulating cooperation with ICTY and replacement of high-ranking officials in the Interior Ministry and State Security service. The rebellion ended with most of the demands granted and a guarantee that JSO would not be ordered to participate in law enforcement but would become a special antiterrorist unit under direct control of the Serbian government rather than the Interior Ministry. Soon afterward most of the Zemun clan members held on various charges were also released.

The 2001 rebellion taught the "Zemun clan" and JSO several lessons: (1) that the government was likely to tolerate rebellions by armed forces over which it did not exercise secure control; (2) that patriotic rhetoric derived from the recent war continued to offer a public cover for criminal activity not related to any current military or political goals; (3) that the group had political supporters willing to declare their support—including the federal president Vojislav Koštunica;[15] and (4) that the group had political opponents unwilling to protect them—chief among them Prime Minister Djindjić. In short, they found that they could make use of sympathy for existing and potential ICTY indictees, and that whether the issue was organized crime or war crimes, they had easily identifiable political allies and enemies.

When Djindjić's government began to escalate the fight against organized crime in late 2002,[16] the campaign to portray Djindjić as a traitor who was himself a criminal also escalated. By early 2003, media close to the "Zemun clan" joined in, as did Koštunica's advisor Aleksandar Tijanić. On 1 February Tijanić predicted in his column in the paper *Nacional*, "If Zoran Djindjić survives, Serbia will not."[17] On 23 February, Tomislav Nikolić, vice president of the Serbian Radical Party, addressed a farewell rally for the party president Vojislav Šešelj who was leaving to face charges at ICTY; referring to a sports injury Djindjić had received not long before he offered a darkly prophetic joke, noting, "Tito also had problems with his leg before he died."[18] What conspirators knew, but Djindjić and media audiences did not know, was that a plan was under way that was intended to put an end to both state action against organized crime and cooperation with ICTY.[19]

"Stop the Hague": The March 2003 Conspiracy

According to the first indictment filed against suspects in the murder of Djindjić,[20] forty-four people engaged in "terrorism" and "conspiracy to commit enemy action" in a project with a specific goal:[21] "The goal of organizing this criminal group was to commit illegal acts, including automobile theft, grand theft, extortion, kidnapping, murder, illegal trade in narcotics, and other criminal acts."[22] In developing the plan the members of the group "had completely regulated 'connections' with various personalities from state institutions, the police, the judiciary, the prosecutors' office, the Security Information Agency [BIA], with the president of the Serbian Radical Party Vojislav Šešelj, with military security commander General Aco Tomić, and with the entire command of the Unit for Special Operations [JSO] which was, in fact, under their strong influence, that is under their command."[23]

The conspiracy had political allies and a political character, according to the indictment: "In order to accomplish their terrorist-criminal interests described above, they aligned themselves with quasipatriotic interests, the so-called patriotic or anti-Hague political bloc in Serbia. The concrete decision, according to information currently available, to carry out the killing was made by [Dušan] Spasojević and [Milorad Ulemek] Legija. Legija named the terrorist plan 'Stop the Hague.'"[24] Additional details of the conspiracy, published in the media in the days following the murder, indicated that the conspirators intended not simply to remove Djindjić, but to take over the government. As the plan was described, "The following day, their intention was that the capital city should be massively covered with posters carrying the message 'Stop the Hague'; that rumors should be released claiming that Djindjić was killed because of his criminal connections; that the government should be portrayed as a group of traitors with criminal connections."[25] Following that:

> On the third day after the murder several more members of the government were to be killed as well as some other prominent politicians, in order to provoke panic and then as saviors and forces of order would appear the formations of JSO. On the political front an idea would be proposed for the formation of some kind of "unity government" (its membership is not specified). At the same time several second-rank leaders of criminal groups would be liquidated and thereby the impression would be created that crime has been eliminated quickly and efficiently, with the message that Djindjić's government could have done the same had it wanted to do so.[26]

The descriptions of the conspiracy offered above are derived from what police and prosecutors offered to a restricted press during the state of emergency immediately after the killing. While the extent of the conspiracy that prosecutors were later able to prove was less than what the initial charges outline, the fundamental elements remain clear: the conspiracy involved close cooperation between organized crime groups and political forces close to the Milošević regime, it involved an attempt to take political power, and it counted on opposition to ICTY for its rhetorical force.

The Murder and Its Aftermath

The murder went according to plan, but the remainder of the conspiracy did not. On 12 March 2003, at about 12:25 in the afternoon, Djindjić was exiting his car to attend meetings, one with the Council Against Corruption at 1:00 and another with Swedish diplomats at 3:30,[27] at the side entrance to the government offices in central Belgrade. JSO Colonel Zvezdan Jovanović, from the window of a building nearby, fired a Heckler and Koch G3 sniper rifle, killing Djindjić immediately and injuring Djindjić's bodyguard Milan Veruović. Though Djindjić was certainly already dead he was rushed for medical treatment, and doctors confirmed his death at 1:30. Deputy premier Nebojša Čović informed journalists at 3:45 that the prime minister had been killed.

The murder was not followed by additional killings, "Stop the Hague" posters, or a "unity government."[28] Instead, acting president of Serbia

Nataša Mićić[29] declared a state of emergency,[30] closed the Belgrade airport, stepped up control of border crossings and road traffic in and out of Belgrade, and announced the beginning of a large-scale criminal investigation. Meanwhile the conspirators burned the Volkswagen Passat they had used to reach the scene of the crime and buried the sniper rifle that had been used to kill Djindjić. They scattered themselves to hiding places throughout the city, and a few hours later an arrest warrant was issued naming the members of the "Zemun clan."

"Operation Sabre": The State of Emergency

Within days of the declaration of the state of emergency, leading members of the "Zemun clan" were arrested, and some who accepted witness protection began to provide details leading to the resolution of cases that had remained open for some time. On 23 March police found an armored Audi A8 filled with rocket launchers and infantry equipment, and quickly established that this was the "car of death" that had been used in a number of drive-by killings over the preceding years. On 25 March new premier Zoran Živković announced that police had identified Zvezdan Jovanović as Djindjić's killer and that he had been arrested the previous day. The same day JSO was disbanded and its functions returned to the oversight of the Interior Ministry. On 27 March police failed to arrest "Zemun clan" leaders Dušan Spasojević and Mile Luković, killing them in the operation instead (Milorad Ulemek evaded arrest for another fourteen months).[31] The arrest of Ulemek's bodyguard Nenad Šare at the end of March proved more useful to police: he confirmed the involvement of Ulemek and JSO in the kidnapping and murder of former Serbian president Ivan Stambolić and the attempted murder of opposition politician Vuk Drašković in Budva in 2000.[32]

The Interior Ministry released a statement as the state of emergency continued confirming that: "As this investigation goes on, police receive new information every day that clearly demonstrates that the murder of the prime minister of Serbia was part of a conspiracy comprised of the so-called patriotic forces led by war criminals, war profiteers, the patrons and inspirers of a policy of crime from the ranks of the parties of the regime of Slobodan Milošević."[33] The statement continued: "Those false patriots, in cooperation with criminal bands, above all the Zemun band, in the name of the couple Milošević-Marković, but also to meet the needs of [Mirjana

Marković's political party] JUL, [Milošević's political party] SPS and [Šešelj's political party] SRS, killed political opponents and people who disagreed with them, beat members of opposition parties and abused citizens who stood against them."[34] As the state of emergency continued, the connection between crimes deriving from state policy and ordinary crimes was illustrated through the narcotics trade. A protected witness offered testimony at the Milošević trial that Serbian State Security had organized in 1993 a "special operation" to transport large quantities of heroin to Croatia, presumably to depress morale by increasing the rate of addiction.[35] And in Serbia, with supply and distribution networks disrupted by police action against organized crime, a rising wave of local addicts sought treatment for withdrawal symptoms.[36] Acting president Nataša Mićić described the activity of the crime groups as "selling drugs to our children, and using the money from that for political activity, killings, and hiding from the Hague."[37]

Some mild effort went into separating the Hague pretext from the criminal context. While Zvezdan Jovanović confessed to the killing,[38] he sought to defend his motives:

> he said that he had killed the premier out of conviction and not for money and that he does not regret the crime, that he did it on the order of Legija who had told him that all [the JSO members] would be extradited to the Hague, that JSO would be disbanded, and that the killing of the premier is supported by some high-ranking people in the Interior Ministry and some politicians. He said that he did not know that criminals were involved in the crime, and that as a patriot he regrets only that.[39]

Even if it could be believed that the connections between JSO and the "Zemun clan" were unknown to the members of JSO, there remained the connection between the murder conspiracy and the previous regime. The human rights lawyer Vojin Dimitrijević formulated the link to reporters as, "This is not just an attempt by gangsters to take power: this is an attempt by gangsters to get the kind of state that suits them best, like the one that they had until 5 October 2000."[40] The association was strengthened by the revelation of another element of the conspiracy: the killers planned after taking power to return Milošević's director of state television, Dragoljub Milanović, to his previous job.[41]

Initial responses to the state of emergency and police action indicated both relief that action was being taken and suspicions as to the continued power of the previous regime. The weekly news magazine *Vreme* argued in an editorial:

> The killing of prime minister Djindjić, the leader of this country, leaves us with the feeling that we are hostages of dark forces that do not even bother to hide themselves much. The murder of the premier was already attempted once, which he did not take too seriously, but what is worse than that is that it was not taken seriously by the people whose job was to protect him. And when that attempted murderer was caught, then released and disappeared, the proper conclusion was that the people in power in Serbia are not the ones we see, but a criminal-political underground that has the strongest influence on the police, prosecutors, and courts.[42]

Cultural figures, including ones not associated with Djindjić's politics, joined in the call for a confrontation with the "criminal-political underground." The poet Ljubomir Simović told political parties, "If they do not do this then they do not even have a reason to exist."[43] The novelist Milorad Pavić listed a number of political killings in Serbia's history and observed, "The killers have always had the same goal: to prevent the opening of Serbia to Europe and the world."[44] Some commentators were explicit in identifying the moment of opportunity and necessity that had arisen from the murder. Writing in the semiofficial *Politika*, Ivan Torov demanded: "That they finally, without hesitation and calculation, reveal that machinery of evil, that powerful symbiosis—created and nurtured since 1990—of politics, public and secret police, criminals, war criminals, profiteers, and thieves. In short the humiliation and destruction of Serbia, all under the pretext of 'patriotism' and 'defense of national honor.'"[45] Writing in the liberal *Danas*, Miloš Minić was more categorical still:

> The regime that was born on 5 October 2000 neither wanted nor dared to arrest those killers. Among other reasons this is because into the front lines of the regime broke some people who had assisted the leaders of Bosnian and Croatian Serbs during the war to put "all Serbs in one state," in a "Greater Serbia." The regime never found the will, readiness or courage to break with that past.

Only Zoran Djindjić had the courage to send Milošević to the Hague. That is why they killed him.

If the government does not begin now to arrest the leaders of all the paramilitary formations, they will not achieve anything. The death of Zoran Djindjić will have been pointless. Now or never— they must do it. And not just to confront the "Zemun clan of killers."

The hundreds of thousands of people who followed Zoran Djindjić to his burial have given their support and obligated the government to act. If the government does not understand this, the moment of massive public support will pass, If they do not do it, they will be leaving them for the next crimes.[46]

As if to confirm that the source of the crime required looking further than a group of criminals operating out of Zemun, the continuing investigation produced further details. Not only did it lead to conclusive evidence regarding the Stambolić and Drašković cases, but it established the existence of networks. JSO and the "Zemun clan" coordinated the trade of stolen property with officals of the Serb parastate in Croatia, and maintained connections after that parastate ceased to exist in 1995.[47] The members of the "Zemun clan" met and coordinated with officials of the Security Intelligence Agency (BIA).[48] Vojislav Šešelj, leader of the Serbian Radical Party, acquired the compromising documents he was known for displaying at press conferences and publishing in his frequent books, via the "Zemun clan" who received them from their allies in BIA.[49] It did not take a look too far into the past to find motivations: Milošević's SPS had labeled the transfer of their president to The Hague as "treason";[50] SRS had promised, "they will answer for that."[51]

Operation Sabre looked to some like a potential turning point. An online commentator declared that with sustained action finally taking place against criminals it was not a "state of emergency" [vanredno stanje] but a "fantastically good state" [izvanredno dobro stanje].[52] *Politika*'s commentator Ljubodrag Stojadinović foresaw an end to "the fatal variant of patriotism, a characteristic reflex of massive war psychosis, which is unsustainable without constant tragedy."[53] Referring to a popular rhetorical figure where people complained that power had changed hands on 5 October 2000, but that "6 October"—the beginning of the new period unmarked by Milošević—had never come, deputy premier Nebojša Čović promised that "6 October has started now."[54] A public opinion survey in March 2003 found that the state of emergency was supported by 73 percent of respondents.[55] When the state of emergency ended after 42 days, acting president Nataša Mićić averred that a pattern of corrupt and dysfunctional state institutions had been broken by state action: "The past 42 days have changed Serbia permanently. For the better. From the report of the Serbian government it is clear that the police have achieved meaningful results. Now the focus is on the judiciary. I hope that everyone who works in judicial institutions understands that they have before them a great opportunity to recover respect for their profession, which some irresponsible individuals among them have stained."[56] Mićić was right, as it turned out, to condition her optimism on the future functioning of institutions. Among the sets of close connections revealed by Operation Sabre was collusion between law enforcement officials and criminal groups, including a deputy state prosecutor who received regular payments to obstruct investigations and reveal evidence to suspects.[57] As the panic following the murder of Djindjić receded, these networks would reactivate, not just to obstruct prosecutions but to discredit the police action that led to them.

The Campaign Against Operation Sabre

The funeral of Zoran Djindjić indicated a level of popularity and support that he had never enjoyed as a politician. An impromptu memorial in front of the government offices attracted thousands of offerings of flowers and written messages of support for the murdered premier. On 15 March the funeral procession attracted hundreds of thousands of participants to follow Djindjić's remains for a liturgy at the church of St. Sava, before the coffin was brought to the Alley of the Great in Belgrade's New Cemetery.[58] Djindjić's successor Zoran Živković[59] addressed the mourners with words calculated to express popular outrage. Referring to the nicknames by which members of the "Zemun clan" were known—Vladimir Milisavljević-Budala (the Fool), Dragan Ninković-Prevara (the Scam), Mladan Mićić-Pacov (the Rat)[60]—Živković set out to proclaim a national identity for respectable people:

You were killed by a group of people that included the Fool, the Scam, and the Rat. Not just in that group, but in other groups there

are still fools, scams, and rats and they have been our greatest enemies, they were ten years ago and they have been in these two years
we have been trying to change Serbia. . . .

I would say to the citizens around us, whom we have never seen
before in numbers like this, people who are honest, hardworking,
fair, who love Serbia: defeat the fools, scams, and rats! This is too
small and too beautiful a country for us to share it with people like
that.[61]

As succinct as it may have been in combining the themes of respectability,
political change, and crime, Živković's address is not the funeral speech
that is most widely remembered.

The best-remembered funeral speech was delivered by the Orthodox
bishop Amfilohije (Risto Radović).[62] Amfilohije had a long history as a "political bishop" and would tell people who questioned his engagement that to
the Church, "nothing human is foreign."[63] His long political activism was
specifically in favor of extreme Serbian nationalism, paramilitary formations,
and in favor of Milošević. He had used his ecclesiastical authority to bless
adventures ranging from the siege of Dubrovnik in 1991 to the paramilitary
outings of Željko Ražnatović-Arkan.[64] When Milošević was arrested he came
to the prison to give him a Bible,[65] and when Milošević was transferred to
ICTY he cursed the government that did it.[66] Addressing the mourners of
Djindjić, he came forward with an accusatory mixed message:

Today we bid farewell to Zoran Djindjić. Nearby stands the monument to the leader Karadjordje, whose head was also cut by the hand
of a friend and brother and was displayed on a stake, stuffed with
straw, in Istanbul two hundred years ago. . . .

In a moment when above the head of his people hung the sword
of Pilate's justice—Zoran Djindjić set into motion the renewed flow
of national and social life. The renewal of the unity of the state
and of the state community of Serbia and Montenegro, of broken
connections with the world. But, he was killed by the hatred of
brothers, shortsighted and blind, which prophesies the eternal
truth—he who lives by the sword shall die by the sword.[67]

Surrounding faint praise for the departed prime minister's achievements
(he had renewed a flow) were some jarring assertions. Were Djindjić's killers his "friends and brothers"? Had his killing, like Karadjordje's, been a

vassal's act of tribute? Had Djindjić lived "by the sword"? Amfilohije was reviving the smears that Djindjić had been a criminal himself, placing the victim on an equal footing with his killers, and reducing the finding of political conspiracy to the level of political competition—violent but nothing special, something to be expected for a person who lived "by the sword" and that had been happening since Djordje Petrović (called Karadjordje) was murdered by agents of Miloš Teodorović (called Obrenović) in 1817.

There followed a campaign to displace responsibility for the killing. One popular thesis was that Djindjić had been killed because he tried too hard to please the West, provoking rage at home. Stojan Cerović brought the threads together in his column in *Vreme*, offering the rhetorical accusation that he was killed by "Slobodan Milošević and Carla Del Ponte."[68] A subhead in the daily paper *Večernje novosti* made the connection implicitly: "The world's recognition—that there was too much pressure and conditionality placed on Belgrade even after 5 October—came too late."[69] The implicit blame placed on other countries for the murder carried a barely hidden political message—if the rest of the world would stop expecting things of Serbia, in particular a recognition of responsibility for what its previous regime had done, then the political violence would also stop. The message suggested an implicit threat as to what would happen if, conversely, expectations were to continue.

The second strategy of displacement cast the murderers not as enemies of the state but as competitors, the state having allied itself with the "Surčin clan" whose leader, Ljubiša Buha-Čume, was to be the principal protected witness in Djindjić's action against (other?) organized crime groups. This recapitulated the story that had been promoted in some media before Djindjić was killed. A more moderate version of the story has Djindjić not choosing one of the criminal groups but mediating among them:

> Let people tear me apart, but the death of Zoran Djindjić was announced. Or rather, a confrontation was announced between him and Milorad Luković [Ulemek] Legija. The object of the confrontation was the very purpose of 5 October: if it was won by of the criminal underground, just those parapolice structures from Milošević's time that Luković personified, that was meant to confirm that what happened that day was a palace coup in which the only reason that Milošević was removed was that he was such a notorious loser. If the state won, that would affirm that there had been deep social

change and fundamental political change, and establish the fact that Serbia was truly dissatisfied with Milošević, and not with his defeats. Unfortunately, for two years Serbia drifted between those two options. At one time it even tried to establish rules for the coexistence of the two, but it did not succeed.[70]

In this version of events, the murder had little to do with law enforcement, or indeed with policy or politics of any kind, but rather represented an internal settling of accounts involving no public interest.

Finally there was displacement coming from critics—principally in Koštunica's DSS—who saw organized crime and political-criminal networks being used as a pretext for unfair political competition, and regarded Operation Sabre as an illegal effort to use instruments of law enforcement as political campaign tools. DSS opposed "Sabre" from the beginning, and on its first day offered a statement insisting on the formation of a "unity" government, arguing that the introduction of a state of emergency was illegal, and suggesting that the new measures "could very easily provoke complete lawlessness, the violation of all political, human and labor rights, and in the final instance anarchy."[71]

DSS remained mobilized and continued its attack on Operation Sabre well past the time when the operation ended. In a television appearance DSS official Obren Joksimović argued "that the 'goal of the extraordinary measures was the destruction and Satanization of political opponents of the government, principally DSS,' that the liquidation of Spasojević and Luković was extremely dubious because 'it is unlikely that somebody who is escaping would carry such a heavy machinegun,' and that 'the state of emergency was introduced irregularly, unconstitutionally, and unnecessarily.'"[72] A more moderate version of the interpretation was offered over a year later by DSS official Dragan Jočić (who became interior minister after the December 2003 elections), casting the state of emergency as a political campaign: "Researching and digging through 'Operation Sabre' is a devilish job, everything is incomplete, everything was done in a rush, either there are few facts or the facts are hidden. 'Operation Sabre' was a massive event that lasted eighty-odd days and from the field of fighting against organized crime entered into the sphere of political struggle and struggle against political opponents."[73] Most at stake in the campaign to discredit Operation Sabre was a fear that the investigation and prosecution could widen beyond the people who carried out the crime and into the network of people who provided information, operational details and ideas, involving people who were still politically active and held public office.

Charges of Abuse in Operation Sabre

As Operation Sabre came to an end it could point to concrete achievements. Some major crimes, including political killings from the Milošević period, were solved. The network of organized crime was meaningfully weakened, while connections between organized crime and war criminals who continued to be defended by the "patriotic bloc" in politics became clear, dealing a major blow to the credibility of actors who upheld the legitimacy of the previous regime. By doing so, a major rhetorical dispensation for war criminals, which operates by placing the environment of war outside the everyday moral universe in which non-political crime is condemned, was also weakened. The government stressed common crime in its statement ending the state of emergency: "During the state of emergency and the police action 'Sabre' in Serbia, from 12 March to 23 April, over 10,000 people were arrested, of whom 4,500 were kept in custody. 3,700 criminal complaints were filed against 3,200 people for 5,600 criminal acts. Among those acts were 28 killings, 15 kidnappings and 208 cases of trade in narcotics."[74] The achievements of the state of emergency were shadowed by allegations of abuse and torture of prisoners. In September 2003 Amnesty International released a report detailing torture allegations made by sixteen former prisoners and suggesting that there might have been "widespread" abuse beyond what their evidence showed.[75] A local newspaper quoted the author of the report, Hugh Poulton,[76] as speculating that "while it is true that we only know of 15 to 20 cases, considering the large number of people arrested in 'Operation Sabre' this could be just the tip of the iceberg."[77]

Amnesty's evidence coincided with information that the Interior Ministry produced in May 2005. At that time, of 11,655 people who had been arrested: "The general inspector of the Interior Ministry Vladimir Božović said at a meeting of the Commission [for Defense and Security] that his office had received 37 complaints of abuse and torture during "Sabre," of which 20 were rejected as unfounded, six were found to be justified, while 11 cases were still being investigated."[78] Bound to affect the credibility of the operation, the allegations of abuse and the government's subsequent recognition of some of the allegations provided rhetorical ammunition to political actors who claimed the state of emergency had provided cover for violations of human rights.

In some cases the government paid damages to people who had been unjustly arrested. Dejan Kuzmanović, a musician who had been incorrectly identified as Djindjić's killer before Zvezdan Jovanović was identified, was paid 400,000 dinars. The same sum was awarded to Dejan Arandjelović, who had been mistakenly arrested because his name was similar to the name of "Zemun clan" member Dejan Randjelović.[79]

It would have difficult for anybody to object to clearly innocent people like Kuzmanović and Arandjelović receiving compensation. The post-"Sabre" government, however, defined the universe of people entitled to claim compensation more broadly. In their formulation: "the right to sue the state can be claimed by anybody who was deprived of freedom and had no charges filed against them, as well as people against whom criminal charges were filed but later withdrawn. In addition, the right to compensation can be claimed by people who were convicted but whose convictions were reversed on appeal. On the basis of this rule, the right to compensation for arrest during 'Operation Sabre' can be claimed by 62 people."[80] Under the compensation scheme, complainants could claim 10,000 dinars (about 50 U.S. dollars) for each day spent in custody.[81]

While the torture allegations involved, as Amnesty International's report put it, "people perceived as relatively low-level criminals and thus to a large extent out of the public eye and so unlikely to have their allegations widely publicized," the promise of money attracted a more prominent class of claimant.[82] A judge, Života Djoinčević, had been arrested amid claims that in exchange for bribes he had released criminals associated with the Milošević regime and the "Zemun clan."[83] But no charges were filed—Djoinčević also had a conviction for illegal ownership of firearms reversed.[84] He sued the state, demanding 20 million dinars,[85] and subsequently refused an offer for 740,000 offered under the formula of 10,000 for each day of custody.[86] Eventually a court ordered that he be paid 4 million.[87]

The most prominent claimants against Operation Sabre were military and intelligence officials allied with DSS. Koštunica claimed that DSS was targeted by the operation—his statement regarding mistreatment of political opponents applied specifically to General Aco Tomić, former head of the military intelligence service, and Rade Bulatović, his security advisor, both arrested in April 2003.[88] Neither Bulatović nor Tomić was charged, and both filed lawsuits. They were joined by several members of JSO, who demanded 40 million dinars,[89] and by political-financial operator Borislav

Mikelić, who demanded 22.8 million.[90] The JSO members' prospects were constrained by their murder convictions, but a court awarded Mikelić 620,000—a decision he appealed as he felt he was entitled to a greater sum.[91] Koštunica's advisors fared better: Bulatović received 669,700 dinars in compensation,[92] while Tomić received the richest compensation of any person arrested in Operation Sabre with a take of 6 million in 2008.[93]

Some of the charges related to the conduct of Operation Sabre—the torture charges in particular—should have and did damage the credibility of the action. The charge that the action constituted a political campaign disguised as a law enforcement operation, though, appears specifically aimed at the original conspiracy indictment. The compensation policy allowed claims by anybody against whom there did not exist an active charge in mid-2004. Considering that 44 people were named in the original indictment for the Djindjić killing and 12 were tried, it might be possible to ask about the remaining 32. Of these, some (like Milorad Ulemek and Dejan Milenković) had not been arrested. Some (like Ljubiša Buha) became protected witnesses. Others, including Borislav Mikelić (named suspect 37) and Aco Tomić (named suspect 38), were named as a part of the conspiracy that prosecutors decided not to try. The eventual criminal case concentrated on individuals directly involved in the murder itself but not on the preparation of the political terrain for an attempted seizure of power, nor on operational assistance or inspiration coming from serving and recently serving state officials.

Limiting the investigation had two principal consequences: (1) it assisted the claim by some political forces that claimed that the state of emergency was a political operation directed against them; and (2) it obscured the connection between domestic organized crime and organized violations of international humanitarian law that became apparent in the immediate aftermath of the murder, and was apparent in the slogan "Stop the Hague." It meant that 42 days of intensive action under the state of emergency would not be sustained, and that documents would not be produced describing the extent of the criminal nexus that had been established in the preceding decade.

Decline, Defeat, Displacement

The government of Zoran Živković, appointed to replace the murdered premier, did not see out the end of 2003. Operation Sabre gave way to the conflicts and scandals characteristic of the everyday life of a weak government in an unstable state. Two senior government officials resigned over the summer amid allegations of money laundering.[94] In September attention was consumed by a scandal about falsified votes in the Serbian parliament.[95] In October, renewed demands from ICTY for the transfer of indictees—four generals from the "Kosovo Six" indictment—led Živković to angrily accuse the Tribunal of violating an understanding with the Serbian government and predicted that the indictments would turn out to be "a political blow to reform in Serbia."[96] Živković predicted that renewed confrontation over issues of command responsibility would hurt his party in upcoming elections, in which Koštunica's DSS was building a campaign on "national" issues and grievances arising from Operation Sabre.

Whether because of ICTY indictments, exhaustion, scandals, or nationalist resentment, the December 2003 elections were catastrophic for the Democratic Party. The Serbian Radical Party gained 82 seats for its 1,056,256 votes,[97] forcing all other parties to unite against them. Koštunica was named as premier, and set about to undo much of the work of Djindjić and the caretaker government that succeeded him. The plebiscitary support apparent for confrontation with crime in March had given way to doubt, counterclaims, and exhausted hope.

The outrage apparent after Djindjić's murder had clearly faded. In its place were lingering doubts about the intentions behind Operation Sabre and a feeling that Djindjić's successors were not likely to carry on the positive part of his legacy. What had seemed clear during the state of emergency had become muddled: Was the problem not criminals but Djindjić's insufficient patriotism? Were the criminals who were caught only a part of the picture? Were the military, intelligence, and political figures originally listed as conspirators innocent victims of dirty politics? Weren't the ongoing scandals simply evidence that there was no end to dirty politics?

After a period of action in which the connections between state crimes and organized crime were revealed, a period of squalor at the end offered to people who wanted to take it the impression that Rade Bulatović and Aco Tomić were innocent victims. Clarity gave way to confusion and complexity to a manufactured impression of equivalency. The way that was open to a turning point was closing off. The pattern would be repeated in later events.

Chapter 6

Denial, Avoidance, Shifts of Context: From Denial to Responsibility in Eleven Steps

Evidence from the "moments" that have been discussed here indicate that incidents that could have been revelatory turned out, for a whole complex of reasons, to be inconclusive. The arrest and extradition of Milošević permitted a set of issues to be introduced, but mostly sketched out the lines dividing participants. The murder of Zoran Djindjić appeared to confirm long-suspected links between war crimes, political crimes, and crime committed for more customarily criminal reasons. But a set of decisions at crucial moments by politicians and police meant that prosecutors concentrated on operational details of the killing rather than the structure of the conspiracy that brought the killing about.[1] Where openings might have been made, confusion was created instead.

In the space of confusion grows the potential for denial. This chapter offers an overview of denial—its motivations and forms, and some rhetorical strategies that look like recognition but have the same consequences as denial. In the following chapter we will examine another "moment," in which denial was deployed specifically in relation to Srebrenica.

Varieties of Denial

There were strong and obvious motivations to deny crimes at the time when they were being committed, and when they began to be investigated and prosecuted. These did not disappear when the regime that was directly associated with the crimes left power. It is possible, from the perspective of guilt, to understand this on an individual level: people who could be charged with offenses—in addition to people who had been charged—either remained in positions of official authority or laid claim to protection from the state.

A quick review of the members of the government that took power after Milošević's departure suggests levels of engagement with the former regime that might have suggested complicity in some cases, but more often suggested the likelihood that people might be called on to explain themselves or face embarrassment. To offer a few examples: Vojislav Koštunica, elected president of SRJ, argued during most of the war years in favor of intensified engagement with the Bosnian Serb parastate, against the Dayton Peace Agreement, and against cooperation with ICTY. Nebojša Čović, one of the deputy prime ministers of Serbia, was an SPS official and mayor of Belgrade under Milošević. Momčilo Perišić, another deputy premier, was chief of staff of the Yugoslav army during most of the war years.[2] Dušan Mihajlović, the minister of the interior, was a vice premier under Milošević. General Nebojša Pavković, who remained as chief of military staff after the change of regime, was convicted by ICTY of crimes against humanity as one of the "Kosovo Six" in 2009.[3] In the period of "cohabitation" between Koštunica's election in October 2000 and the formation of the Djindjić's government in January 2001, continuity with the old regime was especially visible in certain areas: while continuing in his position as director of state security, Radomir Marković destroyed 11,490 documents, or 35,753 pages of material recording the activities of the previous regime.[4]

But the issue does not reflect only on high public officials or people likely to face criminal prosecution. When the discussion shifts from guilt to responsibility, it encompasses a large number of people with previous engagement that may not have been criminal but was also not praiseworthy from a later perspective. It also encompasses risk at the social level—whether this is conceived as risk to the reputation of the state or its dominant ethnic group, or as an implicit charge that an elite or a generation can be blamed for any misery that continues. The number of people who could be said to carry some degree of political and moral responsibility is potentially enormous, and encompasses a large number of people in a large number of institutions—from media and education to industry and trade. Some of this responsibility might be described as passive responsibility or failure to act, but not all of it. To a certain degree, activities in which people engaged for profit or survival, such as producing media content, teaching "history," or importing and selling consumer goods, can be regarded as having made serious crimes possible.

Nor, although after his death he became a kind of icon of resistance to the remnants to the regime, would Zoran Djindjić have been immune. Observers of his career as a Europeanizing liberal never let him forget about the efforts of his Democratic Party (DS) to appropriate some of the war rhetoric of the ultraright Serbian Radical Party (SRS) after the latter party fell out of favor with Milošević in 1993. The phrase "roasted ox" (*pečeni vo*) is enough to remind people of Djindjić's highly publicized visit to Pale to show support for Radovan Karadžić in 1994, when he was greeted with that festive rural specialty. Satirical columnist Vojislav Žanetić reminds readers of the incident in a sardonic parable which does not mention Djindjić's name:

> Somewhere at Pale there is a fire pit. On it once, long ago, there was a fire, above which, once, long ago, there was a grill. On that grill was an ox. Which they ate. Once, long ago.
>
> People say there is a legend that the spirit of that ox often appears at that place at Pale and gazes toward Sarajevo, to catch a glimpse of at least one of the people who then, once long ago, ate from that grill. People swear that they can now hear the spirit of the eaten ox as it sadly lows from Pale.
>
> You wouldn't believe it.[5]

The parable offers a bitter reminder that people took, not so long ago, political positions they would probably now prefer to disown. It is also a reminder that any serious effort to engage the recent past is bound to touch on people who are not on the consensually approved list of scapegoats.

Approaches to Responsibility

What follows is an initial typology of the approaches to the theme of responsibility I have found in political debates in Serbia so far. While the placement is not always entirely clear, what is offered here is meant to resemble a continuum—from affirmation of evil and denial to positive engagement with questions of responsibility. The selection is by no means exhaustive of all the existing variants or possibilities. Rather it represents a typology of the most frequent and visible approaches.

1. Celebration of Crime

Though the active endorsement and celebration of crime is hardly a majority perspective anywhere in the world—not even in places recently emerged from violent conflict—neither can it be said to be entirely absent. Certainly images of criminals have been widely used for publicity and for provocation. Occasional poster and media campaigns celebrating indictees as heroes have attracted international media attention. A 2006 incident involved posters with portraits of Ratko Mladić and the slogan "SrbIn," an effort to combine an ethnic denominator (*Srbin*) with an international colloquial term for fashionable things (*In*).[6] Similarly, occasional notice is taken of the sale of T-shirts with images of indictees, mostly at flea markets and railway stations.[7]

In other instances the affirmation of crime has taken on a more unsettling character. Occasionally in the context of political clashes but more frequently at international football matches it is possible to hear the slogan "*nož, žica, Srebrenica*" (knife, wire, Srebrenica), together with others praising or encouraging acts of ethnic violence—an iconic example is "*Ubij, zakolji, da Šiptar ne postoji*" (kill and slaughter, so the [derogatory term for Albanians] will not exist). The first slogan was developed further in an anonymously recorded rap song using the slogan as its title. The unknown artist generates the theme:

> Srebrenica mesto moje drago
> Nikad u životu nisam bio tamo
> Ali zato mesto mene nešto veže
> Tamo muslimanu vrat se nožem reže
> Za Srbiju brate a s verom u boga
> Srebrenica mjesto ponosa srpskoga
> Zbog srpskog junaka našeg Radovana
> Tamo braćo više nema muslimana
> Bajonetom svojim klao ih je glatko
> Jer samo je jedan
> Djeneral Mladić Ratko.

> Srebrenica, my dear place
> I have never been there in my life

But still I feel connected to it
Because there they cut Muslims' necks with knives
For Serbia, brother, with faith in God
Srebrenica, place of Serbian pride
Because of our Serbian hero Radovan
There are no Muslims there anymore
He slaughtered them with his bayonet
Because there is only one
General Mladić Ratko.[8]

And so forth. When a nongovernmental group unveiled a billboard campaign in Belgrade in 2005 to commemorate the tenth anniversary of Srebrenica, many of the billboards were quickly vandalized both with the *nož*, *žica* slogan and with the ominous promise *biće repriza* (there will be an encore).[9]

Campaigns and countercampaigns of the type described above do occur. When they do, they are met with the expected near-universal condemnation and with international media attention that offers the impression that a popular sentiment is being expressed. More likely such expressions are the property of a few extremist political groups whose memberships number in the dozens rather than the thousands,[10] and additionally of some larger groups (particularly organized football fans) seeking to shock and provoke their opponents and people nearby by approaching a taboo transgressively.[11] In Serbia like in any other place in the world, the enthusiastic embrace of ethnically motivated violence is a fringe phenomenon. At the same time the groups that promote such views are, while not numerous, undoubtedly visible. The public expression of sympathy for large-scale crime nonetheless resonates because (1) its frequent recurrence suggests either that no successful strategy to control it has been adopted or that it is widely tolerated; and (2) there is a fundamental homology between the slogans and sentiments expressed by far-right fringe groups and the stances advanced by state media and through educational institutions under the regime that was in power up to 2000.

2. Pure Denial and Impure Avoidance

One way of pardoning crimes short of celebrating them and their perpetrators is to deny that they occurred. Pure denial promotes the belief that nothing has taken place for which any person might be held guilty or made to feel directly or indirectly responsible. Pure denial may depend on a lack of information, or on a system of values that recognizes facts but justifies or downplays them. Returning to the example of Srebrenica, while the earliest information available in Serbia presented the 1995 events as the liberation of an occupied city, reports that followed the presentation of evidence that more than 7,000 residents were massacred by the Republika Srpska military concentrated on denying earlier revelations.[12] An unadulterated denial is offered by Momčilo Cvjetanović, president of the Serbian Democratic Party (SDS) for Srebrenica: "In Potočari nothing else happened except that assistance was offered to the Muslim population while they were being evacuated, certainly no crimes occurred. Muslims, like Serbs, died in the battles for Srebrenica. Aside from the battles, they also died here and there escaping through the forests because of land mines they had placed themselves beforehand, and many of their armed soldiers also died attacking our observation points."[13] In another version of the denial, the crime is attributed to a shadowy outside conspiracy. Though the theory survived much longer, an early iteration was offered by Goran Matić, federal minister for information in the Milošević government: "that massacre was engineered by the French intelligence service and the intelligence service of Izetbegović's government in Sarajevo, along with the members of the 'Spider' group with the goal of making possible the arrival of NATO to Bosnia and the assumption of other steps by the West toward Yugoslavia."[14] The claims put forth by Matić represent a step from denying the facts to sowing confusion about them. This is a space in which much of the denial discourse would hover for several years. While there were more instances of claims that the victims of the massacres had been "extremists" and "Alija [Izetbegović]'s fundamentalists and their sponsors,"[15] there were still occasional revivals of the claim that people listed as victims had not died at all, sometimes accompanied by claims they had acquired new names and residences.[16] The claims represent alternative ways of reaching the conclusion that "the genocide against Muslims in Srebrenica—never occurred!"[17]

Pure denial of this type has always been an untenable position, was rarely found even during the war years in Serbia, and to the extent that it exists any longer is diminishing. To the degree that it conflicts with known facts, pure denial has a fundamental vulnerability to the revelation of information. However, as Jelena Obradović-Wochnik points out, "Individuals with access to information do not necessarily accept it and the availability alone of evidence of war crimes does not lead to their acknowledgement."[18]

Short of pure denial, there are several variations of impure avoidance, which are not difficult to find at all.

Probably the most common of these in the past years have been empirical unclarity as denial and equivalence as denial. The first approach argues that not all facts are known or that there are disagreements about responsibility for some events, and uses this to dismiss or minimize those events. The second argues that in the conflicts some measure of guilt may be attributed to all sides, and therefore no unique obligation can be attached to any one side. These approaches are discussed in greater detail as separate varieties of denial later on in this chapter.

One essential corollary of denial is metadenial: the denial that things are being denied, and correspondingly to claim that accusations (which are not being denied) are rampant. A newspaper commentator argues: "Serbs are pretty much every day confronting so-called Serbian crimes—in the media, in cinemas, at various exhibitions, in debate halls. . . . And yet nobody can recall that in the last four and a half years anybody has publicly denied or approved even a single crime for whose existence even one bit of evidence has been offered."[19] Metadenial is especially useful for newcomers to denial, as it allows them to reject evidence presented earlier that they had not reviewed.

3. The Ideology of Forgetting

Immediately at the end of the Milošević era many people rushed to demonstrate their new loyalties, to claim that they had always been opponents of the regime, and to deny any connection with the events of the previous ten years. As Petar Luković described the spectacle, "In the invisible rhythm of the still invisible changes, everything which was Black is now White, everyone has, at once, become anti-Milošević, and millions of citizens, in twenty-four hours, changed their favorite color uniforms and in hypnotic amnesia erased the past as though it never existed."[20] This current was noticed by a member of the Theater Artists' Union who requested in an open letter, "I ask my colleagues who did not participate, even in words, and more importantly not in actions either, in the fall of the regime of Slobodan Milošević, that in their current shifts to the winning side, if they are not capable of behaving morally, that they at least behave in good taste."[21] Ridiculing figures associated with the old regime who were shifting

their positions, a local branch of the Otpor! youth resistance group in Kru-
ševac distributed tubes of Vaseline to SPS members, to help them slide
more easily to the other side.[22]

There is probably no need to dwell on the number of cynical political
reasons people might have had for claiming at an opportune moment never
to have supported the regime. But what is of more interest here is the effect
of this rhetorical strategy on discussions of responsibility. What it allowed
people to do was to disavow association with the regime and its activities—it was an unfortunate period, an aberration, one they struggled to
end, when it ended the people responsible went with it. This rhetorical
strategy offered an invitation to declare a new starting point with no
detours into the past. For obvious reasons this invitation had broad popular
appeal, and many people found it easy to accept it automatically. The number and type of these people was always bound to be limited: bystanders
have greater motivation than victims to "forget and move on."

The need to "move on" was sensed acutely by members of Milošević's
political party, SPS, when that party, after a partial rehabilitation as a silent
partner (voting to sustain the government but not a member of the coalition) in Vojislav Koštunica's government, received full rehabilitation as a
member of the governing coalition formed under prime minister Mirko
Cvetković in 2008. The leaders of the two principal governing parties, DS
and SPS, issued in the context of this political sea change a "Declaration of
Political Reconciliation" explaining the transformation of their party interests. The declaration promised "overcoming conflicts from the past" and
"the construction of a state of law, free of resentments from or denials of
the past and without either accusing or exonerating people on the basis of
their political affiliation."[23] This required SPS president Ivica Dačić to
explain that the agreement "does not indicate forgetting, does not indicate
amnesty," going on to argue that "nobody can be given amnesty from guilt
on the basis that they are now a member of one of our two parties."[24] The
rejection of amnesty immediately appeared ambivalent, as it is figuratively
offered (to be immediately withdrawn) both to members of SPS, a party
that did commit major crimes while in power, and of DS, a party that did
not.

The limited invitation to self-amnesty was taken up by Slavica Djukić-
Dejanović, a vice president of SPS who was also the presiding officer of the
Serbian parliament. Telling a Sarajevo magazine that Milošević's rule "had
both positive and negative achievements" but that she as a member of "the

leadership of SPS did not necessarily participate in taking decisions," she rejected the reporter's questions about her responsibility:

> Q: Do you at least feel responsibility for the crimes that were committed in the period we are talking about? You teach ethics to students after all.
> A: I do not have a feeling of guilt, and in the period you are interested in, just like today, political killings, the repression of media, all types of crime are unacceptable and I condemn them.
> Q: Although you were a high official of SPS, you did not know about all of the things that were done by Milošević, his security service, and his army?
> A: Like with all other citizens, the discovery of the political roots of all the evils in our society has created in us a resistance toward those individuals who committed and instigated those acts. Only the agencies that carry out investigation and justice—and then only on the basis of evidence—can identify with certainty the people responsible for each crime. So, I do not deny the crimes you are mentioning, but that happened in a period when there were half a million people in SPS. It was the largest political party in the Balkans and people trusted it unreservedly, so you cannot generalize and simply accuse all those people. I do not accept in any situation, and also not in this one, collective lustration and collective labeling.
> Q: We are not talking about collective guilt but about responsibility. So you have no personal problem with having been a member of a party that brought so much evil both outside Serbia and within it?
> A: I don't know whose conclusion it is that SPS brought any kind of evil to anybody.[25]

For people with connections to the recent past, forgetting and moving on means absenting from concrete consideration of the period anybody whose direct involvement in it cannot be or has not been demonstrated before a court of law.

4. Transference as Avoidance

The invitation to consider guilt as an individual phenomenon arises from a long legal and philosophical tradition. Among the most important and most frequently stated principles that have developed out of the years of war and the international discourse on accountability for human rights abuses has been a distinction between individual and collective responsibility. A broad and justifiable general consensus exists in favor of establishing individual responsibility, and against concepts of collective responsibility.

In favor of this consensus are solid legal arguments, as indicated in the discussion on guilt in Chapter 1. There are also strong theoretical arguments to be made against the imposition of collective responsibility. First among them is the widespread perception that notions of collective responsibility resemble nothing so much as stereotypes about the mindset and behavior of whole societies, which are as untenable as they are likely to be offensive.[26] As Nenad Dimitrijević explains:

> It is not possible to think in terms of the collective responsibility of Serbs, because that implies defining a collectivity as a being, which would have to be recognized as the Serbian Nation. That would be a much more far-reaching step than simply identifying a nation as a sociologically recognizable group . . . it would mean ontologizing the nation. More than this, it would mean agreeing to a nationalistic discourse, since it is precisely in the discourse of nationalism the quasi-ontological construction of the nation is of fundamental importance.[27]

Collective responsibility can be perceived as the enemy of efforts to establish individual responsibility: if everybody in a society is equally responsible, then no individual is particularly responsible, which allows actual criminals to hide within a collective. This represents not only a logical problem—in this version, collective responsibility means generalized punishment and no prosecutions. Just such an argument was periodically offered, for example, with regard to the ongoing fugitive status of indictees, whose surrender for international trial had been postulated as a condition for benefits related to the accession of Serbia to the EU. By refusing to face accusations for individual crimes, the argument went, fugitives caused the entire population of Serbia, including the overwhelming majority who are not criminals, to be punished in their place.

However, the principle of individual guilt in its pure version amounts to a type of transference that in a sense permits people who are not guilty to avoid questions of responsibility. In this construction, bystanders and (former) supporters of the institutions that were involved in crimes are absolved by the direct attribution of crimes to perpetrators. Vojislav Koštunica implied as much when he told *The Independent* after his election in 2000, "The moment we get rid of Milošević, the poison will be taken out of the body politic."[28] By implication, there exists no other poison. Rade Vukosav summarizes the position: "We cannot put an equal sign between the people who pushed us into this horrible fratricidal war and our people. That would mean spitting on ourselves and our people. They dragged us onto the international seat of shame. By denying them we will free ourselves from that shame, and they can keep it as they deserve to."[29] A similar point was argued by the singer Djordje Balašević, a figure of unparalleled popularity throughout the region whose antiwar engagement earned him recognition by the United Nations as a "goodwill ambassador," and whose name is widely regarded in the region as a synonym for human decency. Discussing his concert in Sarajevo in 2000, one of the first visits to the city by an artist from Serbia, he raised the question of responsibility and forgiveness:

> When I went to Sarajevo, the papers here asked, "does he have the right to ask forgiveness in the name of the Serbian people?" Nobody here broadcast the recording of that concert, but it is obvious there that I did not ask anybody for forgiveness, quite simply because I do not have anything to ask for forgiveness for. The people who need to ask for forgiveness have to go there themselves and do it. I can apologize in the name of the human race to a city which was bombed and mistreated, where children were shot by snipers. As a person I feel that pain, but not the need to ask for forgiveness in the name of the people who caused it.[30]

In this version, the demand that people who have not committed crimes feel responsible for the actions of people who have is seen as unreasonable.

Serbian prime minister Zoran Djindjić responded to a reporter's question about degrees of responsibility with laconic sarcasm. The journalist asked whether he felt pangs of conscience for having visited and supported the Bosnian Serb leadership during a period when crimes were committed that he either knew or should have known about:

> That sounds like Leibniz: "Everybody knows everything and if they do not know then they ought to know." But in that case we are all

responsible. Why didn't you, as a journalist who should have known at that time when people were being killed, publish the information and set public opinion in motion? So, you are as responsible as he is. But I think that is not realistic. It is realistic to identify who is individually responsible. Who gave orders, who knew about the orders and had the ability to stop them, and who carried out the orders. If we go after people who should have known but did not know because they were somewhere else, if we go after command responsibility in war, then 20,000 people should be in jail now. But I don't know who would guard them because the guards would be in jail too. That is simply an unrealistic approach.[31]

Practically speaking, Djindjić's argument is probably sensible—if there is an a priori obligation to know, then the distribution of guilt is probably unbearably wide. Prosecution and punishment would function more easily according to a principle of individual and concrete culpability. On another level, his mixing of the categories of guilt and responsibility confused rather than clarified the question.

As legally defensible as the pure individualization of guilt seems, it translates poorly to the level of responsibility. Can the trials of a few individuals really free everybody else from the need to confront what these individuals did in their names? One of the chief arguments against a strictly individualized conception of responsibility is that the people who committed crimes in the name of the Serbian nation would not have been able to do so if they did not have some degree of popular support or acquiescence—that is, if they were not successful in using popular ideas about the identity and interests of the nation as a pretext. Djordje Balašević's denial of personal responsibility clashes with another thesis he put forward in a song as the wars were beginning: "We are guilty because we let them do it (Krivi smo mi što smo ih pustili)."[32]

5. Transference as Ritual Apology

Debate over whether postwar apologies for crimes were in order began before Milošević left power in 2000. Several interested parties, from human rights groups and liberal politicians in Serbia to representatives of victims and previously hostile states insisted that an apology constituted a basic condition for reestablishing relations. Among the contentions behind the demand is that in taking aggressive actions in the wars, Serbia acted as a state and therefore took on responsibilities as a state. These responsibilities are not regarded as having ceased when a new group of people came to power in the state. Similar legal arguments have been made successfully in the past with regard to the imposition of debt obligations and with regard to demands for war reparations. Of course some earlier apologies have become celebrated historical cases, from German chancellor Willy Brandt's apology in Warsaw to the more recent apologies by countries such as Canada and Australia for the treatment of indigenous populations, and by the United States for a variety of abuses including the internment of Japanese civilians, the firebombing of the African American quarter in Tulsa, and the Tuskegee experiment.[33] That there are both legal and political grounds that would compel official bodies to demand and offer apologies is not really a matter of dispute.

What can be disputed is whether anything concrete is accomplished by apologies. The demand for an apology is, of course, not a material but a symbolic demand. It requires that somebody take on the obligation to speak for the group in the name of which crimes were committed, and to express a desire to satisfy the symbolic needs of a group of victims. Since the only currency exchanged is symbolic, we can ask what is represented in the ritual of apology. Taking the example of Willy Brandt's silent kneeling at the Warsaw Ghetto monument in December 1970, probably the most well-known apology in recent history, three facts are striking: (1) the apology was offered decades after the events for which it was made, (2) the apology was made by a person who had no involvement in the crimes, and (3) no words were spoken, so that formal semantic disputes over what was meant were unlikely to arise—public sentiment and consciousness in Germany were likely clear enough by 1970 that the intended meaning was understood. In that regard Brandt's apology may be better understood, not as a statement of regret for something he had done, but as a representation of the state of German public opinion after a long public process of discussion of responsibility. If it were anything else, it would have been a senseless act: an individual offering an apology for somebody else's past deeds.[34] A later initiative, the South African Truth and Reconciliation Commission, codified and rewarded apology: penitents willing to offer a public account could receive immunity from prosecution and the opportunity to request forgiveness from their victims.[35]

The period after 2000 was marked by many apologies and declarations of regret.[36] Montenegrin president Milo Djukanović started the ball rolling in July 2000 with an apology to Croatia for the attack against Dubrovnik in

1991.[37] In 2002 there was an unmet expectation that a regional summit of heads of state would be preceded by an apology to Bosnia-Herzegovina from both Croatia and Serbia.[38] The year 2003 saw mutual apologies exchanged by the presidents of Serbia-Montenegro and Croatia, though this shared contrition met criticism both for its instrumentality and for its extremely general phrasing.[39] Federal president Svetozar Marović continued the process two months later in Sarajevo with an apology to Bosnia-Herzegovina—and also continued to couch the issue in nonspecific terms, apologizing for "any evil or misfortune" that might have been caused by a citizen of his country to a citizen of Bosnia-Herzegovina.[40] Serbian president Boris Tadić followed in late 2004 with an apology to Bosnia-Herzegovina.[41] This came shortly after an apology the previous month from the government of the Serb entity in Bosnia-Herzegovina occasioned by the report of the Srebrenica commission.[42] Tadić's statement in 2004 echoed one by Croatian president Stjepan Mesić in 2003, indicating the limits of apologies by insisting that one was expected in return. As Tadić couched the matter: "However, these crimes were not committed by the Serbian people, but by criminals, individuals. It is not possible to charge a whole people because the same crimes were also committed against the Serbian people, so in that sense we all owe one another an apology. If I have to start first, well, here I am."[43] Another effort to compose an acceptable but not overly incriminating apology on Serbia's part would follow around the tenth anniversary of Srebrenica in 2005, but this effort would fail in the parliament and result in a hurried declaration by government ministers.[44] Tadić would make another effort at the Srebrenica commemoration that year, this time declaring:

> Somebody committed a crime in the nation to which I belong, in the name of the Serbian nation and that fact has got the attention of the entire world, not only our neighbors and the victims against whom the crime was committed. I want to show that Serbia shares responsibility for the future of the entire region, that it accepts the values of Europe as its own values and I want to demonstrate my respect for the victims. If that does not happen today, we will find ourselves in the circle of crime once again.[45]

A mildly worded declaration (it did contain an apology) on Srebrenica did pass the Serbian parliament in 2010 by a slim margin.[46] Not long afterward, incoming Croatian president Ivo Josipović would offer his own apology to Bosnia-Herzegovina,[47] after which he would lead a whirlwind campaign to bring regional leaders to various localities at which they would exchange apologies.

Little satisfaction seems to have come from any of the apologies offered and exchanged. To take the example of Tadić's visit to Srebrenica in 2005, victims' groups belittled the gesture, with Nura Begović of the Women of Srebrenica group arguing: "Sure, go ahead, kill people then apologize. What kind of tactic is that? Why hasn't Tadić delivered Karadžić and Mladić to the Hague? He knows where they are hiding, and by coming to our commemoration he is just trying to extend his term in office so that a more honorable person will not come to power in Serbia who would deliver them."[48] Neither were figures from the other side of the postwar ideological divide receptive to the gesture. Radomir Pavlović, a local politician in Srebrenica, saw conspiracies behind the effort: "Of course if he comes, that means that he accepts that genocide was committed. If he does not come, that means that he gave up because of threats. What does Tadić have to do with things that happened in the past and under the Milošević regime? He wants to extend the hand of reconciliation, but the Bosniaks do not want reconciliation but revenge."[49] On the far side of the ideological divide, the gesture was ridiculed. The tabloid *Nacional* ran a photo of an uncomfortable looking Tadić sweating under a bulletproof vest and reported him worrying about whether his security gear made him look fat, while another article in the same issue claimed that the town's mayor, Abdulrahman Malkić, had himself committed crimes against the local Serb population.[50]

Why do apologies require so much effort and yet provide so little satisfaction? The comparison to Willy Brandt's gesture in Warsaw remains apt. Brandt made his gesture after a long and broadly based public discussion in Germany had already produced concrete results. His kneeling reported the outcome of a process rather than substituting for one. The most charitable interpretation of postwar apologies in the former Yugoslav states is that they indicated the intention of a political force to begin a process in which they were certain to be opposed. An apology standing alone, as Drinka Gojković points out, bears a striking resemblance to the ideology of forgetting:

A person from whom an apology is demanded would have every reason to see an indulgence in it. He could imagine with a clear conscience: I will apologize, and then I can breathe easily! I will not be guilty any longer! Whether he is guilty or not, whether he feels guilty or not, is not important in terms of this demand, nor is it important what those feelings depend upon. Certainly some sort of guilt is implied by the demand itself, but the demand also offers a way to fairly easily put it aside.[51]

In this context, as many apologies can be demanded and offered as any parties care to think of. But they will not represent anything meaningful by themselves. A rushed and opportune apology could instead function as a substitute for what the parties on either side of the process want and need.[52]

6. Tu Quoque

A constant contention in discussions of crimes and responsibility in Serbia is the perception that while crimes committed by Serbs are a source of discussion and international activity, crimes committed against Serbs are systematically ignored. While no objective observers contest the broad consensus that the largest number of crimes with the most systematic character were committed by forces armed and commanded through Serbian agencies and their clients,[53] there is active contestation of the equally widespread thesis that these were the largest crimes. To the destruction of urban spaces in Sarajevo, Vukovar, and Dubrovnik, a response is offered that NATO caused extensive damage to nonmilitary targets in the 1999 bombing campaign.[54] To charges of genocide in Srebrenica, the response is offered that the forced migration of hundreds of thousands of Serbs from Croatia in 1995,[55] and from Kosovo in 1999,[56] constituted a crime on a larger scale. To the massacre of civilian populations in Kosovo, the response is offered that charges of trafficking in the organs of prisoners were more horrifying.[57]

In law the effort to justify one set of crimes with reference to another set of crimes is generally rejected as a *tu quoque* (in Latin, literally, "and you too") argument. *Tu quoque* arguments have no relevance to the charges, as they raise a set of facts that are not under consideration.[58] In politics as opposed to law *tu quoque* could have some resonance, both as a criticism of choices made by ICTY in its decisions regarding who should be charged, and in a broader context as an argument that one group is being treated unfairly.

Slobodan Milošević attempted a *tu quoque* defense at his trial, arguing fundamentally that the reason he was charged with crimes was to provide legitimation for crimes committed by others. While he had almost certainly received legal advice that this type of legal defense would not be accepted, it is entirely possible that he calculated that he had no chance of acquittal and was best off using the television coverage of the trial to argue for his domestic political rehabilitation. And so he began at his arraignment by declaring, "This trial's aim is to produce false justification for the war crimes of NATO committed in Yugoslavia."[59] He would expand the argument in a marathon statement opening the presentation of his defense in 2004. First, seemingly unaware that the charges against him did not include destruction of the Yugoslav state, he argued that the trial represented an effort to cover a conspiracy against Yugoslavia: "Senseless, vulgar theories about bad guys and rough state cannot serve to explain historical facts and provide the historical responsibility for the destruction of a state. The joint criminal intent existed but it didn't proceed from Belgrade, however, nor did it exist in Belgrade at all. Quite the contrary. It existed through the joint forces of the secessionists, Germany and the Vatican, and also the rest of the countries of the European Community and the United States."[60] As the rambling statement went over two days, during which Milošević ranged over a number of topics from Austro-Hungarian and Nazi history, debates from the 1950s over the definition of genocide, and the collected works of Smilja Avramov, he returned to two points. The first was that his trial was not legitimate if all participants in all other wars were not tried:

An international court can have authority only if it was created by a lege artis act and if it is of a general nature. This Tribunal lacks both elements. The act of the establishment of this Tribunal is of an individual nature. It's a political nature. The elementary legal principle is equality. So then we have the question why were not courts formed for all the wars that are being waged throughout the world and that had been waged at least in the past decade of the 20th century. Although there are no principled reasons for not doing something like that and to apply to everybody if such a thing were legal. In other words, this Tribunal represents the most serious form of discrimination against one country, and it is a violation of the protection against all forms of discrimination.[61]

The second was that his prosecution was designed to paper over crimes committed by other parties in the conflict, including NATO, which he regarded as a sponsor of the Tribunal:

> I would just like to point out a paradoxical situation in which you have brought yourself into by bowing down to the daily merciless policy of the Clinton administration. Reality was falsified in the name of a pragmatic political programme. All three indictments were issued after 19 NATO countries carried out an open aggression against the remaining part of Yugoslavia, Serbia, and Montenegro, with banned weapons implementing new forms of tyranny through high technology. Is there any greater cynicism? The indictment for Croatia cites ethnic cleansing of Croats, and this was conceived before the 1st of August, 1991, and lasted until 1992. I must say that one has to be extremely arrogant to place such a lie on paper. As is well known, this was a period of mass crimes against Serbs, and the first major exodus of Serbs from Croatia. A hundred and fifty thousand of them, precisely in this time period. The Kosovo indictment was issued, and I am quoting, "because of the expulsion of a substantial number of Albanian citizens from Kosovo." Well, you saw what it says in [Wesley] Clark's book, but you will see many other also more interesting things. You cannot cite one single village from which someone was expelled while Kosovo was under the control of the Serb state organs.[62]

The line of defense he adopted was not likely to persuade the trial panel and most certainly did not. Presiding judge Patrick Robinson admonished Milošević several times to try to make relevant points, while the lead prosecutor, Geoffrey Nice, openly stated at one point that he could not see what the defendant was talking about. But Milošević had a different goal—to persuade the television audience that he was right when he declared after his electoral defeat in 2000, "they are not attacking Serbia because of Milošević, they are attacking Milošević because of Serbia."[63] In doing so he would provide a set of arguments that came to provide a frequent tool in the arsenal of denial.

One application of the argument was the thesis that a strong emphasis on crimes committed by Serbia and Serb forces was designed to discourage Serbs from raising their own grievances. As one newspaper commentator put it: "The constant repetition that Serbs need to confront their own crimes, while at the same time remaining silent about crimes committed against Serbs, has no foundation neither in reality nor in elementary morality, but it does have a goal—that the Serbian people should understand and accept that they are wasting their time if they try to remind people or to point out their own suffering or crimes committed by others."[64] To the degree that an imbalance is perceived as discrimination, in the view of another newspaper commentator, it detracts from any genuine acceptance of responsibility:

> The heteronomous psychological fear of great powers whose crimes it is forbidden to condemn always creates in the small and weak a strong mental resistance to condemning their own evils. The psychological truth that moral judgment only functions if it is applied universally (because only under that condition are there no "smaller" or "bigger" actors) is more than evident here in our Serbian postwar era. The leaders of the Bosnian Serbs are condemned, but not the leaders of massacres against the Palestinians.[65]

While the reference to Palestinians might suggest that the writer has in mind both a particular great power and a particular body of conspiracy theory, the message functions on another level: confrontation with the past is not expected of all people for universal reasons, but of some people because of their weak position.

This perhaps explains some of the appeal of *tu quoque*, and also why as a rhetorical strategy it tends to cross over from denial to resentment. Turning again to Srebrenica, we will see in the next chapter how commemoration of the Srebrenica killings were answered by countercommemorations for Serb victims of attacks by the Bosnian army on villages surrounding Srebrenica between 1992 and 1995.[66] After a memorial center was opened in Potočari a competing memorial center was opened in Bratunac, and after an annual ceremony in Potočari became a regular and widely publicized event a parallel event was set for Bratunac. The original event was more widely visited and covered than the counterevent, and continued to be for years. An observer responded with charges of discrimination designed to imply equivalence between the objects of commemoration:

> One cannot help but notice that the commemoration in Potočari, beginning in May when preparations began, began to take on very

clear political connotations. Diplomatic representatives in B-H began to announce to the government that they were coming to the meeting. As was expected, they were led by the American ambassador. Although just a day after the meeting in Potočari a commemorative meeting, that is a memorial to the victims in the Serb villages of Biljača, Zalazje, and Sase was announced, the foreigners generally ignored that one. Victims are victims, and however many there are all of them deserve human sympathy.[67]

Defenders of the strategy of equivalence might argue that *tu quoque* is not so much a strategy of denial as an effort to establish a context. To the degree that it establishes a context it sets up a comparative one in which one given set of facts has the same weight as any other that is placed next to it. The effect is to obscure distinctions between crimes emerging from policy and crimes occurring episodically, and between victims and aggressors.

7. Broadening the Context Beyond Recognition

A broader way of postulating a context for understanding crimes has the effect of making all individual crimes disappear. That is to place particular crimes in the context of all crimes—in some instances all crimes committed during the course of the recent war, and in others all crimes committed in (recent?) human history. If it is possible to accept the moralistic proposition offered by advocates of *tu quoque* that all victims, regardless of number or national identity,[68] deserve human sympathy, then it is likely to follow that no crime is more important than another. The use of this type of argumentation predates the conflict that gave rise to its present popularity: while the controversial book *Wasteland of Historical Reality*, by historian Franjo Tudjman, who would soon afterward become president of Croatia, was primarily attacked as an exercise in denial of crimes from the World War II period, it had another principal argument aside from its empirical claims minimizing the number of victims. Genocide, in Tudjman's view, was a constant in human history, dating back at least as far in recorded history as the Old Testament and continuing on through contemporary political conflicts.[69] The argument has two important implications: (1) in the context of human history no particular crime stands out as unique, and (2) engaging in mass violence places a political community within the current of global history rather than outside it.

Probably not many of the people in Serbia who employ this line of argument would happily admit to borrowing a rhetorical device from Franjo Tudjman. Nonetheless it is possible to recognize a line of argument that begins with particular events and by broadening the context causes them to recede to a vanishing point. During the failed effort to pass a resolution on Srebrenica in the Serbian parliament in 2005, this effort became clear. A group of eight nongovernmental organizations came forward with a proposed text according to which "Serbia obligates itself . . . to honor the verdicts which have clearly defined the legal character of the crime of genocide committed in Srebrenica."[70] They were joined in clarity of position in the text proposed by the Serbian Renewal Movement (SPO), which inclined toward religious rather than legal language: "Because that crime was committed by Serb hands and weapons, it also represents a crime against the Serbian people, its history, tradition, and culture. Both as people and as a nation, we regret the massacre in Srebrenica, we bow to the memory of the victims and we offer our deepest condolences in the pain of their loved ones." The DS then in opposition, proposed a less specific wording to "condemn all crimes committed in the course of the wars on the territory of the former Yugoslavia"—implying but not stating that the condemnation came regardless of who committed the crimes. Nonetheless the DS proposal still specified that Srebrenica was to be "especially condemned."

The Democratic Party of Serbia (DSS), which led the government at the time, came forward with a proposal that altered the sense of the resolution. The condemnation of the crime in Srebrenica was accompanied by a shift of context and a list of other crimes that as the text developed began to read more like an accusation than a recognition:

First among victims, Serbia must also be first in the condemnation of all crimes. The Democratic Party of Serbia in this declaration condemns all war crimes, without regard to who committed them, in the conviction that no crime is subject to statutes of limitation and no crime can be forgotten. . . . It is of fundamental importance in the condemnation of crime we do not make distinctions on the basis of the place where a crime was committed or the religion or nationality of the victim. Therefore we unreservedly condemn the crime committed in Srebrenica. Most severely condemning all war crimes committed against the Serbian people, the Democratic Party of Serbia on this occasion draws the attention of domestic and international public opinion to the fact that massive war crimes, like the crimes committed in Operation "Flash," Operation "Storm," Sarajevo, Tuzla, Bratunac, and elsewhere, remain uninvestigated and unpunished.

The broadened context is intended to put forward a moral question. If one set of crimes is wrong, why is another set of crimes not equally wrong? Is there a legitimate reason to set apart particular victims—whether these are victims of large-scale crimes or of the force that the institution making the declaration symbolically represents—rather than commemorating all victims of all crimes?

It might be possible to suggest that there are two reasons. The first is that the broadening of the context has the unstated consequence of diminishing the event at issue. This consequence is, at least usually, unstated. One of the rare articulations of it comes in an article by the philosopher Aleksandar Jokić, insisting that "genocidalism"—his label for the effort to define a particular crime as constituting genocide—is illegitimate if it does not encompass all genocides:

> If my hunch (to be argued for elsewhere) is right, genocidalism of commission has as its ultimate aim or at least its consequences inevitably lead to the silence and cover up of real genocides. Hence, the genocidal use of "genocide" is ultimately an instrument of denial. Concretely, what has been accomplished by those who engage in the widespread genocidalism of commission about Bosnia in the 1990s is precisely genocidalism of omission regarding a real genocide of the 1940s committed by the Ustashe regime in the Independent State of Croatia (NDH). For narratives giving intense attention to the former while remaining completely mute about the latter abound.[71]

The implication is unmistakable: one genocide trumps another. And if it makes sense to compare genocides according to size, certainly Srebrenica (7,475 victims, according to ICTY researchers)[72] will pale in comparison to the World War II-era genocide (460,000–590,000 victims, according to Srdjan Bogosavljević).[73] Differences in context produce differences in meaning.

But in that case, why stop with regional and contemporary examples? The logic of comparison suggests a second reason why shifting the context empties the argument of content. Either example will pale in comparison with the Rwandan genocide of 1994 (1,074,017 declared victims and 934,218 accounted for, according to the Rwandan government),[74] or the Armenian genocide beginning in 1915 (1,500,000 victims, according to Gerald Libaridian).[75] These two examples hardly come close to exhausting the possibilities. Bring in examples on the scale of the Nazi genocides or the Stalinist terror and they all appear to be smaller. Combine them all to bring together all the victims of all the organized outrage in human history and the victims of any particular one fade into tiny parts of a history of human civilization that looks like little more than a maelstrom of starvation, disease, cruelty, torment and slaughter. If that is what all history looks like, to paraphrase Bismarck, is a little conflict in the Balkans worth the bones of a Pomeranian statistician?[76]

Some efforts to dilute the meaning of commemoration tended in just that direction. As a first contribution to the abortive 2005 parliamentary debate over a resolution on Srebrenica, the presiding officer of the parliament, Predrag Marković, ordered a minute of silence in the chamber—dedicated to the victims of both Srebrenica and Bratunac but also, he noted, to the victims of a recent terrorist attack in London.[77] A memorial proposed for a skyscraper development sought design ideas for "a memorial to victims of war and defenders of the Fatherland, 1990–1999."[78] The idea of commemorating participants on all sides together with their victims marks an effort by politicians to forge a compromise—one strikingly similar to the compromise that Franjo Tudjman had proposed in Croatia, whereby Ustashe and their victims would be buried together at the memorial site of Jasenovac, an idea apparently inspired by Francisco Franco's model of national reconciliation after the Spanish civil war.[79] As Lea David observes: "The participants in the war do not have a clear master narrative because they are not succeeding in unifying all of the wars into one 'metawar' . . . in the first place, there does not exist even a minimal consensus about what 'has to be' remembered, and in the second place, different groups continually attempt to legitimate their own narratives and have them included in collective memory."[80] The result is a policy of memorialization that looks very much like the public efforts to determine a context for understanding the recent past—confused, overly broad, with ongoing disputes about which event means what according to what criteria.

Reasonable on its surface, the strategy of broadening the context is designed to appeal to the desire to apply principles universally and to take history into account. But it has the consequence of postulating a universe in which the numbers of victims and perpetrators are potentially infinite and hence indistinguishable from one another—a kind of denial by dilution.

8. The General Position That Not Everything Is Known

If there is a position that minimizes facts by postulating that too much is known, there is a corresponding one that downplays them by claiming that nothing is known with certainty. Returning to Srebrenica again, a discourse has developed seeking to cast doubt on evidence produced by investigators who have exhumed and analyzed human remains seeking to establish the scope and structure of the mass killings that took place in July 1995. While this effort is led by individuals from the region with associations that indicate a political interest in diminishing the scale of the crime in Srebrenica, there is some degree of international participation as well. This international participation comes from figures who regard intervention, especially by the United States, in the former Yugoslavia as a part of a wider imperial ambition, and in that context argue that the killings in Srebrenica were inflated in order to justify intervention.[81] Fundamentally the line of argument offered from this perspective is that the existing evidence cannot be accepted with absolute confidence, and that therefore space is created both for doubt and for the introduction of alternative narratives of events. To the degree that they do not persuasively demonstrate anything concrete, this does not detract from the central purpose of the project, which is to raise confusion about facts that have been demonstrated.

Perhaps the fullest and most comprehensive statement of the perspective offered in this discourse comes in a 2011 publication by the Srebrenica Historical Project. The publication is presented, probably accurately, as representing the state of the art in historical revisionism related to Srebrenica. However in rejecting the label of revisionism the editor, Stefan Karganović, also sets out the thesis to be demonstrated: "The issue of 'revisionism' does not even arise in the case of Srebrenica. Since the Bosnian War ended a decade and a half ago, no fundamental aspect of the matter has been clarified. Therefore everything is open. A provisionally acceptable narrative of

Srebrenica has yet to be written. Hence, at this point there is literally nothing to 'revise.'"[82] The authors seek to put into doubt all the facts that are
known and that have been presented in judicial fora, raising the possibility
that no element of the events is genuinely known. Endeavoring to put
themselves on an equal footing with people carrying out investigations, they
describe a "relentless drive to stifle debate about Srebrenica."[83] Therefore
the "deconstruction" of the evidence is accompanied with a (political)
explanation as to "why the high priests of the Srebrenica cult keep such a
sharp eye out for the slightest stirring of critical thinking, anywhere, about
their false construction. They react invariably with the threat that 'any
attempt at revision of historical facts' concerning Srebrenica is strictly for-
bidden."[84] The authors portray themselves as subject to a "militant medie-
val dogmatism."[85] Within this context they seek permission to enter what
is referred to in multiple instances as a "game"[86] in order to see, not necessarily whether they can score some points, but perhaps persuade a referee
to deduct some from their opponents.

The critique of the Srebrenica evidence offered by the Srebrenica Historical Project is based on the following arguments: (1) not all prosecution
witnesses agree on details, (2) DNA identification is unreliable, (3) aerial
reconnaissance photos may not have used the newest available technology.
The rest of the argument relies mostly on insinuation and attribution of
motives to institutional and individual actors. It also offers a frequently
repeated claim that people presented as victims of mass executions were in
fact not civilians but members of retreating armed units who were killed in
combat (alternatively, sometimes, as executed prisoners of war—indicating
a war crime but not genocide).[87] Failing this, they offer the thesis that a
"holistic" view of events would regard the mass killings as (justifiable?)
revenge for attacks on Serb civilians in an earlier stage of the war.[88]

Without going into great detail on particular claims, which are presented over 321 pages of text, the general tone of the argument can be
presented in a few instances. First the authors claim: "The basic problem
confronting every Srebrenica researcher at the outset is that essential data
are accessible only with great difficulty, or not at all. Almost as daunting is
the fact that the sources of much of the data that are accessible are so
poisoned with fabrications that even the most experienced researchers will
find it difficult to find their way in the labyrinth of contradictions and false
leads."[89] While the question whether the material is difficult to master is

perhaps a matter of opinion, the claim that it is not accessible is demonstrably false. All evidence presented before ICTY is available at the online home of the Tribunal, and a documentary film presenting the evidence *Beyond Reasonable Doubt/Izvan razumne sumnje* was distributed free as a DVD by the Belgrade daily *Danas* throughout 2006.[90]

Most of the empirical material presented is designed to cast doubt on the forensic evidence produced for the use of the Tribunal. On exhumations the claim is offered that "one is not sure if they are speaking of whole corpses or of pieces of corpses."[91] Much of the effort to reject forensic evidence revolves around raising uncertainty about the cause of death for bodies that were exhumed. In the report's discussion of forensic evidence, Ljubiša Simić argues: "It must be made clear that no expert, regardless of skill or reputation, can state with absolute certainty whether an injury was the result of execution or combat merely on the basis of a bullet or an injury to some portion of the body, especially if the body is in an advanced state of decomposition or has been reduced to a skeleton. Unqualified assertions are always a sure sign that the expert is overstepping the legitimate bounds of his or her mandate."[92] In a sense the strategy represented in this argument could stand as representative of the entire project: (1) the plea for a "holistic" analysis offered to encourage readers to think of Srebrenica as being balanced by other crimes is rejected in order to ignore consideration of environmental factors (such as the existence of mass burial sites) in determining the cause of death; and (2) though this is not mentioned in the analysis, much of the decay and damage done to forensic evidence in fact resulted from efforts after the killings to hide evidence (especially by shifting bodies from their original burial sites).

If the arguments offered to suggest that killings did not occur do not, therefore, come off as persuasive, this is not a problem for the authors. They have other arguments in reserve, though these ones rely on insinuation rather than analysis. Chief among these is the contention that "There are reasons to believe not just that the dimensions of Srebrenica 'genocide' have been purposefully inflated, and not only that it was a staged event, but also that it occurred by political arrangement."[93] This contention involves surmises about intentions, the character of planning, and in the final instance, an insinuation that somebody other than the parties charged may have committed the crime. Readers who are not persuaded might be reassured that the authors do not claim that any of this is the case, but rather that "there is reason to believe," just as in principle there could be reason to believe anything else. Though there is an implied caution against believing, in one case, "the abundance of fantastic details provided by prosecution witnesses who seem to have been well coached by the Moslem intelligence service AID for that purpose."[94]

The publication is prepared to resemble a genuine academic work; it has footnotes, charts, appendices—at one point there is even a brief discussion of methodology![95] But among the factors that distinguish it from an academic work is that it has the purpose not of determining anything independently but rather of raising doubt about findings determined by others.[96] Crucially, the authors declare that their purpose is not to establish that events did not happen—they make an effort to deny that they are engaged in crude denial of the facts and reject crude denial as extreme.[97] Rather, in the tradition of the legal defenders of the police officers who beat Rodney King,[98] and in the group of writers who seek to subject the Nazi genocides to "historical review,"[99] they seek to raise doubt about established facts by suggesting that not all existing evidence is determinative. If nothing is known with absolute certainty, alternative assertions and recontextualizations have the same standing as the existing empirical record. In that case the empirical record can be dismissed as propaganda or reduced to one contention among many that can be chosen according to a person's predisposition. Or in the authors' words, "Srebrenica is a big Rorschach drawing and everyone viewing it is free to read into it the meaning that is in accord with his or her own indoctrination on the subject."[100] That indoctrination is the source of understanding is perhaps the point that was to be demonstrated.

9. Contesting the Procedure by Which Guilt and Responsibility Are Established

Not all approaches to denial rely on putting facts into question. A frequently used approach concentrates instead on the people and institutions concerned with finding facts, diffusing knowledge about them, and promoting their discussion. Obviously the Tribunal itself is an object of critique for many reasons, from the conditions of its founding, charges of bias and incompetence, to the unusual way it creates rather than following legal precedent. This dimension of the critique is amply covered in existing literature and so will not be an object of extensive attention here.[101] What has received less attention in the literature is conflicts over the establishment of a documentary record and promotion of discussion of responsibility in domestic politics and culture. In an influential 2003 article, Vojin Dimitrijević drew attention not only to ways facts are subjected to "requalification, where facts are probably being acknowledged, but are marked as something of a secondary nature, permitted, nonpunishable, and not as criminal acts," but also ways some groups offer resistance to "the idea that [the] international community and foreign actors in general can make judgments."[102] The resistance is not, however, directed exclusively toward international actors.

On the domestic terrain the principal targets of attack are nongovernmental organizations concerned with transitional justice and human rights. Especially frequent targets are the Fund for Humanitarian Law (FHP) and its director Nataša Kandić; the Helsinki Committee for Human Rights (HCHRS) and its president Sonja Biserko; the Women in Black and the group's cofounder Staša Zajović; and the Lawyers' Committee for Human Rights and its director the late Biljana Kovačević-Vućo. Advocates of human rights in general, but these three women in particular, are the objects of charges that they are anti-Serbian, that they are traitors, and that they represent a domestic fifth column standing for foreign interests.[103]

In more moderate versions of the attacks human rights advocates are put on an equal footing with defenders of criminals as representatives of two extremes in a debate that lacks a middle position.[104] An article in the popular news weekly *NIN* promises to explain "how the essence of debates about war crimes is lost in battles between extreme nationalists and 'specialists in confrontation with the past' from nongovernmental organizations."[105] Other versions of the attack abandon the pretense of balancing between extremes and simply opt for one, as in a broadside against "Those false humanists and enlighteners [who], these days, shamelessly and soullessly seek their pot of gold in the tragic fate of six murdered Bosnians. And they do it all in the service of their political-dilettante goals or the money and status they can receive for slandering, beheading, and euthanizing the Serbian nation and its national institutions."[106] While the above example relies on avarice for attribution of motive, political attacks are generally more specific. For example, DSS deputy Dragoljub Kojičić called for a parliamentary investigation into whether "some nongovernmental organizations, which currently carry out an anti-Serbian campaign, receive their financing from foreign sources, which would be easiest to confirm by an inquiry into their business records."[107]

In 2003 sociologist Slobodan Antonić provoked a polemic with an article that attacked a group he defined as the "missionary intelligentsia" (the group was largely a conceit of the author, who identified seven individuals writing in six publications, though he would quote a few more in the text),[108] as opposing the society in which they operate, and in an interesting projection, turning themselves into self-declared enemies of their country. Antonić accuses his missionaries of bringing rejection upon themselves by threatening "important values, basic beliefs that form the identity of the community."[109] Since public response to such a threat is negative, Antonić argues,

some domestic enlighteners who want, for the good of their co-tribalists, to "enlighten" them, "modernize" them, "bring them into the modern world," can be wholly infuriated by their resistance. . . . So they look without understanding upon every refusal in the community to accept their values. Then they can often become entirely enraged and begin to behave irrationally. They begin to chasten their co-tribalists and to advance their ideas in an increasingly incendiary and nervous way. And since this ardor and nervousness leads to exaggeration and crudeness, those new values appear to the community in an ever worse light. And so the resistance of the community to the domestic missionaries—because they really have by now become missionaries in their country, since they experience some other city or country as their spiritual home while they sense the place where they live as alien—this resistance keeps growing, and with it the passion and exasperation of the missionaries.

Eventually, the domestic missionaries will all too often have to confront the complete rejection of the community. When that happens they experience it as a personal blow, a defeat. They begin to believe that something is wrong with their co-tribalists, that the whole community is somehow defective. They are embittered with their environment, they hold it in contempt, and in the end they come to hate the whole community.[110]

It is not difficult to identify, in this description of angry, defeated missionaries, elements of influence (though these are not explicitly applied) of postcolonial theory, alienation theory, and pop psychology. Leaving aside the question of whether any actually existing person fits the description that Antonić offers, or whether the public is made up of "co-tribalists" (*saplemenici*), he goes on to describe the "new values" the promotion of which leads to the diagnosis of extreme frustration.

In short, the group Antonić postulates is made up of "self-styled missionaries of the Atlantic Council and its values in Serbia."[111] Their task is analogous to what agitprop and cultural workers may have done in the Communist period, with one essential difference:

> Of course there no longer exists a Party to dictate the line. But now, serving the same function, there are certain nongovernmental organizations for human rights or institutes for democracy and transition from Washington or Bruxelles. By means of their financing of local media outlets, NGOs, unions, etc., they determine the priorities that are foisted in various campaigns on the domestic public: confrontation with Serbian crimes in Croatia, Bosnia and Kosovo, construction of Serbia as a multiethnic and multicultural state, the struggle against (anti-American, it is understood) terrorism, Romani people, homosexuals, children with special needs, humanizing stray dogs and cats, etc.[112]

In a few short sentences, then, he offers a dismissal of advocates of human rights and democracy, but on interesting grounds: (1) they are associated with foreign powers; (2) they are brought into the same category as groups like Roma, homosexuals, and the disabled, against whom discrimination is still very widely tolerated in Serbia; and (3) the importance of their cause is diminished by the association with causes like the care of stray animals, a concern associated with prosperous environments, do-gooders, and Brigitte Bardot.[113]

The polemical descant on the "missionaries" offers three fundamental critiques. First, they are presented as so obsessed with nationalism and confrontation with the past that they are blind to the progressive and democratic potential of Serbian society.[114] Second, they are presented as intolerant of disagreement and inclined to advocate repression.[115] But, third and most important, they are presented as producing effects opposite to what they intend. Antonić makes the last point with a complex image that combines a description of compulsive cleanliness with an image of fundamentalist dictatorships:

> It is good to maintain hygiene, but if you begin obsessively cleaning everything in the surroundings the result will be defeating for two reasons. First, you will not have the time or energy for anything else, because you will have become a slave to hygiene. And second, your obsessive behavior will compromise the very idea of hygiene and offer new arguments to the advocates of living in filth. Nationalism is an evil, which should be opposed. But a fixation on nationalism, finding nationalism where it does not exist, making a nationalistic donkey out of a mosquito, and a general obsession with nationalist exorcism, can only end in a pathetic social extravagance which will provoke the ridicule of the majority, or—if it comes to power—in one more dogmatic tyranny over the society in the name of a fixed idea.[116]

Regardless of the unique stylistic and humoristic devices used here, which could give an impression of moderation, the critique directed at the opponents of nationalism is in fact quite encompassing. Antonić depicts them as a counter-elite opposing a more authentic one, which at the same time that it fails to gain public support also threatens the public with repression and a possible ideological dictatorship. At the same time the suggestion that antinationalists could oppose nationalism more effectively by declining to oppose it leaves his opponents in the polemic little place to stand.

The broadside provoked a wide reaction and a debate that lasted from February, when the initial article appeared, to May, when novelist Vladimir Pištalo weighed in with the last contribution. Of several thematic threads in the discussion, a few stand out. Both columnist Velimir Ćurguz Kazimir and law professor Vojin Dimitrijević pointed out that in not using a representative sample Antonić had failed to demonstrate that he had described a phenomenon that really exists. The political scientist Dušan Pavlović argued that rejecting the critique of nationalism was effectively equivalent to advocacy of it. Consistent with that last insight, Velimir Ćurguz Kazimir saw in the text "the appalling spirit of conspiracy theory and xenophobia," while Miloš Stanojević described the article as "paradigmatic of the whining of right-wing nationalists about how everybody is after them."[117]

Whether or not the "missionary intelligentsia" actually exists, the polemic seems to suggest some meaningful movement in terms of denial. In the first place, the goals and ideas of such projects as confronting the past might be belittled, but they are not questioned on their own merits. In addition, neither facts nor arguments are contested; the polemic is directed toward their source(s) and the spirit in which they are made. Much of the debate that was inspired by Antonić's salvo seemed to concentrate on the issue of what personage was associated with what competing portion of the academic and political elite. In that sense, the campaign to discredit human rights advocates represents an important step along the path from denial to responsibility: crimes are no longer being celebrated or denied, contexts are no longer being shifted. The object of attention is no longer outrage but the competition for political power. Maybe lurking behind that is also the possibility of a debate on the political future.

Forms of Responsibility?

If conflicts over the question of responsibility are moving to the field of competition for political power, then it is time for the presentation to move from denial to responsibility. The final section of this chapter considers two variants of responsibility: one that concentrates on the past, using guilt as the springboard from which discussions of responsibility begin, and one that concentrates on the future, postulating that "answerableness" regarding the past constitutes the basic condition for a path forward that is neither beholden to authoritarian legacies nor reliant on authoritarian leadership.

10. Backward-Looking Responsibility: Responsibility as Self-Accusation

There is an approach to responsibility—confined to a limited group of activists in Serbia but presented more often from political actors outside the country—that has a slightly psychological, slightly metaphysical character. In its mildest version it calls for a "catharsis," while stronger versions seem to call for a collective acknowledgment of guilt and some effort to bring a sense of guilt into part of a national consciousness. Some outside commentators use terms like "denazification,"[118] provoking an intense and for the most part bitter reaction in Serbia.[119]

This approach may be advanced by a limited group in Serbia, but it is not absent from the scene. Some prominent artists, feminist groups, and antiwar groups began discussing this sort of responsibility while the wars of succession were still ongoing, particularly in Bosnia-Herzegovina. Although the Serbian Orthodox Church generally appears in public as a force supporting the nationalist right, there were some actors within it who saw the need to oppose violence, protect people regardless of nationality, and actively seek forgiveness as consistent with their religious mission— most prominent among them Sava Janjić of the Dečani monastery, who sought to shield civilians from abuse during the conflict and told an interviewer shortly afterward, "We in Serbia need an Adenauer but also a Nuremberg for the whole Balkans which will try all the Balkan butchers from Zagreb to Belgrade, from Sarajevo to Pristina."[120] Representatives of all these groups at one time or another declared a need to recognize responsibilities and obligations on the level of society, and some spoke of the need for penance.

Language related to penance and shame did enter into the discussion around domestic trials for crimes against the civilian population. A news headline announcing the arrest of police officers for the 1999 Suva Reka massacre put the case succinctly: "They murdered women and children, they shamed the nation."[121] In delivering the first verdict of Serbia's special judicial chamber for war crimes, judge Vesko Krstajić addressed perpetrators of the Ovčara massacre using an aphorism from nineteenth-century Montenegrin chronicler Marko Miljanov: "Heroism is defending yourself against the enemy, while honor is defending your enemy against yourself. Sirs, here we did not judge your heroism, the verdict on that will be given by history. We judged you for the things you were charged with."[122]

The statements around the trials bring into the discourse the theme of regret. In the judge's statement to the convicts the suggestion is offered that guilt constitutes a failure of honor. The scope is broadened in the journalistic account that pictures the "nation" as having been brought to shame.

It is not entirely clear what is achieved in the formulation that a "nation" participates in shame. At first glance it seems to be a very strong, almost morally fundamentalist position. Concretely, however, it puts forward a vague demand: what are people expected to do with their shame? Express it through statements of regret or self-accusation? It is difficult to see what might be gained by an extended period of expressing or feeling a generalized and atmospheric sense of guilt, except perhaps the prospect of steady employment for psychotherapists. In practical terms, then, while this position seems to offer the prospect of a sort of moral satisfaction for victims, it is in fact far weaker than the position advocating individual engagement with responsibility.

Perhaps the backward-looking form of responsibility makes only a certain amount of sense as a freestanding position, and greater sense in conjunction with another position. One of those other positions would be the insistence on specifying individual responsibility and punishing the guilty, as a way preventing the attribution of guilt to entire social collectives. This is the perspective advanced by Serbian politician Nataša Mićić:

> It is not possible to escape responsibility for crimes, criminals, and criminal policy. The only possibility is that our generation will transfer that responsibility to future ones, to the ones that are coming, and that will have nothing to do with the misdeeds of which we are contemporaries. I think that would be very cowardly. That obligation has to be carried out by us, because the people who committed crimes in our name would like nothing more than for that responsibility and repentance to be left to our children. That way they would escape responsibility for their own lives, while also succeeding in leaving it for the entire people in the future. That is their real intention, because now they have only one goal, to escape responsibility.[123]

Implicit in this point of view is an alternative orientation—the contention that the past matters because of the future. In that alternative might lie the fundamental value of the discussion of responsibility, and it is to that perspective that the final section of this chapter turns.

11. Forward-Looking Responsibility: Responsibility as Engagement?

A variation on the theme of responsibility is not principally about accusation or the possibility of punishment. Most of the discussion so far has been about establishing responsibility for the past, but the present moment offers at least the possibility of people in Serbia taking on responsibility for the future. The discussion about the past may very well be a basic condition for any effort to develop a model of responsibility as active engagement—or it may constitute the first instance of this kind of responsibility in action.

Some of the motivations behind the various approaches to responsibility involve retribution or strategic political positioning. This is neither surprising nor terrible, but it is limited. If we ask why the question of responsibility needs to be posed at all, purely strategic or retributive answers would appear incomplete. Something more fundamental is at stake: the possibility of assuring that the events that provoked the discussion of responsibility do not occur again.

It might be suggested that if there is one factor which made the rule of Milošević possible, and which continues to make controversial the efforts of people associated with him to retain their positions, it is the persistence of an authoritarian political culture that can be dated back to the Communist period or, if one prefers, earlier.[124] While authoritarianism is often condemned from an ideological point of view, at least one functional characteristic makes it enormously appealing: as long as citizens are not consulted about or involved in major decisions, they are the fault (or possibly the achievement) of the person in power. On the one hand this translates to a negative freedom from responsibility for citizens: whatever the state does is done without their involvement. On the other hand, the possibility of shared responsibility—active engagement in the construction of a political future and social order for which all citizens are responsible—is also precluded.[125]

This sort of argument, when it is made in Serbia, seems to be made more often on the theoretical level than in the context of practical politics. In this context the basic point of reference for the discussion is *The Question of Guilt* by Karl Jaspers.[126] Though parallels can be exaggerated, Jaspers wrote the book at a similar political moment and with motivations that echo the motivations of people dealing with the question in Serbia. Germany had just exited a historical period that had permanent consequences on the international reputation of the country, and was faced with the twin challenges of building a new democratic order and assuring that the horrors of the recent past would not be repeated. One of Jaspers's principal arguments is highlighted by Drinka Gojković:

> [Jaspers] draws his chief distinction between societies with political dictatorships and societies with political freedom. In the first the majority of people does not feel responsible for the political life of

the community, while in the second "a politically free life . . . is made possible by the task and the opportunity of shared responsibility on the part of all of us." Political freedom postulates "a political ethic . . . as the principle of the existence of the state, according to which everybody participates by means of their conscience, knowledge, beliefs and will."[127]

In this regard the basic purpose of a discussion about retrospective responsibility for crimes is to catalyze the kind of social change that might lead to active responsibility for the future of the country. The basic thesis behind this is that people who feel as though they have some power over their own lives and the environment they live in are not likely to be susceptible to rhetorics of recrimination or to allow crimes against humanity to be committed in their name.

The category might seem vague, and might be dismissed as visionary, but it may also come closest to the tantalizing goal stated by Otpor! spokesperson Vukašin Petrović as the political transformation of Serbia was just beginning: to "eliminate the last possibility that some new Milošević may appear in Serbia."[128] This approach requires understanding Milošević not just as the sum total of his positions and interventions, but also as the product of a system that generated resignation, powerlessness, and frustration. In a context where ordinary citizens could not meaningfully influence decisions made in their names, those decisions could take any form, including war, repression, and crime. Hannah Arendt described a similar contribution of intellectual disillusionment to an earlier acquiescence to criminality, when many people came to believe that "history, which was a forgery anyway, might as well be the playground of crackpots."[129] If history is not a forgery, of course—if it is a foundation for recognition, knowledge and understanding—then alternatives become possible.

So along the broad continuum from denial to the potential of responsibility, what has been the direction of movement? Again we have to move from the general to the specific. The following chapter will trace discourses around the crime that is generally considered[130] to have been the greatest abuse of the wars of Yugoslav succession, the massacre of a large proportion of the male population of Srebrenica in July 1995.[131] In this respect while it may be the case from a legal perspective that a court is a finder of fact and arbiter of guilt (but not of responsibility), it appears increasingly clear that the publication of facts and the operation of judicial processes may not be sufficient to promote the kind of discussion that puts denial and avoidance into question. This requires processes close to people, about which people are informed through an open dialogue in which they are engaged.

Chapter 7

Moment III: The "Scorpions" and the Refinement of Denial

Many examples of denial discussed in the last chapter relate specifically to the large-scale organized killings that followed the conquest of Srebrenica in 1995. The crime has taken on an emblematic character, serving as a shorthand for the ways armed force was directed against civilians, the coordination between military and paramilitary forces, and the parallel processes of development and denial of evidence. This emblematic character has its critics: Srebrenica was not the only crime in Bosnia-Herzegovina and Bosnia-Herzegovina was not the only place where crimes occurred. In Serbia a broad current of belief regards the emphasis on Srebrenica as tendentious, stressing instead the three years of conflict that preceded the massacre and crimes in which Serbs were victims. Nonetheless, for better or worse, Srebrenica has come to represent the key through which the wars of the 1990s are understood, particularly from outside. It is the only event in the wars for which there exist convictions for genocide.[1] In Serbia, perceptions of Srebrenica stand for orientations about the wars of the 1990s more broadly understood.

In 2005 a development in the Milošević trial briefly played a role in the public discussion of Srebrenica in Serbia—which transformed the discussion for a short period, but ended in confusion and trivia. To show to the judges that Serbia was not connected with the Srebrenica killings, Milošević brought onto the stand a former assistant interior minister, Obrad Stevanović. Stevanović was there to "completely reject any thought that I knew that some paramilitary units had crossed over from Serbia into Republika Srpska in order to perpetrate crimes."[2] In rebuttal, the prosecutor showed a film made by a member of one such paramilitary unit: it showed members of a Serbian interior ministry unit transporting and then executing a group of six prisoners in July 1995, concurrent with the Srebrenica killings.[3] The film and responses to it are described further on in this chapter; first it is necessary to describe the discursive context into which it entered.

Immediately after the Army of the Serb Republic (Vojska Republike Srpske, VRS) forces, commanded by General Ratko Mladić, took control of the Srebrenica "safe haven" in July 1995, there was no public indication of the crimes that took place.[4] International and domestic interest did not develop until August 1995 at the earliest, when it became clear that a large number of people from the area could not be accounted for. At the meeting of the UN Security Council on 10 August 1995, Antonius Eitel of Germany pointed out that "Several weeks after the fall of Srebrenica and Žepa we still do not know about the whereabouts and the fate of about 7000 to 8000" prisoners.[5] Madeleine Albright of the United States suggested that the number unaccounted for could be as high as 13,000.[6] The Security Council responded by passing Resolution 1010, demanding that representatives of international agencies be provided with access to displaced people and that prisoners be fairly treated and released.[7] At that point it had not yet been established that prisoners had been murdered. Investigation would quickly find that they had been, and Radovan Karadžić and Ratko Mladić were indicted for genocide in November 1995.

From that point on dominant media in Serbia engaged extensively in denial regarding Srebrenica, especially (1) to deny that the events occurred; (2) to direct blame away from Serbian authorities, whether this meant blaming VRS, uncontrolled paramilitaries, international actors, or the victims themselves; (3) to minimize the number of victims; (4) to present victims as combatants rather than civilians; and (5) to postulate an equivalence between the killings in Srebrenica and other crimes committed during the wars, especially crimes not committed by Serb forces. There is perhaps nothing surprising about media being engaged on this level while Slobodan Milošević, who would face genocide charges arising from the involvement of institutions under his authority in the killings, remained in power in Serbia.[8]

However, the denial did not end with the change of regime in 2000. One explanation followed the screening of the BBC documentary *Cry from the Grave* in 2001, which provoked a largely negative reaction. Writing in the weekly *NIN*, Petar Ignja described the film as "one-sided" and noted responses from call-in shows after the broadcast that included the assertion that "they had to be killed" and that the murders were a "sacred act." Ignja sought both political and cultural contexts to explain the response:

> Those people probably regarded the film as Western propaganda, with the goal of once again satanizing the Serbian people. . . . One also has to respect the fact that morality in the less civilized world differs from morality in the civilized world. It produces a collective and introverted form of thinking that tries to frame facts in an already existing picture, or even to ignore them, in order to keep developing a fantasy picture. That fantasy is as a rule mythical, and has its origins in a dark archaic picture—an archetype. For an archetypal picture of something, facts, even unassailable evidence of the crime in Srebrenica, are of secondary importance.[9]

A similar line of argument, relying on political and social factors rather than psychological extrapolations of mythology, was offered by Velimir Ćurguz Kazimir:

> How is it that, in spite of the great volume of information, the truth about Srebrenica was hidden? That requires a fundamental and serious answer. A part of the answer lies in a certain shame about the events, but also in some way testifies to national loyalty. Since what is done is done, the best thing is to deny it. That is the position not only of people who were witnesses and participants in the war but also of people who have absolutely nothing to do with wars and violence.[10]

Faced with a crime as horrifying as Srebrenica, denial appeared to offer a defense against the threat to national honor and self-perception.

So deny they did. One of the first issues taken on was the question of how many of the victims were civilians and how many were soldiers killed in battle or executed afterward. The distinction matters because battle casualties, while unfortunate, are not crimes under international law, while execution of prisoners is a war crime but not a crime against humanity or genocide.

The finding of the first Republika Srpska investigative commission in 2002 fit the most convenient legal outcome. This report found that the number of people killed was between 2,000 and 2,500, and that most of these were battle deaths:[11]

> 1800 soldiers of the Army of Bosnia and Herzegovina were killed in battles with members of the Army of Republika Srpska, which lost up to 500 soldiers in those battles. In the course of escape another hundred Bosnians died from physical exhaustion, while, according to the report, about a hundred Bosnian soldiers were killed after the fall of Srebrenica either out of personal revenge or because some RS soldiers were not acquainted with international law.[12]

Though the report received extensive publicity and promised to provide a "new truth about Srebrenica,"[13] it was generally rejected. The international High Representative in Bosnia-Herzegovina demanded the appointment of a commission to conduct a broader investigation[14]—the one that produced the fuller 2004 report that was followed by an apology from the Republika Srpska government.[15] While the 2002 document was intended to be used for the legal defense of indictees, it was introduced into evidence just once, in the trial of Miroslav Deronjić. The chamber determined that the report was "one of the worst examples of revisionism" it had seen, and dedicated a section of its verdict to "prevention of revisionism."[16] Interestingly, though the 2002 report from RS followed on the report from the Netherlands Institute for War Documentation (NIOD) that found that of 7,500 victims 6,000 had been liquidated (and led to the resignation of the Dutch government), it mentions neither the latter report nor its findings.[17]

The version of events portraying the deaths in Srebrenica as battle fatalities remained current despite its being debunked by other sources. In the classic version, "a large number of people fell in the effort of the Bosnian army to break through lines in order to establish contact with the territory under the control of the so-called Army of Bosnia and Herzegovina."[18] Among the most prominent advocates for this interpretation was the late Milan Bulajić, who also blamed the killings on the people who were killed: "The enormous suffering among the Muslims came primarily and mostly because of the attempt to break through the lines, and also because they refused to surrender their weapons when Srebrenica fell, because they had been ordered to carry out a suicidal mission toward the Muslim territory and that is where the largest number of them died."[19] Aware that combat fatalities could account neither for the number of victims nor their demo-graphic characteristics,[20] Bulajić maintained an alternative account of events in which Western powers (personified by French president Jacques Chirac), needing an atrocity to justify planned future intervention, staged the mass slaughter using a combination of French intelligence agents and Serb mer-cenaries not under local command.[21]

The value of the battle fatalities story (or the French intelligence story) is that it offers a reminder that Serb forces were not the only armed forces operating in the Srebrenica region. Attention would frequently be drawn to Serb victims of attacks carried out by local forces, particularly those under the command of Naser Orić,[22] between 1992 and 1995.[23] In 1995 Ratko Mladić referred to those forces as "Muslim fundamentalists."[24] Later they would come to be associated in the denial discourse with Al Qaeda, after that group became universally known following the terrorist attacks in the United States in 2001.

Together with the association of the Bosnian military with feared global terrorists came fantastic stories of cruelty, meant to establish that genocide in Srebrenica had been committed against Serbs rather than by them. One story in a lurid Belgrade tabloid involved prandial prizes for murders: "The reward of 25 kilograms of flour for every murdered Serb was publicly announced by the Muslim government in Srebrenica in 1992. Kemal Mehmedović from the village of Pale got twelve of those bags of flour and he was not the only one. Why has no nongovernmental organization raised its voice about the genocide against the Serbs in Bosnia and Herzegovina."[25] The "25 kilos of flour" story is unconfirmed and could hardly be expected to be true. It appears to originate in the media coverage that followed the taking of the city in 1995.[26] Its principal utility is to suggest the brutality of opponents in the Bosnian War.

There were also currents of ordinary factual denial. Among these were stories suggesting that people listed as missing or dead were still alive. One story had a person listed as killed escaping from a prison in Serbia, with the headline ridiculing him as a "vampirized Srebrenica martyr," and the article claiming that this instance illustrates a large number of people claimed as dead, "whose names are used in the most dishonorable way to fictively increase the number of victims."[27] Occasional stories would claim that people listed as dead had moved and changed their names (always to a Serbian name) and place of residence (always to place in Serbia), as in the assertion about "Hazim (Rašida) Čelebić, born on 10 October 1971 in

Cerska near Vlasenica, is on one of the lists of victims, the so-called Sre-brenica apocalypse list, both on the list of 'AOP Tuzla' and on the list of the International Red Cross. However, investigation has proved that Hazim is alive and well in Novi Sad, with a new name and surname—Srećko Pav-lović."[28] These stories echoed similar ones from the war period seeking to establish that stories of victimhood were fabricated.

Media efforts notwithstanding, the campaign for denial weakened through 2003 and 2004. Confessions by Momir Nikolić and Dragan Obren-ović before ICTY both confirmed elements of the crimes and provided details of them.[29] With the opening of the memorial center for Srebrenica victims in Potočari in 2003, a regular system of observance was put into place.[30] In 2004, the Republika Srpska investigative commission released its report on Srebrenica, which included a list of 7,800 people counted as miss-ing (and a list of perpetrators in an unpublished annex).[31] The report's publication was followed by a public apology from RS president Dragan Čavić in June, and a declaration from the entire government in Novem-ber.[32] The head of the commission regarded the report as meeting the need to "finally . . . remove the anathema from the Serbian people, so that finally there will be an end to stories about the guilt of a whole people, which is the reason for the existence of this commisssion."[33]

The RS commission report was greeted with some controversy, how-ever. A columnist in *NIN* described it as "the extraction of confessions by any means."[34] Other critics were more categorical, including one who declared that "the truth is, after all, that the 'Srebrenica case' has been transformed into an American-Islamic-Muslim weapon for the satanization of Serbs."[35] Some attention was paid to a minor scandal in which the first head of the investigative commission, Marko Arsović, resigned claiming that the high representative Jeremy Ashdown had sought to manipulate findings to show that Serbs were "the only ones guilty" of crimes.[36] As to who else might be guilty, a thesis was presented that the documentation of the crimes represented an attempt "to cover up the monstrous crimes committed by members of the notorious Al Qaida against Serbs in Srebrenica."[37]

The high point of denial came in May 2005, when the law students' group Nomokanon hosted a panel presentation,[38] "The Truth About Sre-brenica: Ten Years After the Liberation of Srebrenica,"[39] at the Faculty of Law in Belgrade. The meeting began with cheers for Radovan Karadžić, charged with genocide in the killings and still a fugitive at the time.[40] Little that was said by panelists at the meeting was unexpected or new. A retired army general, Radovan Radinović,[41] repeated the thesis that the massacre had been staged to encourage international intervention. Dragoslav Ognja-nović,[42] a legal advisor to Milošević, presented the numbers that had been offered as findings in the rejected 2002 RS report on Srebrenica. Journalist Ljiljana Bulatović[43] got an enthusiastic response from the audience by congratulating them on "the tenth anniversary of the liberation of Srebrenica."[44] On balance what was spoken by the panelists would have been anticipated by anybody who had been following denial discourse from daily media.

What attracted far more attention was the activity that surrounded the meeting. It was hosted by a University of Belgrade faculty, a site where public discourse potentially gains the stamp of scholarly authority.[45] It was condemned by representatives of human rights groups, who having failed to prevent the meeting from taking place showed up to it en masse—where their presence was countered by members of far-right groups, most prominent among them Obraz, associated with the Serbian Orthodox Church. The evening was marked by shouts and insults directed toward the representatives of the human rights groups, both from participants in the meeting and from private individuals who appeared to have been engaged for security at the event. Most of the people who came to protest the panel left shortly after it began, when the atmosphere of confrontation had become intense. At the end, one participant spat on the director of the Fund for Humanitarian Law.[46]

The organizers of the meeting were compelled to backtrack after an evening of provocation and disorder. The law faculty's official statement began with an effort to reassure readers that humanitarian law is indeed taught at the faculty.[47] The Nomokanon group told one set of journalists that no denial took place at the meeting and that their student organization was not tied to any other ultraright groups,[48] while telling another that the panel had been "a scientific conference based on facts."[49]

Condemnations, explanations, and justifications notwithstanding,[50] the Nomokanon panel revealed some dimensions of the state of denial in post-Milošević Serbia: (1) there were still some institutions willing to offer it support; (2) there was an audience for denial discourse, but at the same time (3) receptiveness to the version of events that was dominant before 2000 was hardly universal; and (4) there were people willing to make the point dramatically on both sides. Opinion was harshly divided in an atmosphere of controversy and uncertainty. A few weeks later, a shocking intervention into the discourse would appear, however briefly, to upset the balance of uncertainty.

Initial Responses to the "Scorpion" Film

On 1 June 2005, at the Milošević trial, portions of a film were shown to rebut the testimony of a defense witness that forces from Serbia had not been involved in the crimes in Srebrenica in July 1995. The film showed, in gruesome detail, members of the "Scorpions," a paramilitary unit under the command of the Serbian interior ministry, receiving a group of prisoners and executing them.[51]

The document first shows the "Scorpions" at a mountain house where they receive the prisoners. The prisoners are briefly seen lying face down in the back of a truck with their hands bound behind them. The truck sets off, and at an isolated roadside the prisoners are ordered out. At this point it becomes apparent that they are six teenage boys. One of them has no shoes. They are forced to lie face down by the side of the road, their hands still bound. One of them asks for water and is brusquely refused. As they wait for further instruction, the "Scorpions" ridicule the bound boys and fire the occasional gunshot into the air. After several minutes the boys are directed to walk single file into the woods, with a pair of armed paramilitaries on each side and another group of armed paramilitaries following them. When they reach a meadow, four of the boys are shot at close range and killed. The remaining two are instructed to carry the bodies to an abandoned house at the edge of the meadow. Then they are brought to the house where they too are shot. We see the "Scorpions" walk away from the scene, and the film ends with some later scenes of the paramilitaries enjoying a dinner, listening to music at a ski resort, and shopping at a market.[52]

The film's value as evidence was limited: it demonstrated that killings had taken place and showed that units under Serbian command participated in massacres that were at least contemporaneous with the Srebrenica killings.[53] In fact the film was not admitted into evidence by ICTY and has not been used in other trials. Its impact upon being broadcast, however, appeared at first to be enormous.[54] Its force was magnified by the testimony of relatives of Smail Ibrahimović, a victim of the murders whose fate was unknown until he was recognized in a broadcast of the film.[55]

Leading political figures came forward immediately to express their shock and condemn the crime. Both president Boris Tadić and prime minister Vojislav Koštunica offered statements, bridging one dimension of the political gap in the country. More surprisingly, so did spokespeople for parties that had been involved in the crimes of the period and engaged in denial afterward, such as the Socialist Party of Serbia (SPS) and the Serbian Radical Party (SRS). Polling suggested that public support for cooperation with ICTY was rising.[56] The presiding officer of Parliament, Predrag Marković, introduced a discussion of the film by declaring: "I am ashamed that crimes were committed by Serbs. I am also ashamed that some of them have found refuge in my country. There is no way that it can be permitted that somebody should try to gain political points at the expense of victims who should rest in peace. They will rest in peace if justice is established."[57]

A few people drew attention to the manufactured character of shock and surprise, noting that facts about Srebrenica were hardly unknown before the broadcast. The historian Predrag J. Marković (unrelated to the politician of the same name) told an interviewer:

> It will be very difficult to minimize [the weight of Srebrenica]. There it is as the first item in the news, nobody reads the denials. The crime is impossible to deny and there is a question of whether it is moral to relativize it. Unfortunately, Srebrenica will remain a dark spot in our history. And we will be perceived not as a nation of victims but as a nation of executioners. The people who committed the crime in Srebrenica also committed a crime against Serbia and our history. . . .
>
> There is something hypocritical in the claims to be shocked by the video recordings of the massacre in Srebrenica. As if there were no massacre until the recording appeared. I do not know what people imagine a massacre looks like that is different from the way it appears in that recording. Why so much shock all at once because of that recording? It could have been done without that piece of evidence.[58]

In a short time after the film was made public, it began to appear that public opinion was rapidly moving in a direction it had not appeared to be headed for the previous five years.

Questioning the Film: Film Critics and "the Truth"

The initial response would not be sustained. Already in July an article would appear arguing that that the material in the film was falsified. The article would recirculate through various web sites for a long while afterward. In the article, Ivona Živković argues that all documentary films are constructed,[59] and also:

> The civilians who are present at the shooting of their friends watch it with no emotion. Then they move the bodies with the same blank facial expression. After that they stand peacefully and wait to be shot themselves.
>
> The scene in which the shootings take place has the sound of rifles being fired three times before the body in civilian clothing, who is being shot from close range, reacts. Instead of the shot person responding with great motions, he succeeds in peacefully staying on his feet with two bullets in his back. Only after the third bullet, without spasms, he falls on the grass and very gently at that, almost slackening, more like a drunk falling. There is no blood.
>
> So, if this were the work of a professional documentary filmmaker, the assessment would be that the director did not create the scene with enough drama or psychological logic!
>
> In the whole sequence, there is no human drama, no fear for the fate of the condemned, no face shows any emotion, there is no kinesthesis, and it is about moments when life is cut short, where emotional tension should be apparent from both sides.
>
> Simply put, the killings we have seen on television and in films are more lively, brutal, and dramatic than the set of scenes shown in the video recording that has been declared an authentic killing.[60]

Not content to comment on the deficient skills of the dramatis personae, Vojislav Šešelj, in an appearance as a defense witness for Milošević, declared that the film was falsified for political purposes.[61] Pressed for evidence, however, Šešelj merely promised to provide materials "when I get them from the expert team."

Outside of a narrow group, the thesis that the film was falsified did not catch on. A larger part of the campaign to reply to the film did not involve contesting the evidence but matching it. On 9 July 2005, in the large performance hall in Belgrade's Sava Center, SRS organized a showing of a film they had produced themselves. Titled *Istina* (The Truth),[62] it offers an hour-long montage of footage of a long list of horrible things that had been done to Serbs by other participants in the wars of succession in the former Yugoslavia.

The audience for the screening, which included SRS supporters brought in by bus but also certainly included interested members of the public,[63] filled the large hall and spilled out into the lobbies where the event could be followed on video monitors. In the front row sat leaders of SRS, and also a selection of leaders of the Serbian Orthodox Church, including Patriarch Pavle (Gojko Stojčević),[64] together with some of the most prominent intellectual lights of the nationalist right, among them former law professor Smilja Avramov,[65] philosopher Mihailo Marković,[66] and humorist Branislav Crnčević.[67] SRS official Aleksandar Vučić read a letter from Vojislav Šešelj,[68] sent from custody in the Hague, charging that with the publicity surrounding the "Scorpions" film domestic and international media "are trying to portray the entire Serbian people as genocidal . . . they see victims on only one side while the Serbian helpless, women and children are treated as if they do not exist." With this letter the tone was clearly set to regard the film as responding to a charge.

SRS deputy leader Tomislav Nikolić reached for a more balanced tone than the one suggested by Šešelj's letter. He began his address combatively, accusing other actors of wanting to "place the burden of historical responsibility on us and our children." Then in a departure from his customary rhetoric, he presented a formulation of responsibility: "On the territory of the former Yugoslavia there were many crimes. They were committed by individuals of every nationality. We Serbs as members of the nation that has suffered the most must condemn all crimes. All crimes. Those that were committed by members of our nation but also those that were committed against Serbs. We had to do this in order to be able to forgive. We had to do it in order for it not to be forgotten." The rhetorical formulation was clearly intended to offer a key for interpretation of the film: it was repeated by the narrator of the film twice, once at the beginning and once at the end. As large a step as may have been represented by Nikolić's recognition of crimes—in a first, he mentioned Srebrenica—it was compensated by the step in the other direction, accusing the world of representing (all) Serbs as criminals and ignoring crimes committed against them.

None of the balance implied in Nikolić's statement was apparent in the film itself. Most of the material presented was recycled from television war coverage of the 1990s, offering a montage of familiar scenes of mutilated corpses and mourners, interspersed with compromising footage of various regional politicians. The crimes presented in the film mostly involved mistreatment of prisoners of war, undermining the repeated claim that genocide was at issue. The previously unseen material presented in the film consisted of some footage from interrogations of Croatian and Albanian prisoners and a segment showing some executions of prisoners by a group presented as mujahedeen in Bosnia-Herzegovina.[69] The most gruesome images were repeated at the end of the film, which wraps up to the World War I-era patriotic song "Tamo daleko." There are no credits at the end indicating who may have been the director or editor.

If the film was meant, as SRS leader Tomislav Nikolić indicated before the screening, as a "reply" to the film that had shocked public opinion the previous month,[70] it was not a direct reply. The effort to balance the rhetoric that was apparent in Nikolić's speech was undercut by the propagandistic tone of the film itself, while the promise of new and transformative evidence remained unfulfilled. To the degree that *Istina* did function as a reply, it was oriented toward consolidating the political bloc that had been jarred by the "Scorpions" film, setting the stage for a campaign not to deny the evidence presented the month before but to alter the context in which it would be understood. There would be three currents in the effort to shift the context: (1) to elevate the prominence of the counter-commemoration in Bratunac to rival the commemoration of the Srebrenica victims in Potočari; (2) to downplay the role of official institutions in the Srebrenica killings, concentrating instead on the "Scorpions" while insisting that they operated independently; and (3) to partly acknowledge the commission of crimes in Srebrenica while raising doubt and fear on the question of whether they constituted genocide.

Bratunac = Srebrenica

The first major intervention into the context of Srebrenica was an effort to draw a line of equivalence between the 1995 massacre and earlier violence in the surrounding villages. In this context the killings, however regrettable, blend in with killings that took place at other places and times. Manipulation of numbers is essential to the effort. The general argument was most succinctly stated in a petition circulated by the "Srebrenica Historical Project" urging the Serbian parliament not to pass a resolution acknowledging the Srebrenica killings. Representing its hypotheses as conclusions, the petition argued:

> The execution of Moslem prisoners in July of 1995, after Bosnian Serb forces took over Srebrenica, was a war crime, but it is by no means a paradigmatic event. The informed public in Western countries knows that, at that time, forces attributed to the Republic of Srpska executed in three days approximately as many Moslems as Moslem forces, raiding surrounding Serbian villages out of Srebrenica, had murdered during the preceding three years. There is nothing to set one crime apart from the other, except that its commission was more condensed in time. In a vicious civil war, in which all sides commit crimes, all innocent victims are entitled to compassion but the victims of one ethnic group should have no special moral claim to unique recognition. Putting the suffering of one group on a pedestal necessarily derogates from the right of the other group—in this case Serbian non-combatants in the devastated villages surrounding the enclave of Srebrenica—to an equal measure of sympathy.[71]

The power of the argument depends on maintaining the empirical premise that the numbers are roughly equal and the difference lies in the timing. The empirical premise is difficult to maintain as it conflicts with all available evidence. On the symbolic level, however, there remains a consistent effort to draw attention to the parallel commemoration of Serb victims in Bratunac, and to make it competitive with commemoration of Srebrenica victims in Potočari.

Beginning in 2005, the military cemetery in Bratunac became the site of an annual commemoration for Serb victims from the region. The ceremony was set for 12 July, one day after the larger Potočari commemoration.[72] When Serbian president Boris Tadić established a precedent in 2005 by attending the Potočari commemoration, he faced pressure from the opposition to come to Bratunac as well. SRS made the point by sending its representatives to Bratunac.[73] In 2005 the memorial site in Bratunac listed the names of 301 Serb civilians killed in 1992 and 1993.[74] In 2009 the commemoration (and the number of victims) was expanded with the addition to the ceremony of local victims from the Second World War,[75] as well as the construction of a cross commemorating 3,267 victims of the more recent war.[76]

The construction of images of equivalence generates pressure on regional politicians and internationals to give recognition to one set of crimes as a part of the process of giving recognition to the other. When they decline they are condemned for lack of balance. The bishop officiating at the 2005 ceremony, Vasilije (Ljubomir Kačavenda), phrased it dramatically: "What happened in the most recent historical period can never be repeated, not for the Serbian people nor for anybody else. Today there are no representatives of the international community here, to give their respects to these innocent victims. Let them not come, we do not need them, because they are unjust to those people who gave their lives for truth, for the good of their family homes."[77] In a similar vein, the far-right intellectual Kosta Čavoški told a journalist that Serbian officials did not come to the Bratunac commemoration on instructions from "world powers."[78] The Bratunac counter-commemoration provides an annual source of charges that political leaders who do not attend "are ashamed of Serb victims," "silence the other side," or "step on all Serb victims."[79] Inflating the Bratunac commemoration represents a strategy for contesting the importance of crimes without directly denying them.

Scorpions = Independent Operators

Another alternative to denial of facts is denial of involvement in their creation. The "Scorpions" shown in the film were as good candidates for scapegoats as were likely to be found. They had never been noted for their fighting ability, and the film footage indicates that they were hardly model soldiers: their discipline is poor, they have difficulty maintaining a line whether for inspection or to receive a benediction, and commanders clearly did not entrust them with sensitive or demanding tasks. They were chiefly used during the wars in Croatia and Bosnia-Herzegovina to exploit oil reserves and support smuggling operations in northwestern Bosnia.[80] Members of the unit had already been charged with another serious crime, and one of their members, Saša Cvjetan, had already been convicted of killing fourteen civilians and wounding five in Podujevo in 1999.[81] There would be no difficulty in portraying the "Scorpions" as criminals and undesirables, as this had already been confirmed by a domestic court. What would be more difficult would be demonstrating that they acted without official orders.[82]

Clear evidence existed tying the "Scorpions" to the Interior Ministry. They were named as a State Security unit in the ICTY indictment filed against high-ranking security officials Jovica Stanišić and Franko Simatović.[83] In 1999, they were identified as "reserve units" of the Special Anti-terrorism Unit under Interior Ministry command. If there was confusion as to whether they became Interior Ministry forces in 1995 or later, it would make sense to ask who, if not the Interior Ministry, had moved them from Croatia, where their base was located, to Bosnia, where they were filmed in action.[84]

Already at the first trial of members of the "Scorpions" they distinguished themselves by making scenes. At the Cvjetan and Demirović trial in Prokuplje,

> The prosecutor, for example, did not succeed in confirming the names of most of the victims, or even their approximate number, nor did he try to expand the indictment in spite of clear indications that in addition to Cjvetan and Demirović at least a few other "Scorpions" had participated in the killing. With regard to the motive, he was satisfied to affirm that "motives for such behavior are unexplainable and difficult for a normal person to understand." During the trial, members of the "Scorpions" made up a majority of the public, encouraging the accused who, for his part, did not hold back from entering into verbal duels with witnesses and with journalists who covered the trial. In such an atmosphere, it was logical that none of the witnesses could remember who fired in the garden in Rahman Morina street.[85]

That trial was moved from Prokuplje to Belgrade. After the showing of the film four more "Scorpions" were arrested and charged, including the commander, Slobodan Medić. The subsequent trial showed similar behavior from the now larger number of accused, and it showcased both the inexperience and ineptitude of the unit of the unit and the vulgarity and vanity of its commander, who explained the film by declaring that he "would kill the cameraman like a rabbit."[86]

The distasteful behavior of the "Scorpions" provoked an effort to reduce the crime to the members of that unit, denying any role for the forces that supplied and commanded them. The effort is visible in one postfilm statement by a politician tied to the previous regime:

> The general secretary of the Serbian Radical Party Aleksandar Vučić condemned the crime against the Muslims in Srebrenica and declared that those who committed "those horrific crimes and who killed in cold blood" should be condemned to the most severe sentences.
>
> He said that Serbs as a people are not guilty for individual crimes that some people committed and announced that he would soon make public details about crimes against Serbs in the former Yugoslavia. He said that the members of the "Scorpions" were not from Serbia and did not have connections with any agency in Serbia, and that there would be more shocking footage which show crimes committed by members of other nationalities. Vučić declared yesterday that "the goal of the media campaign that is being conducted against the Serbian people and state is the unobstructed arrest of Ratko Mladić and the formal abolition of Republika Srpska."[87]

While it might be possible to separate the political commentary from the rhetorical effort to isolate the "Scorpions," they go together. Isolating the "Scorpions" implies that a judgment can be made on the crimes without making a judgment on the policy of which they were a part.

The lawyer and human rights activist Vojin Dimitrijević identified and condemned the strategy that was under way, stressing that

> responsibility for the monstrous crime against six Muslims from Srebrenica cannot be reduced merely to "punishing some psychopaths," but that it is necessary to establish the responsibility of "the sane people who sent them there. . . ."
>
> "We will not be able any longer to offer the defense that ethnic cleansing and genocide were the product of a regime that did not have much to do with us, because it seems that, although they are aware of all the facts, many people continue to stand behind those crimes or do not understand that they are crimes," declared Dimitrijević, adding that "pathetic declarations that we were only defending ourselves and that others did the same will not be of much help."[88]

In that same spirit a declaration was offered by the group Dimitrijević headed, the Belgrade Center for Human Rights, in which they "call upon domestic public opinion, politicians, all social elites, the media, and citizens not to make meaningless the remembrance of the Srebrenica victims. Everybody should make an effort and should clearly recognize the difference between war and crimes, between soldiers and innocent civilian victims, between the national interest and senseless killing."[89] Establishing the nexus that would prevent the isolation of the "Scorpions" from the policy of which they were a part involved documenting the relations between the unit and military and security structures. This was one of the roles taken on by the director of the Fund for Humanitarian Law, Nataša Kandić, in her role at the "Scorpions" trial representing the interests of the victims' families. In many instances, however, when she put forward questions moving beyond the details of the crimes to the issue of how the criminals got to be where they were and on whose instructions they acted—the judges disallowed the question.[90]

If the amplification of Bratunac represented one way of limiting the damage done by the "Scorpions" film—by arguing that there were victims an all sides—the concentration of blame on the "Scorpions" represents another. A consistent line of defense in several ICTY cases, including the Milošević case, was that political and military authorities had issued orders for international humanitarian law to be followed. The implication is that if anybody did not follow the law they were doing it on their own account.[91] The point to be demonstrated was that the facts represent isolated events and not the existence of a policy.

The Genocide Debate

As the discourse on Srebrenica shifted from factual denial to alteration of context, the stake of the debate became clearer: what happened may have been revenge, may have been a massacre of prisoners of war, or may have been a set of spontaneous acts by irresponsible forces under no formal command, but could not be recognized as having constituted the implementation of a policy. There were concrete motivations for this strategy: many people charged before ICTY were charged not with having carried out crimes personally but for participation in a "joint criminal enterprise" that had the commission of crimes not as its *consequence* or as a *by-product* but as one of its *goals* and *principal elements*. In addition, a suit was pending before the International Court of Justice (it was decided in 2007) in which Bosnia-Herzegovina charged Serbia with genocide and complicity in genocide.[92] The concern was that if crimes were defined as genocide and tied directly to Serbian authorities, this would create obligations for Serbia as a state that it was unprepared to take on.

In that spirit the lawyer Radoslav Stojanović, who led the defense of Serbia before ICJ, intervened into the "Scorpions" film debate. Seeking to avoid a public declaration that would handicap his defense, he told journalists: "It is the obligation of Serbian institutions to condemn crimes, but not to give a legal qualification—was it genocide or another crime. That would prejudice the verdict of the International Court of Justice."[93] Meanwhile human rights organizations objected to the effort to put into question a matter that they viewed as settled by ICTY's genocide verdicts. Nataša Kandić argued that it was improper for the "Scorpions" to be charged with one offense in a case that an international tribunal had found to constitute another: "It is an issue whether it is legally permissible in the case of the crime committed in Srebrenica to file an indictment for war crimes, rather than for genocide, for which the Hague tribunal has tried and convicted general Radislav Krstić, Momir Nikolić, Dragan Obrenović, all the people who have admitted their guilt."[94] Much of the debate in 2005 (and later, in 2010, when the Serbian parliament again debated a resolution on Srebrenica) turned on the question of whether to call Srebrenica a genocide, to call it another crime, or to avoid calling it anything at all.

Arguments opposed to the genocide label received intense publicity. Milošević's longtime defender Smilja Avramov suggested that while there may have been a crime it was not an extraordinary one: "A massacre can be the extermination of a group, but it is treated as a spontaneous act of the kind that happen in all wars. Genocide, on the other hand, is a crime planned in advance and everybody has to keep that in consideration."[95]

Some international actors also advanced arguments against genocide. American historian Charles Ingrao was quoted comparing Srebrenica with the Nazi genocides: "To characterize Srebrenica as a genocide there would have to exist a precise document which completely clearly shows that it was ordered by the political leadership of the country. The Nazis had such a document in the Second World War and that is why they were tried for genocide."[96] Canadian general Lewis MacKenzie[97] suggested an argument that the killings in Srebrenica could not have been a genocide as only men were killed, whereas women were deported.[98]

At the same time that there was an effort to deny that Serbs had committed genocide at Srebrenica, there was a parallel effort to establish that other groups had committed or intended to commit genocide. Smilja Avramov offered Bosnia-Herzegovina as a counterexample: "If we consider the goal of the war in Bosnia, founded on the 'Islamic Declaration,' we can very easily find evidence of genocidal intent since Bosnia-Herzegovina is envisioned as an Islamic state. In any case, there is not any instance of Muslims attacking a Serb village in Bosnia and saving the women and children, as was done in Srebrenica."[99] Not all participants in the debate agreed on the question of what state ought to be charged with genocide instead of Serbia. Politician Miloš Aligrudić prevaricated a bit before settling on Croatia: "There was no genocide on the territory of the former Yugoslavia committed by any party, but rather ethnic cleansing of particular parts, as a consequence of the civil war, disturbances on the ground and the saving of the bare lives of threatened people. . . . What most resembles genocide is 'Operation Storm' in 1995, because behind that stood the organized activity of the Croatian state, which was oriented toward the expulsion of Serbs."[100] Interestingly there were no imputations of genocide against another major set of opponents, Albanians in Kosovo. Likewise in 2001 the supreme court of Kosovo determined that the actions of Serbian authorities in Kosovo in 1999 also did not constitute genocide.[101]

Aside from concern about the eventual ICJ verdict, two other fears were raised as part of the campaign to avoid the legal qualification of genocide. One was the concern that "Serbs [would be] declared as a genocidal people and punished for all those crimes that were committed by criminals of other nationalities."[102] The other was the belief that a finding of genocide could be used to annul the establishment of Republika Srpska (agreed at Dayton in 1995) as one of the two constituent entities of Bosnia-Herzegovina:

> Republika Srpska was not then [in 1995] called "self-proclaimed" but enjoyed the status of an international creation, as one of two entities with the right of developing special relations with Serbia. Now, since it is said that Bosnian Serbs committed genocide in Srebrenica, and Srebrenica is in Republika Srpska, the impression is

developing that Republika Srpska is some kind of genocidal creation and that it does not have the right to exist, because it was created after an unpunished genocide.[103]

By this point the strategy of denial has shifted from denial of facts to recasting contexts, and eventually toward recognition of the facts accompanied by an effort to avoid their consequences. In this sense it might be possible to regard the "Scorpions" film as having altered the situation by shifting activity from denial to self-interested advocacy.

Antin: The End

As the discourse moved from denial of facts to disputes about contexts and consequences, it also shifted from victims to politicians. The longer it lasted, the less interest was maintained in the topic and the more the discourse deteriorated. There was a flip side to the publicity accorded the evidence of violations of international humanitarian law: attacks on the evidence often took the form of attacks on the advocates of human rights in Serbia, personified in the three women who headed the three most prominent human rights organizations.[104] They would appear in media, including on the shouty "debate" shows on television, to defend the evidence and their positions. This strategy had a pronounced tendency to backfire as it created a forum for further attacks, escalation of rhetoric, and wandering of the discourse about human rights abuses away from the topic.

One event that seemed to set the entire discourse off track was set off by human rights activist Nataša Kandić. Appearing as a guest on a radio interview program, she confronted a leader of SRS, one of the main organizations involved in contesting evidence that was being presented to the public. In her comments she suggested that "there are indications" that "the acting president of SRS was certainly in situations involving weapons and that some civilians in Antin suffered at his hands."[105] In fact there was no evidence that Tomislav Nikolić had participated in armed conflicts or committed crimes against civilians. Military records indicated that he had been in Antin in December 1991 and January 1992, but not that crimes were committed during that period. The available evidence indicated that a massacre of thirty civilians did occur in fall 1991, before Nikolić arrived.[106] For Nikolić's part, his voluntary service did not involve being under arms, and he worked as a clerk in his unit.[107] Croatian police confirmed that they did not have any evidence implicating Nikolić.[108]

SRS used the provocation as an opportunity to intensify its campaign to discredit Kandić, and announced that it was filing libel charges against her.[109] Kandić backed down a bit, telling journalists that the evidence to which she referred was not in her hands but was held secretly by the counterintelligence service.[110] Eventually a court did find Kandić guilty of libel and ordered her to pay Nikolić 200,000 dinars in damages, allowing a newspaper close to SRS to publish an article on the court case with the large headline "Liar!"[111]

The sideshow that developed around Kandić's erroneous remark illustrated how easily the discourse over responsibility could run off course. Instead of concentrating on victims, on lines of command, or indeed on the event in question, the incident allowed Nikolić (together with the entire political right) to present himself as the injured party. The discussion again became reduced to competition among prominent political figures while it offered ammunition to the groups that accused human rights advocates of being deficient in patriotism and one-sided. What began as a cinematic intervention that seemed set to confirm a very large-scale crime in Bosnia-Herzegovina ended as a judicial intervention that sustained doubt regarding a much smaller-scale crime in Croatia. The general effect was to reduce a serious discourse to the level of political trivia.

The "Scorpions" film may have represented the single largest opportunity to open a discussion based on acknowledgment of facts. While some future events—eventual verdicts against Karadžić and Mladić, for example—could produce a similar effect, there have not been public events of a comparable scale since this shock in 2005. What happened in that instance confirms the pattern already observed in earlier events. Briefly, a window was opened. While it was open, the debate shifted. Following sustained engagement by media and political parties, it was closed.

Chapter 8

Nonmoments: Milošević, Karadžic, Šešelj, and Mladić

The previous chapters examined three "moments" that had an element in common. They revealed something about the recent past and about continuity with power structures in the present. What they revealed was often, for various interested actors, threatening, and had to be covered over. Sometimes questions were covered over by denial, sometimes by altering the context, sometimes by trivialization. But in each case protecting people engaged with the past required a refinement of the discourse, maintaining its longevity while at the same time demonstrating its fundamental fragility.

Some events revealed little beyond the extent to which the public was divided. On these occasions conflicts were reperformed and it became apparent that the balance of public opinion had shifted or interest had fallen off. But these were mainly events in which actors played to their core audiences and did not reach far beyond them. Looking at them closely reveals some of the limits of public discourse about the recent past: entrenched interests constitute a hard barrier to the dialogue moving forward, while repetition and forgetting cut two ways, both making conflict more marginal and emptying the dialogue of content and moral force. I have labelled these "nonmoments," not because they fail to illustrate the contours of political and cultural exchange, but because they catalyzed no movement. The death of Slobodan Milošević, the arrest of Radovan Karadžić, the ongoing trial of Vojislav Šešelj, and the arrest of Ratko Mladić reflected symptoms of a stalemate in discourse while throwing back little light about them.

The Death of Slobodan Milošević

After the presentation of evidence had dragged on for two years, the Milošević prosecution completed its case on 25 February 2004. Milošević began his defense on 31 August of the same year. The trial became more complex as he began to bring in his witnesses, since they would frequently (and generally unintentionally) raise issues that the prosecution had not had the opportunity to raise in the first half of the trial. This meant that the pattern of contested rulings and frequent interruptions that had been established from 2002 continued, and the trial showed every sign of developing into an affair that would drag out over several more years. The process was abruptly cut short, however, by the defendant's unexpected death on 11 March 2006.[1]

There was already considerable public dispute over how far the prosecution had succeeded in demonstrating its case and Milošević in contesting it. The judges afforded the defendant considerable indulgence in an effort to assure that the trial could be as fair and complete as possible while he, with no particular legal knowledge or skill, conducted his own defense.[2] As his death terminated the trial before its completion, no judicial chamber would deliver a verdict that could offer an authoritative answer to the question of his guilt.

Milošević's death had not been entirely unpredictable. The trial had been lengthened considerably by pauses taken for medical reasons, indicating that the state of his health was poor and possibly indicating that the defendant manipulated his medical condition in order to control the course of the trial. Media promoted speculation that his death had been caused either intentionally or through the neglect of the Tribunal medical staff. The tabloid *Kurir* quoted a Belgrade lawyer, Svetozar Vujačić,[3] suggesting a conspiracy to put a sudden end to the trial because "[former Montenegrin president Momir] Bulatović had prepared thousands of exhibits and official documents that would put an end to the Hague trial."[4] The daily *Večernje novosti* offered a series of similar features on 12 and 13 March, immediately following Milošević's death. An interview with Milošević's brother Borislav went under the title "The Court in the Hague Killed Him," while a statement from Milošević's wife Mirjana Marković went under the title "The Tribunal Is the Guilty One."[5] The rest of the editions for those two days featured short articles with statements from the likes of Montenegrin rightist politician Andrija Mandić ("Scheveningen has been transformed into a death camp"), lawyer-ideologist Smilja Avramov ("that is not a tribunal, it is a mortuary!"), and philosopher-parapolitician Mihailo Marković ("The Hague tribunal literally killed him").[6] More programmatic was a prediction (unrealized, as it turned out) in a tabloid called *Tabloid*: "There is no longer any doubt that Washington, and Moscow quickly after, with harsh words, will dissolve the Hague tribunal and arrest its employees who caused the deaths of Hague indictees. In that way Serbia will get off its back the parasite and bloodsucker in the form of Del Ponte, who for a monthly reward of one hundred thousand Euros sucks the blood of Serbia, which is already suffering."[7] Similar tabloids behaved similarly. *Svedok* published open letters from Milošević's wife and son, both fugitives inaccessible to law enforcement agencies but somehow available to certain publishers.[8] While an investigation at ICTY came to the unsurprising conclusion that he had not been murdered or subjected to neglect, but had rather succumbed to a heart attack,[9] this did not end the speculation in tabloid reporting.

The rush to develop theories relating the death of Milošević to upcoming witness testimony or other conspiracies pointed to two ongoing dilemmas. On the one hand, the free run of the tabloid imagination affirmed an established stereotype about Serbia in international media:

> The reporting of the tabloids has produced a powerful impression outside of the country. Global news agencies have concluded that Serbian nationalism is still strong, and many foreign reporters have been asking domestic experts whether there would be demonstrations organized in Belgrade against the Hague tribunal or in support of Milošević's political successors. The Western media have already begun to speculate as to whether Serbs would accept the results of the autopsy or continue to believe in theories of his "murder" in the Hague, regardless of what the doctors conclude. All of that returns into currency the old stereotypes about the Serbian tendency to assume the role of the victim and the conspiratorial mindset.[10]

On the other hand, the continued atmosphere of mystery and intrigue mirrored the failure of the trial to resolve questions of central importance for understanding the recent past in Serbia: What had Milošević's trial meant? How was his rule to be remembered? And how widely shared was the perception expressed by a magazine columnist that "there is not the slightest doubt that the indictment against Slobodan Milošević was an indictment against Serbia"?[11]

One place where the conflict over the meaning of Milošević's legacy played out was in sites of media-based commemoration. The daily paper *Blic* offered, as a front-page feature summarizing the life and times of Milošević, a set of photos recording several low points of his rule: the wreckage on the Ibar highway from the attempted murder of opposition politician Vuk Drašković, the murder of journalist Slavko Ćuruvija, the pyramid-scheme "banker" Dafina Milanović, the protests at electoral fraud in 1996 and 2000, and the antiregime demonstrations of 9 March 1991.[12] In the obituaries section of the major papers there appeared the expected messages of sympathy from supporters, but also some unexpected messages. *Politika* published an obituary notice dedicated to "our comrade in arms [*saborac*] in the Hague" and signed by thirty-four detainees of the Scheveningen detention unit in various stages of their trials, including the Croat detainees Mladen Naletelić-Tuta and Ante Gotovina.[13] An obituary in the Novi Sad daily *Dnevnik* offered a backhanded commemoration, "1987–2000: May all of those who suffered because of the political project that was carried out in Serbia rest in peace": it was signed by a pantheon of prominent cultural figures from Vojvodina—the film director Želimir Žilnik, the journalist Marina Fratučan, the popular music legends Slobodan Tišma and Branislav Babić-Kebra, "among others."[14] The most impressive of all the satirical obituary notices came from a nonexistent group of people. Under the customary photo and name of the deceased appeared the text:

> Thank you for all of your lies and theft, for every drop of blood that thousands of people spilled because of you. Thank you for fear and insecurity, for lost lives and generations, for dreams that did not come true for us, for horrors and war that you carried out without asking our consent, for the whole burden you have put on our shoulders.
>
> We remember tanks on the streets of Belgrade and blood on its pavement. We remember Vukovar. We remember Dubrovnik. We remember Knin and Krajina. We remember Sarajevo. We remember Srebrenica. We remember the bombing. We remember Kosovo. There is much we still have to remember. And dream.
>
> We remember the dead, the wounded, the unfortunate, the refugees. We remember our own destroyed lives.[15]

The notice was signed with a fictional name that would have been recognizable to everybody: Mile Ćurčić, the confused and angry victim of nostalgia masterfully played by the comic actor Zoran Cvijanović in the popular television series *Mile vs. The Transition*.[16] Mile's signature was preceded by the suggestive names some invented family members: Nada (Hope), Srećko (Fortune), Živko (Life), Sloboda (Freedom), and Vesela (Joy).[17]

Divisions clearly marked the period immediately following the death. In the daily *Danas*, Vesna Perović offered a long anti-obituary under the title "Guilt does not die," refusing to honor the memory of Milošević:

> All this is covered over by our ultrahypocritical folk expression, only speak well of the dead. Which would mean—do what you want while you are alive, be a cad, a liar, and a murderer, and when you die we will only speak well of you. Then what will we say about people who were decent during their lives? What will we say about the victims of the deceased, what happens to the universal human need to secure the victory of Good over Evil, and Justice over Injustice? If that is really the way it is then everything that is human has lost all meaning.[18]

Similarly in the daily *Blic*, a columnist drew an analogy between the fate of the Milošević family (wife and son hiding in another country, daughter rejecting the family legacy) and the fate of the country: "What Slobodan Milošević did to the country he also did to his family—destroyed and irretrievably divided. Political advantage was more important to him than anything else: than the lives of his friends, than the fate of ordinary people, than territory. . . . That is how it was while he was in power, and that is how it has remained after his death."[19] Short statements from political figures indicated no greater sympathy. Asked for a statement, Dušanka Filpovski of the New Serbia (Nova Srbija) Party simply responded, "the people of Serbia said everything they had to say about the rule of Slobodan Milošević on 5 October 2000 [when he was removed from office]."[20] Čedomir Jovanović of the Liberal Democratic Party was even more categorical: "Don't expect me to lament the fate of Slobodan Milošević on 12 March. Excuse me, but he died in his bed at the age of 65, while Zoran Djindjić was murdered at his workplace at the age of 50 because he wanted to change this country."[21]

Notwithstanding widespread public skepticism, the supporters of Milošević invested effort into producing a ceremony that would see him off with
the trappings of honor. Nenad Bogdanović, the mayor of Belgrade, rejected
an attempt to secure his burial in the "alley of worthy citizens" in the city's
New Cemetery, declaring:

> During the course of my mandate in the Belgrade City Hall I have
> agreed that the Alley of Worthy Citizens should be used for the
> burial of people who have, by their character and engagement, left
> a positive, noble and human trace in this city and in our country.
> The traces that the Milošević regime left behind it are the reason
> that I believe that he in no way deserves the mantle of a worthy
> citizen, neither in the Alley nor in Serbian history.[22]

The government refused to intervene to change the decision, and the military declined to arrange for burial with military honors. Rejected by the
city and state governments, the family briefly experimented with the idea
of a burial in Moscow. Eventually Milošević would be buried in the garden
of his family home in the town of Požarevac.

Deprived of the opportunity for a public burial, Milošević supporters
organized a public rally. The turnout at the final public farewell to Milošević was disputed: supporters say that 500,000 sympathizers came, BBC
claimed 50,000, Belgrade police claimed 80,000 and the daily *Politika*
reported 100,000.[23] Although the military had refused him honors, the stage
did have people in uniform on display. One set of them was a group of
three children brought over by their noncustodial father for the purpose.[24]
Another was a group of retired generals, parading in the uniforms of units
to which they had never belonged.[25] The Ministry of Defense would affirm
after the ceremony that the retired generals, who were not military officers
in active duty, did not have the right to appear in public in uniform at all.[26]
Among the ceremonial presentations that were offered to commemorate
the life of Milošević, "his speech of 2 October 2000 was read aloud, in
which he accused the then leader of the opposition Zoran Djindjić that he
wanted to establish a marionette regime in Serbia in the name of foreign
intelligence services."[27]

Other speakers at the rally spoke to the effect that Milošević, in answering the criminal charges against him, had ended his life defending the country—and of course kept alive the hypothesis that he had been killed by a

malicious judicial institution. In a letter read to the meeting by his deputy Aleksandar Vučić, the Hague defendant Vojislav Šešelj set out the contours of a conspiracy theory:

> Today everybody knows who killed you. It was the people who could not withstand the brilliant defense before their Inquisition of a court, the people who bombed and destroyed us, the people who want today to destroy Serbia. And to do that dirty job they have brought into their criminal ranks their servants in Serbia.
>
> The occupier and its occupational servants in our country acted jointly with one goal and one task, to destroy our Serbia as quickly and completely as possible. That is why they had to kill you. They had to, because you proudly, honorably, and courageously defended our people and our country. They had to, because all that was left of their indictment before that anti-Serbian tribunal was printed words on paper. They had to because it was becoming ever more apparent that the Americans and English and other Westerners caused the crisis in the former Yugoslavia, and your guilt was only that you tried to save your people from a pogrom.[28]

Meanwhile Milošević's leading intellectual supporter, the right-Hegelian Mihailo Marković, argued for the historical significance of the deceased in pioneering a "truly democratic alternative to Stalinism" in the wake of the fall of European Communist regimes in 1989, but contended that his

> mortal sin was lack of submissiveness to the one remaining global superpower, when it began to subdue the Balkans to create a path to the greatest world reserves of petroleum in the Middle East and on the Caspian Sea. Slobodan did not want for elasticity and diplomatic flexibility, but that was not nearly enough. They required absolute obedience, colonial subjection, and that is incommensurable with the Serbian national character. Slobodan had the confidence to say to the greatest power in the world—no! By itself that meant that he would receive a death sentence. Everyone who is free to think knows that Slobodan is not guilty for any of the wars he was charged with.[29]

Given the intensity of the rhetoric and the impressive turnout at the public sendoff, it seemed to some observers that the rejected leader might be coming back into vogue. Referring to a statement at the rally by Milošević supporter Milorad Vučelić that it was a "people's burial," the politician Vuk Drašković called it a "meeting for the burial of the people."[30] Vlajko Senić, a vice president of Drašković's party, feared that "for the first time since 5 October 2000, unfortunately, we are near a situation in which the people who led the state until that date seem to have majority support in public opinion."[31]

Opponents of the Milošević legacy made certain that the rally-cum-funeral would not be unchallenged by another event. On the day that supporters held their rally in front of the parliament, Bojan Kostreš, the president of the Vojvodina Assembly, led a delegation on a visit to the graves of prominent victims of Milošević: they visited the burial sites of the murdered prime minister Zoran Djindjić, the murdered journalist Slavko Ćuruvija, and Milošević's murdered predecessor, Ivan Stambolić, among others.[32] In Belgrade, people scheduled an "antiburial" to coincide with the supporters' commemoration. While one group mourned the deceased, the "antiburiers" planned to mark the event by releasing colorful balloons in the city, while some intended to visit the supporters' commemoration in order to, as their slogan said, "Overi" (Make certain [that he is dead]).[33]

The responses to the death of Milošević suggest that, just as during his life, views regarding him were deeply divided, interpretations of his legacy remained just as divided. Some considered his rule as deserving of praise. Some rejected his rule but praised his "defense of the national and state interest of Serbia" before ICTY.[34] Some blamed ICTY for failing, in a trial that had dragged on for four years and promised to drag out yet longer, to convict him even "in those cases where his guilt was unproblematic and undisputed."[35] Others saw a farcical event that took the shape of a "rally opposed to the majority in Serbia" and promised to end in more crime.[36] These conflicts remained unresolved. There is still a group of people that comes to the Milošević family garden each March to pay respects to the deceased. And one year after his death, one person broke into the garden to honor an old Balkan folk ritual by driving a stake into Milošević's grave.[37]

The Arrest of Radovan Karadžić

In the period after 2000, the status of the remaining ICTY fugitives presented a continual barrier in relations between Serbia and the European

Union. Once Ante Gotovina was arrested in 2005, all the fugitives who were still sought were former officials of Serb parastates and were generally believed to be hiding in Serbia. Radovan Karadžić and Ratko Mladić, the former president and military commander, respectively, of the Serb entity in Bosnia-Herzegovina, were charged with major crimes, among them genocide. Goran Hadžić, a former laborer who had briefly occupied the presidency of the Serb parastate in Croatia, was a far less important figure but the manner of his evasion of arrest was compelling: he slipped away from police surveillance of his house, video cameras recording his departure, and after that no trace was seen of him for years. In frequently repeated episodes, ICTY officials would claim to have evidence that the fugitives were hiding in Serbia, and Serbian officials would claim to have no information about their location. Periodic police raids would prove unproductive. Rumors spread about networks protecting the fugitives—some involved old associates from the war period, some involved the figures who had established themselves in organized crime, and many of them involved insubordinate but powerful elements of the military, police, and (especially) state security services. Concurrently a mythology developed around the fugitives—as heroic figures who had defended the nation, as figures of resistance to an international power that commentators on the right came to describe more often as an "occupation,"[38] as repositories of a residue of otherwise defeated national pride.[39] The belief that they would never be caught was widespread: either they were so well protected that the hunt was futile, or the evidence they could produce was so potentially damaging that the state was determined to let them die as fugitives.

Consequently it came as a surprise when Radovan Karadžić was arrested in Belgrade, where he had been living for some time, on 21 July 2008. The arrest itself was uneventful. Police had been tracking him under his assumed identity for months, and finally apprehended him while he was riding a city tram. Larger-than-life stories about a powerful network of guards and financiers proved to be imaginary. He lived on his own, was able to arrange for publication of his occasional writings by his former press assistant Miroslav Toholj, maintained a largely inactive "Committee for the Truth About Radovan Karadžić" headed by his brother Luka and the multipurpose apologist Kosta Čavoški, a retired professor of the law faculty,[40] and otherwise led a daily existence that, as details of it came to be known, emerged as comical and bizarre.

In the legend that had been built up around Karadžić, he was protected by a well-financed and well-armed network that shuttled him between his family home in the former Bosnian Serb capital of Pale and his native Montenegro through a network of monasteries in eastern Herzegovina. If he had a powerful and well-connected network, however, it must have degraded over time. By the time police apprehended him, he had been living under conditions more burlesque than glamorous. He had lived under the assumed identity of Dragan Dabić, which was traced variously to a retired farmer in the Vojvodina village of Ruma or alternatively to a reservist who was killed in Sarajevo in 1993.[41] In addition to this he had acquired the nickname "David," apparently because his curiosity led him to ask repeatedly "to see" [da vidi] the techniques of his recently acquired profession. The photos made available after his arrest show Karadžić lightly disguised under copious facial hair with a ritualistic braid on top, a combination of monastic tonsure and the American comic actor Wilfred Brimley.

As for his new profession, Karadžić had been in psychiatric practice in Sarajevo before entering politics, and he appeared to have found a related field. He attended a school for "bioenergetics" on the outskirts of Belgrade, where on completion of the course he received the title of "general for poisons, gold, and landmines."[42] He provided mystical healing services to individual clients and at the private "Nova Vita" clinic in the Belgrade suburb of Rakovica, and also offered counseling for fertility and sexual dysfunction with the benefit of "human quantum energy."[43] He wrote a series of articles for an alternative medicine magazine called Zdrav život (Healthy Life), advocating the use of an old religious meditation technique called tihovanje (the name calls up images of gentleness and quiet) as a means of therapy.[44] In the evenings he would visit a bar near his residence, Luda kuća (the Madhouse), which was a destination for devotees of the most traditional Serbian music—epic tales recited to the accompaniment of the one-stringed gusle.[45] There he had the unique pleasure of performing epic narratives about himself while seated under his own portrait.[46]

The marked eccentricity of Karadžić's adopted styles of work and life quickly made him an object of ridicule, easy to discredit and easy to extradite. For detractors it took little effort to develop a narrative that a gambler and liar had found new ways to live as a fraud and a charlatan. Would-be supporters found it increasingly difficult to stand by a person who had been the beneficiary of an engaged fugitive-assistance network but who in the end—unable to resist the temptation to make publicity out of his success as a "bioenergetic healer"—had been uncovered by his "need for attention and his exhibitionism."[47] And so it happened that Radovan Karadžić was arrested, processed for delivery to The Hague, and sent to await trial quickly and without major incident. The complex of characteristics that served to discredit him, however, also functioned to trivialize and undermine his arrest and particularly the reasons an indictment against him had been issued in the first place. Dejan Kožul observed:

> The endearing old fellow who heals people with his own power, or simply by autosuggestion, succeeded in one more of his intentions—he drew the attention of the public away from the crimes of which he is accused and now more attention is being paid to the bars where he played the *gusle*, the yoghurt that he drank, and the messages he sent in general. Who still remembers the messages that the same old fellow sent and submerged just fifteen years ago?[48]

Perhaps perceiving that some portion of the public continued to embrace the crimes of Karadžić, both government officials and media decided to concentrate on Karadžić the person instead. The person was easy to discredit, and less was at stake. An unintended consequence may have been that the public was introduced to the comical side of genocide, where benefits accrue to the state from international organizations but matters of life and death count for far less.

Dispirited Karadžić supporters and some far-right parties managed a small protest in Belgrade, which was attended by about 16,000 people, 1,000 of whom remained afterward to riot and engage in confrontations with police.[49] The meeting was largely interpreted as a performance of the increasing marginality of the parties that organized it—one daily paper titled its roundup of commentaries "The losers of the election use Karadžić as a means for survival."[50] While this assessment of the failed rally may have been accurate as a political diagnosis, it was also illustrative of a pattern that could be observed before. Substantive questions of fundamental importance were reduced to tactical questions involving the competition between political parties and some public figures associated with them. There was no discussion of the charges on which Karadžić would be tried because there was, as far as media and political actors were concerned, no topic to discuss.

The Ever-Ongoing Trial of Vojislav Šešelj

Measured by the time elapsed between arrival at the ICTY detention facility in Scheveningen and the completion of legal proceedings, the trial of Vojislav Šešelj is the longest ICTY has heard. No indictment had been announced in February 2003 when he requested to be informed by the Tribunal whether charges existed against him. On receiving the reply that he was considered a participant in the joint criminal enterprise led by Slobodan Milošević and that independent charges against him would be filed for violations committed by paramilitaries under his command and for contributing the commission of crimes by public advocacy of violence, Šešelj rushed off to Tribunal custody voluntarily. There has been speculation regarding his motivation for delivering himself to the Tribunal—he surrendered on 23 February 2003, just three weeks before Zoran Djindjić was murdered. In the initial indictment for the murder of Djindjić, Šešelj was named as a conspirator, but although he has been questioned by Serbian prosecutors in Scheveningen, he cannot be tried on the charges as the primacy of ICTY over domestic courts prevents the initiation of proceedings against him in Serbia.[51]

The Šešelj case is complex, as the strength of the indictment relies on (1) demonstrating that Šešelj actually exercised command over paramilitary forces nominally under the control of his party, but in fact financed and organized by Serbian state security; and (2) demonstrating the extent of his participation in a joint criminal enterprise led by state officials while his party was nominally in opposition, but in fact heavily sponsored and enabled by the regime. Although ICTY distinguished formal from actual chains of command in earlier cases,[52] it was deemed necessary to include in the indictment the qualification, "By using the word 'committed' in this indictment, the Prosecutor does not intend to suggest that the accused physically committed *all* of the crimes charged personally."[53] Direct responsibility relies on Šešelj having encouraged others to commit crimes through inflammatory speeches in Vukovar, Hrtkovci, and Mali Zvornik. There is a marked tendency in public opinion to ignore both the role of instigation in constituting an accessory to crime and Šešelj's (sometimes informal) role as a public official. Rather, the perception is that he is charged with having made outrageous comments as an individual, an act which while distasteful is not illegal, and which comports with Šešelj's long-cultivated public image as a crass buffoon. The consequence is on the one hand to denigrate the importance of the charges against him, and on the other hand to regard them as charges for "speech crimes" (*verbalni delikt*), calling up associations with discredited show trials from the Communist period.[54]

The perceived seriousness of the trial is further undermined by the Tribunal having granted Šešelj the privilege of representing himself, following the precedent established by Milošević, who brought the right to self-representation into international law.[55] In the Milošević case self-representation meant that the court felt compelled to indulge the defendant in delaying proceedings, wandering into irrelevant topics, abusing witnesses, and using the trial chamber as a forum to deliver televised political speeches. Where professional ethics or the threat of sanction would prevent qualified lawyers from behaving the way a self-representing defendant does, courts often give greater leeway to nonlawyers accused of crimes, partly to prevent defendants from claiming afterward that their ability to present a defense was curtailed.[56]

Šešelj has made maximum use of the opportunity for publicity afforded by his trial, and has declined to offer a legal defense. Well before he moved to The Hague, he claimed in 1994 to look forward to his trial, saying he "would never miss such a show."[57] And his interventions have been very much in the character of a show. They have included sending long and vulgar submissions to the Tribunal, indulging in personal insults, using the court chamber as a forum for disquisitions on nationalist ideology, and indulgence of a number of personal idiosyncrasies, including, in one letter, appearing to demand oral sex from the employees of the ICTY registry.[58] He has made a practice of objecting to translations that use Croatian or Bosnian rather than Serbian idiom.[59] He has objected to the judges' robes on the ground that they remind him of the Spanish Inquisition.[60] Some of his abusive letters to the Tribunal registry have circulated through electronic networks as a type of folk culture. Much of this antic behavior has been tolerated or indulged by the judges, for the sake of assuring that the trial continues. Among the results of this have again been extended delays in the process, dragging a trial with months of substantive procedure over nine years.

While in the ICTY holding facility Šešelj has written and published extensively. He is an extraordinarily prolific writer, possibly among the most prolific in the history of the Serbian language. The National Library of Serbia lists more than 200 titles under his name. Most of his works are polemical in character, explicitly directed toward real and imagined political opponents. In one period many of them were widely read because he published compromising material about his opponents that his party received from the State Security services.[61] Since arriving at The Hague in 2003 his titles have suggested a strong focus on his own situation. After his first custody-era book *Četnički vojvoda pred Haškim tribunalom* (The Chetnik Duke Before the Hague Tribunal), in 2003, his subsequent titles overwhelmingly involved insults directed at Tribunal personnel. The first of them was *U čeljustima kurve Del Ponte* (In the Jaws of the Whore Del Ponte), in 2004, and was followed by a series of works with titles in a similar spirit, six of them in 2009 alone.[62]

Any interest in Šešelj's books would probably be more symptomatic than literary. The use of deliberately provocative personal insults in the titles continues a practice that he adopted in an earlier period when most of the people he perceived as his opponents were domestic political actors. The tone is such that the books seem unlikely to generate sympathy for his cause or an interest in reading among people who are not already his followers and likely to welcome his unique stance. However, this tone may represent the most important element of the written work. Its vulgarity and irreverence is enhanced by folk expressions and insults that, however potentially offensive, are likely to be recognizable to the domestic public. Here Šešelj draws self-consciously on a local tradition, apparent in politics, literature, and folk humor, where a proud but beleaguered weaker party responds to strong pressure with calculated disrespect. In calling on this tradition, Šešelj offers a pronounced invitation to the audience to understand him as a representative of the mythology of resistance—a populist gesture from a person who insists that judges address him as "professor."[63]

Although his indirect connection to most of the crimes with which he is charged might suggest that the Šešelj case is one where competent attorneys could conceivably obtain an acquittal, Šešelj has little motivation to seek acquittal or to return to Serbia at all. He would return to an environment in which he would no longer have access to the support from state institutions that constructed his political career in the 1990s or to controlled media that provided him with nearly unlimited quantities of publicity. The political party he continues to lead in absentia split in 2008, with the much larger proportion of its followers opting to follow the faction that rejects his legacy and policies. He would be likely to face a number of criminal charges including ones related to the murder of Zoran Djindjić. And he would lose access to the source of funding represented by ICTY, which in May 2011 agreed to provide several million euros for the purpose of financing his defense.[64]

As the trial descended to farce and remained there for several years, public interest in the charges and process waned. After the prosecution completed its presentation of evidence in 2010, Šešelj exercised his right under rule 98 bis to request a summary acquittal. The trial chamber declined the request in May 2011,[65] assuring that the trial would continue for however long it took Šešelj to present a defense case. Among the polarized reactions to the unsurprising decision from convinced supporters and opponents of Šešelj, one response that stood out came in the form of dark humor. The popular satirical web site Njuz.net came out with the headline "The Hague Tribunal Sentences Itself to Šešelj." Writing in the voice of the presiding judge, Jean-Claude Antonetti, Viktor Marković summarized a relieved public opinion: "Whatever the result of this trial may be, one thing is clear: we all live in a world in which Vojislav Šešelj exists, and that is a reality we will have to confront sooner or later. We have tried in this way to limit that world to the chambers of this court, conscious of the fact that we will have to listen to and look at that man in the coming years."[66] While Vojislav Šešelj may have adopted the time-honored insurgent strategy of undermining his trial by rejecting the authority of the court, the effect may not have been to encourage sympathy in his favor. The continuous spectacle created by his behavior may have had a more wide-ranging effect, to empty the ongoing inquiry into the character of events of substantive meaning.

The Arrest of Ratko Mladić

Although protests and social unrest have been predicted ahead of every arrest of an ICTY indictee, these have never materialized; the most prominent indictees received token displays of support at best. The last remaining fugitive, Goran Hadžić, was not prominent enough to have either supporters or opponents, and consequently his arrest also did not bring people out to the streets. If mass protest was ever going to happen, it would have happened for Ratko Mladić. His brusque manner—during the war he could be seen barking orders to his soldiers, to nearby journalists, to the hapless commander of compliant Dutch peacekeepers—led celebrants to see in him a promise of bold national leadership.[67] His casual sadism—he would order attacks on civilian targets in Sarajevo by shouting "Raspameti!" (Blow their minds off!), and was famously filmed distributing chocolates to the children of Srebrenica for a moment, until the cameras were turned off, the chocolates were taken away, and the children's male relatives were murdered—made him the face of the monstrosities produced by lunatic politics. It was not possible to be of two minds about Ratko Mladić. And yet his unanticipated arrest in May 2011 produced a weak, brief, and unpersuasive public display by his supporters, accompanied by rather more melodrama and jostling for political advantage.

Much of the drama around Mladić's arrest concerned his long period on the lam and the series of possibly sincere and certainly unsuccessful attempts to secure his arrest. Indicted in 1995, he enjoyed official protection while the Milošević regime remained in power. The protection appears to have lasted longer than the regime did. Until 2001 he lived openly in Belgrade and was occasionally sighted at restaurants and sports matches, though after that he did not appear in public. He remained an employee of the Yugoslav military until he was ordered into retirement by the Supreme Defense Council on 16 June 2001.[68] Various stories circulated regarding how long his whereabouts were known and to whom—some involved a policy to continue his protection and to prevent his arrest and extradition, while others involved insubordinate elements in the military and security services protecting the fugitive and hiding information from other state agencies. Speculation never let up about an incident at the Topčider military barracks in 2004, when two young recruits died of gunshot wounds under unexplained circumstances. An official report that the incident was a murder-suicide persuaded few people, and several groups—among them the families of the soldiers—continually raised the question of whether these two deaths were associated with Mladić's hiding places. The families' request that Mladić be questioned in connection with the incident was declined.[69] Stories circulated suggesting that opportunities had existed to arrest him over a long period, with 2009 the latest date at which it was asserted that his location was known.[70] One story had him taking refuge in a convent in 2006.[71] The actual conditions of his arrest were less melodramatic: he was apprehended in his cousin's village house, under a pseudonym (Milorad Komadić) that was remarkably similar to his name.

While the refinements of the fugitive narrative added a dash of cloak-and-dagger to the arrest story and helped to keep alive a populist image of gallant resistance to domination, they were undermined by an increasing number of details about the actual condition in which Mladić was found. Whatever protection he had once enjoyed had clearly deteriorated, and explanations for this fact varied: either the efforts of law enforcement to restrict his access to financing had succeeded, or, in a continuation of the cloak-and-dagger narrative, his arrest had been agreed beforehand. In any case, when he was found in his cousin's house he was visibly aged, seemingly confused, and in apparent need of urgent medical attention. These details came to be magnified by his legal representatives, who exaggerated the seriousness of his medical condition to delay his transfer to The Hague.[72]

As the focus on Mladić came to be increasingly personal, the details that emerged about him became increasingly trivial. Over the five days spent in domestic custody awaiting extradition, news media maintained hourly updates on his visitors, his requests, his condition, and the progress of his extradition process.[73] Audiences were informed as to whether he was polite toward Bruno Vekarić, the deputy special prosecutor for war crimes (on the first day he was not, and on the second day he was).[74] Much discussion was provoked by his refined and eclectic requests: he wanted some classic Russian novels to read, a television set to watch, and fresh strawberries to snack on.[75] Updates were maintained on whether he would be permitted to visit the grave of his daughter, who had committed suicide using his pistol in 1994.[76] Such stories appeared on the one hand to shift a story about war crimes into a celebrity story, while at the same time altering the picture of Mladić from that of the ruthless force commander to an ill and confused old man with a sad personal story and a set of very ordinary desires.

If the topic of crime did not enter the discussion of Mladić's personal fate, it did not make much of a show in the official discussion of the arrest and extradition, either. Announcing that the arrest had been made, president Boris Tadić lost no time in emphasizing that an EU condition had been fulfilled and that the government would expect reciprocal gestures.[77] In a statement that appeared to have been written out for her phonetically, the monolingual justice minister Snežana Malović announced that extradition had been ordered and that therefore "Republic of Serbia has fulfilled moral and international obligation."[78] As political statements concentrated almost entirely on telling the story of how the arrest was carried out (by way of refuting speculation that it could have been carried out much earlier) and on anticipating beneficial consequences in terms of Serbia's relations with Europe (while leaving out of the discussion any mention of the crimes with which Mladić was charged and their victims), a few observers complained about the "complete absence of the moral aspect" of the Mladić story in most public discussion.[79] The shift of narrative from the level of confrontation with crime to the level of practical calculation made the arrest and extradition of Mladić palatable even for those members of the Serbian public—almost certainly the majority—who held skeptical attitudes toward the Tribunal and doubted many of the established facts regarding his crimes. With substantive matters off the agenda, it was easy enough to calculate that keeping Mladić was unbearably expensive and extraditing him enticingly profitable.

As for supporters and defenders of Mladić, despite years of reports in which he figured as a hero, there were few of these to be found. One news report had the residents of the village of Lazarevo, where the fugitive was apprehended, embittered and seeking to rename the village "Mladićevo."[80] More reports from Lazarevo, however, had locals denying knowledge and shunning publicity. The only large-scale public demonstration for Mladić came in a meeting organized by the Serbian Radical Party in Belgrade on 29 May. Although the meeting was announced well in advance and the efforts of the party organized transport from the interior of the country, only about 7,000 people attended, barely outnumbering the riot police who came in force to prevent disorder.[81] The small crowd listened to Vojislav Šešelj's teenage son Vladimir reading a letter that was more directed to Šešelj's former political associates than anyone else,[82] and heard Mladić's son Darko defending his father as a fighter for the freedom of his people rather than a criminal.[83] As the public withdrew from the square in front of the Serbian parliament, hooligans set into action, and the meeting was followed by confrontations with police and 43 injuries.[84] The poor turnout and desultory quality of the rally did little for Mladić and little for SRS. The meeting was portrayed as an unsuccessful attempt by a declining political party to claim a monopoly on sympathy for criminals, in one of a series of meetings it organized that finished with street violence. The Radicals responded, to little effect, with charges that the rioting was the work of saboteurs.[85] To the degree that the meeting was intended to show a public united behind indictees, it failed; it did succeed in showing that there were still political actors willing to seek profit through controversies over the crimes of the recent past.

Another ongoing controversy would remain current as preparations began to be undertaken for the commencement of the Mladić trial. Mladić, like Radovan Karadžić, was charged with personal responsibility for genocide in several instances in Bosnia-Herzegovina, including the massacre in Srebrenica for which other suspects had already been convicted. As the suggestion began to be circulated about whether his trial would be joined to the trial of Karadžić,[86] speculation grew as to whether all defendants shared an interest in these cases. Just as Mladić had an interest in tracing the origin of crimes to political decisions made by Karadžić, Karadžić had an interest in indicating that crimes were committed by an insubordinate military commanded by Mladić. Both Mladić and Karadžić had a potential interest in suggesting that crimes originated in Serbia via Milošević and his state security apparatus. For each of the defendants charged with participation in the joint criminal enterprise to which a policy of committing crimes was attributed, there was clear advantage in pointing to another participant in the enterprise as the leading participant.

The first representative of the Serbian state to raise the concern about attribution of blame was Radoslav Stojanović, the law professor who had defended Serbia in the genocide case brought before the International Court of Justice by Bosnia-Herzegovina. Stojanović expressed the fear that by presenting evidence indicating that he was following orders that did not originate with him, Mladić could undo the partially successful defense that had been argued before ICJ, in which the court majority found that while Serbia had failed to prevent and punish genocide, it did not carry guilt of commission or as an accessory. As Stojanović assessed the matter: "When the decision was made about Srebrenica there was no contact between Mladić's command and Belgrade. I am afraid that he might say the opposite now, for example that before making the decision he had spoken with Milošević."[87]

The statement confirmed suspicions that among the reasons that a series of Serbian governments may have sought to avoid a Mladić trial was the possibility that his defense could implicate the state.[88] The suspicions were further encouraged by an unusual interview that Aleksandar Dimitrijević, who headed the military security agency until 1999, gave to the Bosnian weekly *BH Dani*. General Dimitrijević repeatedly insisted that the Bosnian Serb military was not formally subordinate to the Yugoslav army, but just as systematically avoided discussion of informal control and the engagement of state security.[89] As discussion of the eventual trial concentrated less on the guilt or innocence of the indictee, and more on the degree to which Serbia might be implicated by his defense, it became more clear that an interest was served by the difference between the level of attention paid to victims and the level of attention paid to the reading material and fruit that Mladić preferred.

It seemed as the extradition passed, the arraignment went forward and the trial approached that the most prominent remaining indictee was also subject to trivialization. Consistent with the legend that had already grown up about the excellent interpersonal relations that existed among detainees in the Scheveningen facility, the recently convicted Croatian general Ante Gotovina—reputed to be the most accomplished cook in the detention facility—was reported to have been ready to welcome his new companion by preparing him scampi.[90] So as dialogue failed to move forward in response to a large stimulus, there was honor among thieves, parsley among murderers, and silence among politicians.

What Makes These Nonmoments?

What makes a nonmoment a nonmoment? Although this study has considered a large number of events, it can be regarded as an investigation into things that did not happen. Instead of a systematic effort to detail elements of guilt, the post-Milošević years saw, at least at many of the top levels of power, a creative development and refinement of denial. Instead of the generation of a discourse on responsibility, the period has seen both efforts to shift the context in which responsibility is understood and a variety of campaigns to put into question the motives of people who promote this kind of discourse. Instead of the development of narratives about and understandings of the past, the last ten years have seen an entrenchment of divisions regarding the character of this period that trace their roots to the political conflicts of the time. The nonevents are incidents that illustrate the lack of motion in public memory.

Lack of motion can be traced to deficiencies in the political culture; there is no shortage of efforts to detail those deficiencies in Serbia and tie the ongoing division in public perceptions to some long-term and fundamental characteristics of the state and society.[91] On the other hand, a larger question can be raised: if we are looking for a process that has not happened—certainly not in a short time—in any other social or political context, could the deficiency reside in the process rather than in the context? To the degree that transitional justice is a moralistic project, it is one that seeks to achieve results in the field of society and culture using instruments of politics and law. It has been assumed in social science that such a relation between cause and effect ought to exist as long as social science has been around to call itself by that name. Emile Durkheim famously argued in *The Rules of Sociological Method* that societies depend on the existence of crime, at least in part because the response to it affirms and strengthens the collective sentiments that bind the members of the society together.[92] In different ways that argument has been recapitulated by transitional justice theorists from Mark Osiel to José Zalaquett.[93]

Durkheim's argument was appealing both for its elegance and for its invitation to think of all elements of the community, even disturbing ones, as being necessary to the functioning of the whole. But it was always marked by tension: proposed as a way of broadening thinking about immorality away from a fundamentalist position, it was also proposed by a theorist whose most enduring idea proposed that society was decaying and moving toward "moral mediocrity."[94] Whether or not we accept the invitation to regard crime as productive or inevitable, the insight that moral sentiments are (possibly? sometimes?) rehearsed when a crime is committed offers strikingly little guidance on understanding crime or ameliorating its causes. The shortcomings of the argument are well illustrated in Serbia, where crime has undoubtedly been productive but can hardly be said (as it also cannot for other places in the world) to have been addressed.

Chapter 9

Politics and Culture in Approaching the Past

The process of transitional justice is predicated on some assumptions that are inarguably noble, if a bit tormented in practice: that truth leads to justice, justice to catharsis, and catharsis to reconciliation. Put another way, it represents an attempt to use the instruments of law to produce consequences on the level of politics, and to expect developments in politics to catalyze processes on the level of culture. It is not surprising that not all these assumptions work perfectly. These are predictable difficulties arising from an effort to treat social practices and interactions as though they operate in a mechanistic fashion when in fact they do not.

And yet it is not the case that nothing has happened. As indicated in Chapter 2, in 2000 there appeared to be a broad consensus of denial and rejection, however much this consensus may have been troubled by doubt, uncertainty, and the desire to know more. During this period, lines of differential understanding and memory began to be drawn, dividing those parts of the public who sought refuge in continuity with the recent past and those who rejected that legacy and sought to build a future based on recognition of the wrong that had been done and mutual rapprochement. While the basic contours of disagreement remain largely the same as they were at the moment of Milošević's arrest, some shifts are nonetheless observable. In particular there are shifts with regard to what people know, what they feel compelled to recognize, and what they feel able to deny. Not all these shifts have resulted in active engagement with the legacy of the recent past or dialogue about it; the desultory response to the arrests of the last prominent indictees suggests that among the results might also be counted exhaustion and apathy.

Over 2010 and 2011, while this book was being completed, ongoing activity offered a picture of just how many things had changed and how many essential questions remained unresolved. Prosecutors made initial gestures toward reopening the investigation of the murder of Zoran Djindjić, concentrating this time on the political background of the conspiracy that had been excluded from the initial investigation and prosecution.[1] While the new investigation may well not get far, the initiative reopened the public discussion that had been cut off by the failure of the post-Djindjić government in 2003.[2] It also began to appear that at least some authorities in some states were beginning to regard crime as a shared regional problem rather than a set of unique national ones. The links between the enormous problem of organized crime in the region and its roots in the state-sponsored crime of the previous period showed, as did the fact that the issue encompassed the entire region and could not be addressed by any single state. Police, prosecutors, and judicial institutions developed ambitious strategies of cross-border cooperation. The most impressive of these was the prosecution of suspects in the murder of the magazine editor Ivo Pukanić and his employee Niko Franjić in Zagreb in 2008. As it became clear that the conspiracy involved a Serbian crime group led by Sreten Jocić ("Joca Amsterdam") Serbian and Croatian police cooperated in the investigation. The trial involved courtrooms linked by video feeds in both countries, allowing evidence to be given with considerably less risk to witnesses and expertise from both sides of the border to be engaged.[3] The conviction of the conspirators in November 2010 represented a powerful demonstration of the necessity and potential of joined forces in generating an approach to crime. Also during this period, some developments in international criminal justice began to undermine the popular argument in Serbia that international institutions were one-sided. In December 2010 the Council of Europe accepted a report from rapporteur Dick Marty advocating investigation of an organ-harvesting operation that implicated prominent political figures in Albania and Kosovo and may have involved political prisoners as victims.[4] And in April 2011 one of the more severe ICTY sentences was delivered against Croatian generals for abuse and deportation of Serb civilians in the 1995 Operation Storm.[5] Similarly, in 2010 Croatian prosecutors began visibly acting against a number of notorious figures from the war period who had previously enjoyed untouchable status, such as the paramilitary commander turned politician Tomislav Merčep.[6] Taken together, it looked possible that some of the pieces of the crime and investigation puzzle, and possibly also of the reconciliation puzzle, might be starting to fall into place.

Still, there was no shortage of indications that tensions remained and that lingering grievances could be mobilized to unravel the developing threads of reconciliation. One of the Bosnian Serb generals convicted in the Srebrenica genocide, Radislav Krstić, was assaulted in an English prison by Muslim inmates, in an attack apparently motivated by the circumstances of his conviction.[7] A series of attempted extraditions by Serbia, while unsuccessful, pointed to failures to investigate crimes attributed to Bosnian forces in the early stages of the conflict. Warrants were executed against former Bosnian politician Ejup Ganić in England and former Bosnian general Jovan Divjak in Austria in connection with an incident in 1992 in which evacuating Yugoslav army soldiers were fired upon in Dobrovoljačka Street in Sarajevo.[8] The case was clouded with uncertainty, in relation to both the chain of command and the number of victims, but this uncertainty could have been resolved. ICTY had received a request to investigate the incident but declined, referring it instead to Bosnian prosecutors, who did not act. A consequence of this sort of inaction is that events frequently raised from the Serbian side as grievances and examples of imbalance in the investigation of alleged war crimes—the Dobrovoljačka Street shootings and the attack on the withdrawing Yugoslav army columns in Tuzla are two prominent instances[9]—remain unexplained and open to reactivation by politicians at any convenient moment. Official exchanges on the topic were marked by public disagreements over jurisdiction, evidence, and the responsibility of states.

For every step forward, there seemed to be a corresponding step back. Meanwhile, the space for stepping appeared to be reduced, as ICTY planned to complete its mandate, domestic institutions displayed their unreadiness, and the memory of crimes receded further into the past. Would the ambitious effort to transform what may have been history's best-documented war into a fatal blow to impunity end in confusion, polarization, and amnesia?

Transitional Justice in Context

Some perspective is certainly in order. It is entirely too easy to allow disappointment with particular incidents to grow into an excessive skepticism regarding the entire process. There have been instances in the past, of course, in which it has been appropriate to talk about guilt and responsibility on a large scale. If postregime transformations are taken into account, the last thirty years have seen a number of initiatives—most of them voluntary, some of them creative—to produce accounts and to generate dialogue on the record of a recently departed regime.[10] Postconflict initiatives are far rarer and more spotty. The most sustained efforts before the founding of the international criminal tribunals for the former Yugoslavia (ICTY) in 1993 and for Rwanda (ICTR) in 1994 were the Nuremberg and Tokyo tribunals at the end of the Second World War. These were not voluntary initiatives but military tribunals functioning against the background of the postwar occupation of Germany and Japan. While the Tokyo tribunal's record is largely neglected, the mythology that surrounds Nuremberg may well be undeserved. The long and exhaustive process of confrontation with the Nazi past in Germany is better traced as beginning from the activation of domestic judicial institutions in the 1960s than to a military tribunal founded by occupying powers in the 1940s.[11]

Viewed historically, limited but meaningful action in the ten years following the departure of Milošević from power is a relatively large and rapid development. Ernst Renan was, after all, thinking of a variety of concrete empirical instances when he developed his formulation that "forgetting, I would even go so far as to say historical error, is a crucial factor in the creation of a nation, which is why progress in historical studies often constitutes a danger for the principle of nationality."[12] Similarly, Stuart Hall points out that most modern nations are the result of "a lengthy process of violent conquest—that is, . . . the forcible suppression of cultural difference," which "have first to be 'forgotten' before allegiance to a more unified, homogeneous national identity could begin to be forged."[13] The motivation to produce accounts and to right wrongs, from the point of view of most political actors, is generally very weak indeed. Rather, as Theodor Adorno observed long ago, "the attitude of forgetting and forgiving everything, which should be the province of people who have suffered injustice, has been adopted by the people who practice it."[14]

So it should come as no surprise that generally in societies, confrontation with uncomfortable facts about the past does not happen, or happens only after an extended period of time. In the United States, one hundred years passed between the end of the Civil War and the passage of the Civil Rights Act, and questions of memorialization of the genocide of Native

Americans remain very controversial.[15] Other incidents in U.S. history remained covered up for a long time—for example, the violent riots in Tulsa, Oklahoma, in May and June 1921, which saw at least 39 deaths and more than 800 injuries, and involved the use of air power by local police in the destruction of the city's African American neighborhood, were silenced to the degree that newspapers from the period of the violence were removed from local archives. Not until 1997 was a commission appointed to investigate the events, with a report recommending reparations produced in 2001.[16] As noted above, in Germany, a generation passed before large-scale interrogation of the Nazi period took place. Meanwhile many events, such as the Armenian genocide, remain the object of energetic denial.[17]

A preliminary conclusion could be suggested that for confrontation with inconvenient experiences of the past to happen at all is rare in human history. That it should happen quickly is something wholly unique. Viewed in this perspective, for all the persistence of denial and all the deficiencies in the process, the accounting that has taken place in Serbia and Southeast Europe over the past decade probably exceeds what precedent might lead a reasonable person to expect. A brief overview of some of the factors behind that process might help in developing an explanation of why it was undertaken at all, and why it has faced some important limitations.

In the first place, much can be said about the role of the international community and a changed international situation in forcing the confrontation. If the conflicts in the former Yugoslavia did not take place in the context of an ambitiously declared "new world order," they at least took place under dramatically changed conditions of surveillance and attention.[18] This was the first set of wars which had an international tribunal overseeing their conduct while they were still taking place. It was the first set of wars in which daily events and developments were reported to such a degree that large and far-flung publics knew about them instantaneously.[19] Maybe more to the point, it was the first set of conflicts to be carried out in a new international environment in which standards appeared to be slowly replacing sovereignty, in which international civil society maintained a constant institutional presence, and in which human rights have become a permanent part of international rhetoric (whether or not they are consistently adopted in practice).[20] While this set of circumstances that may have been relatively unique to the 1990s had consequences for the combatants in the wars of Yugoslav succession, they also encouraged the countervailing argument that standards were applied unevenly and without the benefit of precedent.

At the same time, it would not be accurate to ascribe all the concern about human rights and violations of international humanitarian law to outside influence. The civil societies of the states of the former Yugoslavia participated in the development and extension of standards of humanitarian law, and not exclusively in the role of victims or observers. The wars of succession could also be called the first wars to be carried out simultaneously with a domestically initiated debate on war crimes, international oversight, and responsibility. By the time the Milošević regime came to an end, Serbian civil society had already established institutional structures and intellectual practices that did not permit the new government to set the pace of confrontation by itself. These included a ten-year record of documentation, research, debate, and international communication on the issues involved.

In this respect, while limitations imposed by domestic politics have been a focus of attention here, it would be a mistake not to speak also of limitations from the international side. ICTY offered a promise that the rule of law would be affirmed in armed conflicts, starting in 1993 and into the future. As the limitations of ad hoc tribunals became apparent the sense grew, largely among legal professionals, that a permanent institution with worldwide oversight would address some of these shortcomings. Consequently the ICC was founded in 2002. The ICC cannot be said to have lived up to the promise that greeted its founding. It has been constrained by the resistance of powerful countries, particularly the United States, which have actively sought to restrict its oversight. It has also been constrained by its own prosecution strategy: no fact better illustrates the difficulty of establishing global jurisdiction over states regardless of their power than that to date, nobody outside the continent of Africa has faced a charge from ICC.[21]

On balance, what factors contributed to the development of an effort to take on the question of guilt and responsibility? Much of the existing literature has concentrated heavily on the role of international pressure, either in the form of demands presented by various governments and ICTY or in the form of quid pro quo offers on the part of the U.S. government and the European Union in particular (release of aid for arrests; conditionality related to membership in international bodies).[22] In general the thesis has been well demonstrated that while on the one hand the level of "cooperation" correlates well with the quality of relations between the countries from which cooperation is demanded and international institutions, on the other hand the reduction of the process of justice to mechanisms of "cooperation" detracts from efforts to achieve substantive justice.

At the same time the process cannot be reduced to demands placed on states compelled to "comply." Domestic political instrumentality also played a meaningful role, though this role was limited by other forms of political calculation. Many of the dilemmas described in Chapters 5, 6, and 7 derive from the basic disagreement that divided political forces from the moment that power changed hands in Serbia in 2000: the clash between the forces advocating continuity and a "soft transition" led by Vojislav Koštunica and the advocates of a break with the past, and a "hard transition" led by Zoran Djindjić.[23] The latter group had a strong motivation to encourage the break with the past by making use of information that would be likely to discredit their predecessors, perhaps shocking the public along the way. The ability to satisfy this motivation was always mitigated by the fact that the "hard transition" option did not at any point enjoy plebiscitary majority support. As was most dramatically demonstrated in the 2008 coalition agreement between the Democratic Party (formerly led by Djindjić) and the Socialist Party of Serbia (formerly led by Milošević), compromises with the forces of the recent past were required to enable implementation of even a modest agenda. This meant that to the degree that there did exist any popular desire for revenge against the former rulers, expression of this desire would always be muted by caution and calculation.

This brings us to the puzzle of the "moments" and "nonmoments." There were occasions in which it appeared, at least temporarily, that the revelation of new facts could have profound consequences in provoking major changes in public perception and public opinion. But "moments" lasted a short time before discourse descended into relativism, distraction, and trivia, while "nonmoments" never even reached that initial point. Repeatedly, the impulse for confrontation ran up against the limited capacities of political actors and elites. This blocked process occurred in an environment where there were many forces with an interest in cutting dialogue short, and few actors energetically inviting the public to an opening of the books. The process got as far as rigid procedures and weak will could take it.

On Being Part of the Way There

Even if it has been largely absent from most of the political discussion on processes of considering and reclaiming the past, an implicit assumption of much of the debate around the issue has been that the process of public discussion and mutual recognition not only represents a formal international obligation, but also addresses a genuine social need. The general thesis is that in a period of collapse, dictatorship, isolation, and violence the society was destroyed,[24] and consequently one of the conditions for its reconstruction is a full account of who did what, who suffered in what ways, and why. If what is at stake is a genuine need, then the failure of political processes to address it would be expected to leave traces—either important things will be failing to occur, or sectors outside the political sphere will arise to compensate for the unmet need.

Before proceeding any farther here, it may be necessary to deflate some expectations. It is impossible to engage the discussion without using a number of terms—like "truth" and "justice"—that can only be approached with a maximum dose of caution. Not only is it the case that long traditions of inquiry in a number of disciplines, from philosophy and theology to psychology and politics, have developed labyrinths of discourse around these terms without settling on a final answer, but it is also the case that every claim to hold a monopoly over truth or justice justifiably raises outraged and bitter reactions. Particularly in a part of Europe where fascist regimes were followed by communist ones, there is every reason to be suspicious toward claims about natures, essences, and historical inevitabilities. It might be helpful to consider terms like these as having primarily a rhetorical status; one of the sites in Belgrade where discussion on the topics considered in this work is regularly hosted is called the Center for Cultural Decontamination. Nobody has the least doubt regarding what the name is meant to suggest, even though it is probably the case that nobody can think of a single example in history of a culture that has been "decontaminated."[25]

Moving from the realm of enormous philosophical abstraction to the middle range, however, there are probably some elements of "truth" and "justice" that are less controversial, and where it might be easier to find agreement about their necessity. There is a genuine interest, difficult to contest, in knowing how many people were victims of violence and accounting for their condition today.[26] There is a genuine interest, contested but perhaps not legitimately, in knowing who were the perpetrators of violence, under what command and what pretexts they operated, and whether the violence occurred as unaccountable acts or in the context of official or undeclared state policy.[27] There is probably a need for a generally accepted understanding of how Yugoslavia, the most prosperous and most politically and culturally open state during the Communist period, became a site where repressive regimes and large-scale violence thrived for a period. There is probably a need for assurance that at least the major perpetrators and planners of violence are likely to be tried and punished. At the emotional level, there is very likely a need for the personal experiences of people who suffered from violence to be heard, shared, and to the degree possible understood.[28]

These needs have been neither wholly unmet nor wholly met. Yet it is probably legitimate to raise the point that needs of this type have not been wholly (and often not even partially) met in any other comparable historical circumstance. It may be that unsuitable language has distorted the process. Expressions like "catharsis" and "reconciliation" derive from sources in psychology, particularly clinical counseling practice as it has developed around problems of interpersonal relationships. This is clear from the terminology that is used as well as from the therapeutic frame in which hoped-for social processes are described. Of course it is problematic whether psychological practices and concepts translate to the level of social and political conflict.[29] To move to a more ambitious frame of discussion and speak of such things as the "reconciliation" of collectives or the "cleansing" or "unburdening" of society is a large step—and considering the paucity of concrete historical examples, it may be a step into analogy or fantasy.

How then to approach a goal that has not been achieved, when it is not possible to affirm that the goal was realistic in the first place? It may be reasonable to return to the middle range and to affirm some basic facts that are known. Has Serbian society been transformed by the political changes that followed the fall of the Milošević regime in 2000? No, the change of regime was just a change of regime. Has there been a revolution in international politics and in global consciousness regarding the centrality of humanitarian protection? No, but that is also not especially surprising. Have perceptions developed and been diffused that are radically distinct from the ones that were promoted during the time that violence was being prepared and carried out? No, but it is just as uncertain that perceptions have remained the same. We can, at least, confirm the existence of some (largely expected) absences.

Have there been responses to these absences on the part of society that would indicate that the incomplete response to the recent past is widely felt to constitute a problem? Here it may not be possible to reply with a high

level of certainty, and I have little comfort with the type of "grand sociology" that uses a strategy of synecdoche to draw sweeping conclusions
from scattered evidence. But it is possible to describe some public activity, on both a political and cultural level, that has developed largely or
entirely outside the context of legal and judicial procedures and has been
directed toward compensating for or pointing out some of these procedures' shortcomings.

One initiative, launched by a coalition of human rights organizations in
alliance with some victims' and veterans' groups, is the campaign for a
regional commission for establishing facts about the conflicts on the territory of the former Yugoslavia (REKOM).[30] Aware that international trials
were not producing a complete account of the conflicts or providing victims with an opportunity to have their experiences recognized, that ICTY's
failure to communicate with the publics of the region constituted a missed
opportunity for understanding, and that the domestic trials that will follow
the closure of ICTY are not likely to accomplish more, the coalition proposes a cross-national nonjudicial commission with the task of establishing
the scale and structure of victimization and with investigating events which,
while not illegal, influenced the course of violence.[31] As of the time of writing, the status of the initiative seems uncertain. It is controversial, and faces
accusations in Serbia of being anti-Serb, in Kosovo of being pro-Serb, in
Croatia of being pro-Yugoslav, and in Bosnia of being imposed from outside.[32] The campaign that began in April 2011 to collect a million signatures
by June fell short: the petition drive had collected 477,000, with a very
uneven distribution across the region.[33] Governments have been lukewarm
toward the campaign, while not all human rights organizations support it
and some have charged that it distorts the regional human rights community, overshadowing less ambitious but perhaps more plausible local
efforts.[34] Nonetheless the series of consultations that was undertaken in
the early stages of the campaign represents an important document for
understanding the process of transitional justice as it has developed so far,
with participants underlining both some of the disappointment that judicial
initiatives have engendered and also the shared interests of veterans, victims, and activists.[35]

Another effort points in a far different direction. A cultural intervention, the independent cinematic production *A Serbian Film* was conceived,[36] and remarkably successfully executed, with the intention to shock.

The plot follows a retired pornographic actor trying to return to the profession, and signing on to perform a film for which the production requires his complete ignorance, and which involves a degree of depravation that shocks and threatens even him (to say nothing of the audience). It has been described as "the nastiest film ever made,"[37] and has been treated accordingly. Serbian authorities attempted to ban the film,[38] and Spanish authorities did ban it.[39] In England, the Westminster City Council refused to allow it to be shown at a horror film festival,[40] and the film made a record for having the most content ordered cut from it in order to be assigned an "18" rating of any film since 1994.[41] Addressing the controversy without trying to defuse it, the director, Srdjan Spasojević, issued a statement explaining his intentions:

> The major metaphorical take concerning this film was to treat real life as pornography. In our region for the last few decades we have brought ourselves to the point where we experience our lives as pure exploitation through which we are emotionally, psychologically and creatively raped by the incomprehensible, chaotic, unbelievably stupid and brutal forces of corrupt authority. Through every kind of job you can get in order to feed your family, you end up being viciously exploited and humiliated in the worst and lowest fashion. In this country, beaten and battered beyond belief by both the forces inside and outside of it, spiritual prostitution became the only real currency. We make the allegory of it all come alive by treating pornography as something casual and perfectly normal—our everyday life. The virus of that special kind of pornography has spread to every pore of our existence—political, cultural, and essential.
>
> Through our folklore, the erotic has always been naturally linked and intertwined with the violent. Violence comes out of our everyday pornography as much as it is the other way around. Together, the pornographic and the violent mix into a cocktail that we drink every morning as cheap breakfast. Through centuries, women and children here have been treated as a male property and, as their owners, we are allowed to mistreat them in the most inhuman ways and it all comes off as perfectly normal. This film serves not as a documentary depiction of our reality, but as an X-ray, a diagnosis of the malformed and disease-driven soul of our society. That is the reason for showing the almost unshowable scenes in the film in such

unrestrained and direct manner. The violation, humiliation, and ultimate degradation of our being must be felt and experienced by every viewer so that it cannot be ignored. Those scenes figure and communicate as literal drawings of our disfigured and raped emotions. You may call it torture-porn, but to us, it is our life.[42]

And he located the film in the context of contemporary efforts that do not inspire the same type of controversy:

> The films that preach and enforce political correctness are the dominant form of cinematic expression today. Nowadays in Eastern Europe you cannot get a film financed unless you have a pathetic and heartwarming "true story" to tell about some poor lost refugee girls with matchsticks, who ended up as victims of war, famine, and/or intolerance. They mostly deal with VICTIMS as heroes, and they use and manipulate them in order to activate the viewer's empathy. They make a false, romanticized story about that victim and sell it as real life. That is real pornography and manipulation, and also spiritual violence—the cinematic fascism of political correctness. We can freely tag these pictures as compassion-porn, made to elicit the lowest form of sympathy and compassion and therefore cheapen national, political and personal tragedies. As much as the pornography in our film depicts our lives, it also describes Eastern European cinema today—the pornography of a victim.[43]

While it was easy enough to regard the film as an effort to exploit war-derived stereotypes depicting Serbs as violent and amoral, others encouraged more specific political interpretations. Screenwriter Aleksandar Radivojević argued that the subject was "the monolithic power of leaders who hypnotize you to do things you don't want to do."[44] Critic Damir Pilić in *Slobodna Dalmacija* went farther, drawing a direct association to Slobodan Milošević.[45] The impulse to offer images designed to shock can of course be traced to a number of sources, not all political. Yet it seems plausible that at least in part, the producers of *A Serbian Film* had in mind a political-cultural environment in which distinctions between right and wrong consistently took second place to some other consideration.

It is not quite the case that REKOM and *A Serbian Film* compete for public attention; each of them has its limited audience and the membership of these audiences may not overlap much. Yet each in its own way draws attention to shortcomings of the efforts of the last decade—one in an effort to correct them, and one in an effort to dramatize their consequences through exaggeration. Probably there are lessons for the future in a political and cultural environment that offers both sorts of interpretations. The first involves the need, in accounting for the past, to move beyond law and procedure and engage with society and culture. It is in the spheres of understanding environment and identity, and of relations with others in the region, that the consequences of large-scale violence are felt. To the degree that the process of achieving some sort of justice has involved directives from international actors to figures at the top level of politics, it is necessary to understand that orders delivered to the top reach the top, and not farther. At the same time, extensive communication and outreach is necessary in confronting sensitive events and issues. Not all incidents that open a topic move it forward; some open wounds instead. This is an area in which efforts to explain developments and offer context on the part of influential domestic and international figures would have been extremely helpful. Instead it was absent.

Outside the realm of politics and international relations, culture has been stepping into places where official actors have refused to tread, or have consistently changed the subject. Expressions of bitterness designed to shock—like *A Serbian Film*—represent one type of response. But there have been other instances of cultural production that have stepped in to provide catalysts for dialogue. Novels like *Elijahova stolica* by Igor Štiks have sought to place the siege of Sarajevo into a psychological and emotional context.[46] *Hotel Zagorje* by Ivana Simić Bodrožić similarly sought to encourage sympathy and understanding with victims of the destruction of cities, while *Pad Kolumbije* by Saša Ilić explored political and personal aspects of the criminalization of Serbian society. Works like these are only a small sampling of ways that recent literature has attempted to engage public issues that have remained unarticulated by political sources. Correspondingly in cinema, films addressing the experience of victims and participants such as Jasmila Žbanić's *Grbavica*,[47] Vinko Brešan's *Svjedoci*,[48] Danis Tanović's *Ničija zemlja*,[49] and Goran Paskaljević's *San zimske noći*,[50] to name just a few of the best-known examples, have attracted large audiences and a welcoming reception throughout the region regardless of their country of origin. There is no shortage of related efforts in theater, music, and visual and plastic arts. The consistent and diverse cultural production in the void left by politics speaks to the existence of a considerable public desire for engagement with the open questions of the recent past.

While cultural initiatives rarely investigate and never sentence, they offer some of the keys to understanding that have been missing from political and legal projects: the ability to hear and identify with the lived experiences of individuals, a route to engagement that participants in the public can understand, and an openness to interpretation that constitutes an invitation to dialogue. Many of the refinements on transitional justice—from community courts to the involvement of religious and cultural institutions and the integration of victim testimony and forgiveness in "truth" commissions—have represented ways of integrating these keys to understanding. In other institutions the absence of them is described with the term "democratic deficit."[51] Given the distance between the genuine accomplishments of transitional justice initiatives in the region and the ways in which they have been received, it is hard to imagine any real progress without these forms of engagement.

Notes

Chapter 1. Guilt and Responsibility: Problems, History and Law

1. The formal name of the Tribunal is the International Tribunal for the Prosecution of Persons Responsible for Serious Violations of International Humanitarian Law Committed in the Territory of the Former Yugoslavia since 1991. It is universally referred to by the acronym of the shorter version of the name, ICTY, or by the location of its facilities, the Hague Tribunal.

2. Patrick Robinson and Serge Brammertz, "Letter dated 21 November 2008 from the President of the International Tribunal for the Prosecution of Persons Responsible for Serious Violations of International Humanitarian Law Committed in the Territory of the Former Yugoslavia since 1991, addressed to the President of the Security Council"; and "Report of Serge Brammertz, Prosecutor of the International Tribunal for the Former Yugoslavia, provided to the Security Council under paragraph 6 of Security Council resolution 1534 (2004)." Security Council document S/2008/729, 24 November 2008.

3. UN Security Council Resolution 827 (1993), adopted 25 May 1993, S/RES/827 (1993).

4. The Socialist Federal Republic of Yugoslavia (Socialistička Federativna Republika Jugoslavija, SFRJ), composed of six republics (Bosnia-Herzegovina, Croatia, Macedonia, Montenegro, Serbia, and Slovenia) and two autonomous regions (Kosovo and Vojvodina), ceased to exist in 1991. In 1992 the Federal Republic of Yugoslavia (Savezna Republika Jugoslavija, SRJ) was founded by Montenegro and Serbia. In 2003 that state was succeeded by the State Union of Serbia and Montenegro (Državna Zajednica Srbije i Crne Gore, SCG), which lasted until the declaration of independence by Montenegro in 2006.

5. War crimes are commonly defined as violations of the Hague Conventions of 1899 and 1907, and the Geneva Conventions of 1949 and Additional Protocols of 1977, although there is a growing movement to expand the scope of these documents. The most recent international iteration of war crimes was produced in 2000 for the International Criminal Court. See Preparatory Commission for the International Criminal Court, "Finalized draft text of the Elements of Crimes," PCNICC/2000/1/Add. 2, 2 November 2000.

6. The term "crimes against humanity" was first used to characterize the Armenian genocide. It was introduced into international law by the Agreement for the Prosecution and Punishment of the Major War Criminals of the European Axis (the "London Agreement"), which established the International Military Tribunal ("Nuremberg Tribunal") in 1945. Article 5 of the ICTY Statute offers a list of crimes against humanity, as does the International Criminal Court statute.

7. The only existing legal definition of genocide is in the 1948 Convention on the Prevention and Punishment of the Crime of Genocide, but this definition is the object of scholarly controversy. For different sides of the analytic debate, see Andreopoulos (1997); Harff and Gurr (1988); Fein (2005).

8. Considerable scholarly attention has been given to efforts in Germany to publicly come to terms with and accept the burden of responsibility for the crimes of the National Socialist regime of 1933–1945. A summary of debates is provided in Maier (1988). Controversy continues to confront Japan for its refusal to make similar efforts with regard to violations committed during the World War II period, including the sexual enslavement of women from Korea and China and the Nanking massacres of 1937–1938.

9. Some of the more recent histories of the World War II in Yugoslavia emphasize the point that the complexity of the conflict defies efforts to represent it either as a two- or three-sided civil war or as a domestic resistance to occupation. See Tomasevich (1975; 2001); Pavlowitch (2008).

10. The number of victims of the World War II-era genocide in Croatia remains a matter of historical and, of course, political dispute. It is not a matter of dispute that a policy of genocide was declared and partly carried out by the quisling state in that period.

11. The most notorious instance was the Bleiburg massacre of prisoners of war in 1945. For an assessment of the evidence on this, see Tomasevich (2001: 751–88).

12. Vasiljević (1995: 39–57) documents the various wartime and postwar responses. Although humanitarian laws and agreements became a part of Yugoslavian law, the State Commission for Documenting the Crimes of the Occupiers and Their Collaborators, formed in 1943, eventually produced an incomplete report, which the members of the commission quickly disowned, in 1948. The royal government in exile also declared the formation of a Commission for the Investigation of War Crimes in 1944, but this commission never began its work (55).

13. Among the people who make the argument explicitly is Nebojša Popov, "Traumatologija partijske države," in Popov (1996).

14. Banac (1989).

15. A variety of perspectives on this question can be found in Cohen and Dragović-Soso (2008).

16. For sample arguments, there is the thesis that secessionists destroyed the state (S. Stojanović 1997), the thesis that the Serbian regime made the state untenable

(Magaš 1993), and the thesis that SFRJ was the state that withered away (Jović 2009). There is also a wide variety of positions and interpretations between and outside these.

17. The commission is discussed in Chapter 4.

18. The issue was raised to establish the jurisdiction of the International Court of Justice in cases related to the conflict. The ICJ ruled that the Federal Republic of Yugoslavia was bound by the Genocide Convention as a successor state to Yugoslavia in determining that it had jurisdiction to hear suits brought against it (and its successors) by Bosnia-Herzegovina and Croatia. However it ruled that that state (and its successors) did not have standing to sue the member states of the NATO alliance for aggression in the conflict of 1999, as it was not a UN member at the time.

19. Alternative interpretations rely on alternative counting strategies. While the largest mass killing (of up to 8,000 people in Srebrenica in 1995) was committed by Serbs, the largest forced migration (of about 200,000 people from Croatia) was committed against Serbs. It is not clear exactly how such a calculus could be helpful, as most people would shy away from the effort to determine how many expulsions equal one death, or vice versa.

20. In the March 2004 violence against the Kosovo Serb population, in addition to deaths and injuries about 730 private homes were destroyed and 36 Orthodox religious and cultural sites were attacked. A year later, Amnesty International noted the inadequacy of responses to the violence. See Amnesty International, "Public statement: Kosovo/Kosova (Serbia and Montenegro): The March Violence—One Year On," AI document 70/006/2005 (Public), 17 March 2005.

21. In 1998 Zdravko Mušić, Hazim Delić, and Esad Landžo were convicted (and Zejnil Delalić was acquitted) for crimes committed against the prisoners of the Čelebići camp. All ICTY trial chamber judgments can be found at UN International Criminal Tribunal for the Former Yugoslavia, http://www.un.org/icty/.

22. Of particular interest in the Haradinaj verdict is section 2.2, "Difficulties in obtaining witness testimony" (14–18), in which the judges discuss witnesses who were prevented from giving evidence, but nonetheless conclude they did receive evidence "from more than 90 witnesses" (18).

23. I described this struggle in one of these states in Gordy (1999). There have not yet been similar systematic studies of this phenomenon in other former Yugoslav states, but similar patterns can be observed.

24. On some level it might be considered that they are not out of power. Each of the parties in power during the armed conflict have since either led governing coalitions (as in Croatia) or joined them (as in Serbia).

25. Vladimir Vukčević became the first special prosecutor for war crimes in Serbia in 2003. Bosnia-Herzegovina's War Crimes Chamber was established in December 2004 and began work in March 2005. The situation in Croatia has been mixed: a (partial) "general amnesty" was declared in 1996, and the parliament made a declaration on the legitimacy of the state's military efforts in 2000 (Zastupnički dom Hrvatskoga državnog Sabora, "Deklaracija o domovinskom ratu," 17 October 2000).

However in response to pressure from the European Union special war crimes chambers were designated and the first cases began to be referred to them in 2005. Previously prosecutions in Croatia had been widely perceived as being selective. See Cruvellier and Valiñas (2006). Also Lamont (2007) and Organisation for Security and Cooperation in Europe Mission to Croatia, "Background Report: Domestic War Crime Trials 2005" (2006).

26. Eight crimes against humanity are enumerated in Article 5 of the ICTY Statute, supplemented by a flexible ninth category of "other inhumane acts."

27. UN Security Council Resolution 827, adopted 25 May 1993.

28. The first person to be charged with genocide by ICTY was Milan Kovačević, whose trial began on 6 July 1998 and terminated with his death three weeks later. The first conviction for genocide was handed down by ICTY in 2001 against Radislav Krstić for his complicity in the 1995 Srebrenica killings, though the charge was reduced to complicity in genocide on appeal. Vidoje Blagojević was convicted of complicity to commit genocide in 2005 but this portion of the decision was reversed on appeal in 2007. Several indictees charged with genocide had the charge reduced by making plea agreements. Slobodan Milošević died in custody in 2006. A number of other cases are still in progress at the time of writing; one major case, that of Ratko Mladić, remains in preparation.

29. Civil charges were laid both by Bosnia-Herzegovina and by Croatia against the Federal Republic of Yugoslavia and its successor states for genocide before the ICJ. The ICJ found in the case filed by Bosnia-Herzegovina that Serbia had failed to prevent and punish genocide. The charges filed by Croatia have yet to be heard.

30. The full text of Milošević's 2 April 2001 appeal, "Ki br. 318/01, Istražnom sudiji Okružnog suda u Beogradu za veće toga suda iz člana 23. stav 6. ZKP: Žalba protiv rešenja o odredjivanju pritvora od strane okrivljenog Slobodana Miloševića," was published by the daily newspaper *Danas* on 3 April 2001.

31. The term appears to have entered the language through a squeaky back door carved out by Serbian regime media in 1992. Naimark (2001) describes it as having "exploded into our consciousness" (ouch!) in May that year. Without the "ethnic" modifier, "cleansing" appears to have had a variety of military and propagandistic uses over a much longer period. Naimark defends the term, relying fundamentally on linguistic premises (it resembles some terms in German and some Slavic languages) and on the need (?) for a term to describe something mildly distinct from genocide. The International Court of Justice ruled that the term "ethnic cleansing" has no specific legal meaning, and finds that in absence of specific evidence of intent "Neither the intent, as a matter of policy, to render an area 'ethnically homogeneous,' nor the operations that may be carried out to implement such policy, can as such be designated as genocide." See ICJ, "Case Concerning the Application of the Convention on the Prevention and Punishment of the Crime of Genocide (*Bosnia and Herzegovina v. Serbia and Montenegro*)," 71, para. 190.

32. Marjanović was simultaneously prime minister and head of the import-export firm Progres, which controlled the trade in gas between Russia and Serbia. He died in 2006.

33. A former chemical engineer, Šainović is regarded as having exercised control over the printing of currency during the 1993–1994 hyperinflation, during the course of which hard currency was transferred en masse from private hands to the control of the regime and its allies. He has been in the custody of ICTY since 2002, where he was charged as one of the "Belgrade Six" of high officials responsible for violations of humanitarian law in Kosovo. He was convicted by ICTY in February 2009.

34. As director of the customs service Kertesz was able to control and harvest profit from the lively smuggling trade that developed while the country was under a regime of international sanctions. He is widely considered to have organized the supply of money and materials to paramilitary forces in Croatia and Bosnia-Herzegovina and to have controlled an arsenal of patronage that maintained the regime's core of support. In February 2007 he was convicted of complicity in a political murder (he secured automobiles for the perpetrators) and in September 2007 he was tried for embezzlement of public funds. He is also a defendant in the ongoing case against the "tobacco mafia."

35. Sincere apologies to corrupt individuals who were left off this list. Some of them are discussed in Jelena Cerovina and Biljana Baković, "Nikada nije kasno za sud," *Politika*, 10 August 2008.

36. One charge for which Mirjana Marković failed to appear involved distribution of apartments in state possession to political allies. See I. S., "Mirjana Marković okrivljena i za dodelu stanova: Poternica može i za blaža nedela," *Glas javnosti*, 9 April 2003. The family is also charged with illegally acquiring two residential properties for itself in Belgrade. See Unsigned (Pink), "Sudjenje Miloševićima zbog vile," *Pink vesti*, 13 December 2008. Further charges relate to smuggling and money laundering. See Unsigned (Sudska hronika), "Sudjenje u aferi novci u septembru," *Dnevnik*, January 2007. As Russia has granted asylum to members of the family, there is a low likelihood that the cases will come to trial.

37. Slavko Ćuruvija was shot and killed by two assailants outside his house in 1999. A summary of the intimidation that preceded his murder is offered in the statement by the Association of Independent Electronic Media, "ANEM Press Release: The Heralded Murder of Slavko Ćuruvija," 12 April 1999, and R. V., "Na beogradskom Novom groblju sahranjen Slavko Ćuruvija," *Vreme vanredno izdanje* 6, 17 April 1999. Nobody has been charged with his murder.

38. The murder attempt was carried out on the Ibar highway, where attackers tried to crush Drašković's car and the one accompanying it with a truck full of sand. The case has been tried and appealed three times with a rotating cast of indictees. In the most recent episode those convicted included members of the transport police, members of the Unit for Special Operations (JSO), and the former heads of the state security service and the customs agency.

39. Dobroslav Gavrić, Milan Djuričić, and Dragan Nikolić were convicted of committing the murder. Only Nikolić has actually begun to serve his sentence. The identities of the people who organized and ordered the murder, as well as their motivations, remain a source of widely ranging rumor and popular creativity.

40. An early political patron of Milošević, Stambolić was sidelined in 1987 and later became a critic and was perceived by Milošević as a rival. His disappearance while jogging in a park in 2000 remained unexplained until March 2003, when members of the JSO, charged in the murder of prime minister Zoran Djindjić, revealed that he had been kidnapped, transported in a van to a remote location in Fruška Gora north of Belgrade, and murdered. Former state security director Radomir Marković and four JSO members were convicted of his murder in 2005.

41. The passengers were kidnapped by a group of Army of Republika Srpska soldiers under the command of Milan Lukić. Lukić was tried and convicted in absentia in 2003, and his trial for other offenses before ICTY began in July 2008. Nebojša Ranisavljević was tried and convicted in domestic courts for the case; he received a sentence of fifteen years. None of his accomplices have been charged, although evidence against them was given at the Ranisavljević trial. There is evidence that state authorities, including the directors of the Yugoslav Railways, knew of the crime in advance. See Women in Black, "Fourteen Years Since the Crimes in Štrpci," 26 February 2007; Humanitarian Law Centre, "Abduction at 'Štrpci—Fifteen Years On," 26 February 2008; Marina Grihović, "Regional Report: Štrpci Case Stirs More Controversy," Institute for War and Peace Reporting, 16–21 September 2002.

42. In May 1992, the locally ruling Serbian Radical Party (led by Vojislav Šešelj, with local organization provided by the village's Radical chair Ostoja Šibinčić) organized a campaign to intimidate the local ethnic Croat majority and encourage them to leave the village. Šibinčić was tried and acquitted by a domestic court and returned to active political life as a local official in 2006. Šešelj faces charges related to the forced resettlement of Croats from Hrtkovci before ICTY. See Jovanka Zurković, "Nije se Ostoja vratio, ali ima pravo da radi," Danas, 20 March 2006; J. A., "Povratak Ostoje Šibinčića," Dnevnik, 10 March 2006; B92 vesti, "Godišnjica progona Hrvata iz Vojvodine," 6 May 2003; "Podsećanje na slučaj Hrtkovci," 4 May 2005; and "Potvrdjena optužnica protiv Šešelja," 14 February 2003.

43. The passengers were tortured before they were murdered and their bodies have not been recovered. Milan Lukić, Oliver Krsmanović, Dragutin Dragićević, and Djordje Šević were convicted of torture and murder in the case in 2003. The latter two are in prison in Serbia, while Lukić is on trial for other charges before ICTY and Krsmanović is a fugitive.

44. A detailed summary of the state of domestic law and the condition of the application of that law is offered by Dimitrijević (2000).

45. Milanović was convicted in 2002, but went into hiding rather than appearing to serve his sentence. He was arrested in 2003. The RTS bombing also involves a symbolic debate over responsibility and victimhood. Supporters of the Milošević

regime quickly, and with heavy publicity, built a monument to the sixteen workers who were killed, and argued (persuasively) that the attack constituted a violation by NATO of the Geneva Conventions that specify only military objects may be targeted. The families of the victims take a different approach, agreeing that the bombing constituted a war crime, but regarding the regime as an accomplice since it failed (or deliberately refused) to protect employees in a building everybody knew was a target.

46. In May 2001 a campaign was renewed on behalf of the former Bosnian Serb leadership to contest charges of war crimes, crimes against humanity, and genocide by releasing orders that Radovan Karadžić issued instructing armed forces to observe the Hague and Geneva conventions and to refrain from abusing civilians. It is difficult to see how such documents would help Karadžić's case. At the time of the war he was either: (1) as he previously claimed, not in control of forces which were only partly under the command of his self-proclaimed government, and partly composed of paramilitaries not formally subject to command. In that case, his orders could not have had any force; or (2) in a position to command and order forces operating on the territory of Bosnia-Herzegovina, in which case the legal standard of "superior responsibility" presumes that he had knowledge of events, and imposes a duty to prevent the commission of crimes, to punish those who commit crimes, and to control forces under his command. See Bantekas (1999).

47. Support for the Serbian paramilitary (a self-proclaimed military organization, the Army of the Serb Republic [Vojska Republike Srpske, VRS]) in Bosnia-Herzegovina included paying the salaries of its officers, which would constitute a more direct connection than simply providing money to the organization. Tatjana Stanković, "Čuvari tajni i nacije," AIM, 8 April 2001. In March 2007 the International Court of Justice found that while the Federal Republic of Yugoslavia may have exercised "overall control" over the VRS (143–44, para. 402; 144–45, para. 406), this standard was overly broad and did not fulfill the stricter standard of showing "complete dependence" (140, para. 392) necessary to demonstrate complicity.

48. David Cohen, "Beyond Nuremberg: Individual Responsibility for War Crimes," in Hesse and Post (1999: 53–92).

49. The arrangement and its consequences are discussed in Chapter 6.

50. Unsigned (editorial), "Zadah zločina," Danas, 7 June 2001.

51. For an account of the attempt to hide the truck in the river on the night of 20 March 1999 and the finding and opening of the freezer truck on 6 April 1999, see Jovan Dulović, "Kako su uklanjani tragovi zločina, gde su završili leševi iz hladnjače, da li je postojala 'Dubina 1,'" Vreme 543, 31 May 2001.

52. Filip Švarm, "Leševi iz kamiona—hladnjače," AIM Press, 8 May 2001.

53. Dulović, "Kako su uklanjani tragovi zločina," notes that on 6 April 1999, when the truck was removed from the river and opened, among the people present were prosecutors, judges, police officers, citizens who happened to be there, and passengers on a bus that was going by and was stopped by police. He estimates that on that day about 200 people saw the contents of the freezer truck.

54. Unsurprisingly, the name also led people to wonder whether there was a "Dubina 1" (see title of Dulović's article).

55. B92 vesti, "Počela ekshumacija leševa iz hladnjače," 2 June 2001.

56. Stojan Cerovic, "Zločin i tajna," *Vreme* 540, 10 May 2001. The two "kingdoms" Cerović mentions in the last sentence are a reference to the mythological cycle of the Battle of Kosovo, in which King Lazar loses the battle after choosing "the kingdom of heaven" over "the earthly kingdom."

57. B92 vesti, 11 April 2001.

58. Surprisingly, the term was also been used in the same period by Djindjić's rival, federal president Vojislav Koštunica, although he was then beginning to position himself as opposed to ambitious projects of exploring and explaining the evils produced by nationalism, of which he claimed to be a "moderate" exponent. See his statements in Steven Erlanger, "Admissions by Milosevic Should Speed His Trial, Bosnia Says," *New York Times*, 4 April 2001; and Joshua Kucera, "Serbia Puts the Past on Trial," *Scotland on Sunday*, 8 April 2001.

59. This study will not deal with the concept of guilt as it is used in psychoanalysis.

60. There are of course exceptions to this principle (as with insanity) and expansions of it (such as strict liability).

61. Walker (1980: 544–45).

62. Jurisprudence has also developed the principle of corporate responsibility, though this relies on the legal fiction whereby corporations are treated as though they are individuals.

63. The book first appeared in German in 1946 as *Die Schuldfrage*. For this discussion I am using Vanja Savić's 1999 translation into Serbo-Croatian.

64. Jaspers (1999: 19).

65. H. D. Lewis, "Guilt," in Edwards (1967: 395).

66. Jaspers (1999: 48, 49, 49).

67. Jaspers (1999: 21, 50, 21).

68. Jaspers (1999: 21–22, 22, 23, 57).

69. Jaspers (1999: 21).

70. Lewis, "Guilt," 396.

71. David Fyffe, "Responsibility," in Hastings, Selbie, and Gray (1980 [1905]: 739).

Chapter 2. The Formation of Public Opinion

1. B92's publishing house Samizdat B92 released, in addition to political memoirs and essays related to contemporary themes, a large number of titles calculated to promote public discussion of crimes committed during the wars of succession and responsibility for them. These included collections of interviews and memories, like Ristić and Leposavić (2000), accounts of related phenomena such as translations of

Country of My Skull, a memoir of the South African Truth and Reconciliation Commission by journalist Antjie Krog, and histories of the Nazi Holocaust by historians such as Raul Hilberg.

2. The issue was a frequent topic in the popular weekly political talk show *Peščanik* (The Hourglass) and in the weekly broadcast *Suočavanje* (Confrontation), which was directed exclusively to the question.

3. The criticism refers to more or less all elections conducted since 2000. While the objection could be taken as a reflection of the survey agencies involved, the issue is broader: it has to do with the instability of voter turnout, the frequent short-lived popularity of some "protest" parties, and the uncertain willingness of survey respondents to answer honestly in unstable climates characterized by insecurity and weak trust.

4. "Najviše pitanja gradjana Djindjiću i Koštunici,"B92 vesti dana, 30 May 2001.

5. In public statements, spokespeople for the Tribunal and for the Tribunal Prosecutor energetically rejected the suggestion of a trial anywhere other than The Hague. Apart from the question whether this would have been a good idea, such a proposal was expressly permitted by the ICTY rules. According to the Tribunal's Rules of Procedure and Evidence (Rule 4), "A Chamber may exercise its functions at a place other than the seat of the Tribunal, if so authorised by the President in the interests of justice." There are contradictory interpretations of Article 9 of the ICTY Statute, which claims (1) that national courts and ICTY have "concurrent jurisdiction" for the prosecution of violations of international law, and at the same time and (2) that ICTY has "primacy" over national courts. Section (2) defines "primacy" as meaning, "At any stage of the procedure, the International Tribunal may formally request national courts to defer to the competence of the International Tribunal," which suggests that the initiative in trying suspects can begin with national courts. A similar conclusion is suggested by Article 10 (the *non bis in idem*, or in American legal jargon, "double jeopardy" clause) of the statute, which says that no person already convicted by ICTY may be tried by national courts for the same offense, but that a person already convicted by national courts may be tried by ICTY for the same offense if ICTY finds that "(a) the act for which he or she was tried was characterized as an ordinary crime; or (b) the national court proceedings were not impartial or independent, were designed to shield the accused from international criminal responsibility, or the case was not diligently prosecuted." This version of ICTY "primacy" addresses a serious problem (already apparent in the court-martial of the "Vukovar three" by the Yugoslav army, for example), but also suggests that any national courts wanting to try cases related to violations of international law might have had a motivation to get a head start, so their authority would not be precluded.

6. The instrumental motivations which people might have for opposing their own prosecutions are too obvious to mention here. It may be worthwhile to mention that supporters of the former Croatian regime (and to a lesser degree of the various "entities" of Bosnia-Herzegovina) offered the same arguments and used the same rhetorical

constructions in their opposition to ICTY. Compare, for example, the statements of Franjo Tudjman's former foreign minister Zvonimir Separović (*Slobodna Dalmacija*, 5 December 2000), with the arguments offered by the most visible Serbian opponents of ICTY, such as Kosta Čavoški and, for a time, Čavoški's erstwhile coauthor Vojislav Koštunica. As a legal and political theorist Čavoški coauthored a fundamental study of the origins of single-party rule in post-World War II Yugoslavia with Koštunica (1990). Later he would contribute to the development of nationalist demands in a series of minor works, (e.g., 1995), before releasing a number of polemical works as president of the International Commission for the Truth About Radovan Karadžić, a Karadžić support group (2002, 2005).

7. The survey was published in the online version of the paper on 11 April 2001.

8. For a survey of the major media outlets in Serbia as of 1995, see Gordy (1999), and Thompson (2005). There have of course been changes since 2000 in the mediascape of Serbia, with the ideological role once played by *Novosti* now increasingly played by popular low-price tabloids such as *Press* and *Kurir*.

9. The initial results were released by agency director Srdjan Bogosavljević at a press conference in Belgrade in May 2001. A summary is offered in "Najveći branilac srpstva Ratko Mladić," B92 vesti, 17 May 2001.

10. According to the full survey report, 78.0 percent of respondents were able to name three people guilty for the wars of succession, while 40.5 percent were able to name three "defenders of Serbhood." SMMRI (2001: 32).

11. SMMRI (2001: 4).

12. SMMRI (2001: 15).

13. SMMRI (2001: 22).

14. SMMRI (2001: 27). However, according to the same survey, only 11.2 percent of people who named the Markale attack believed it was committed by Serb forces. This is consistent with the position promoted by state media at the time of the attack and afterward, which argued that the army of Bosnia-Herzegovina manufactured this atrocity and others for purposes of publicity. Similarly, only 22.8 percent of people who knew of the massacre in Račak believed reports of it were true.

15. SMMRI (2001: 28).

16. SMMRI (2001: 31).

17. SMMRI (2001: 30).

18. SMMRI (2001: 73).

19. SMMRI (2001: 72).

20. SMMRI (2001: 71).

21. SMMRI (2001: 68).

22. SMMRI (2001: 69).

23. The case in question is the "freezer truck" incident in which the bodies of massacre victims from Kosovo were apparently removed from the scene and destroyed; see Chapter 1.

24. Petar Luković, "Viewpoint: Serbia's New Capital," *IWPR Tribunal Update* 219, 30 April–5 May 2001.

25. Zoran Slavujević, "Razmere nelegitimnosti političkog sistema i njegovih institucija," in Mihailović (ed.) (2000: 141).

26. Slavujević, "Razmere nelegitimnosti političkog sistema."

27. On the role of the Serbian Orthodox Church in the conflicts of the 1990s and their aftermath, see Vukomanović (2008) and Hadžić (ed.) (2004).

28. Slavujević (2000).

29. On this theme, see especially the recent work of Ana Dević, in particular "Nationalism and Powerlessness of Everyday Life: A Sociology of Discontents in Yugoslavia Before the Breakup," paper presented at conference, "Living with the Beast: Everyday Life in Authoritarian Serbia," Clark University, Worcester, Massachusetts, 2000.

30. Singleton (1976) summarizes several of the most important of the earlier studies. The effect of factors such as the desire to emigrate is evaluated in Milić and Čičkarić (1998). Several related dimensions are also explored in Lazic (1994, 2000).

Chapter 3. Moment I: The Leader Is Not Invincible

1. This is of course the schema developed by Raymond Williams (1981: 203–4) to account for "dynamic forms" of culture.

2. It may also have been possible to choose the date of 28 June 2001, when Milošević was transferred to the custody of ICTY. I chose the earlier date because: (a) the events were carried out publicly rather than secretly; (b) it marked the first dramatic break from the protected status enjoyed by the former ruler; and (c) the events as they took place were relatively less anticipated and hence "newer" as a catalyst for discourse.

3. The genre of the political memoir would expand rapidly over the following years, would come to include writers and memoirists from outside the circle of opposition to the former regime, and would expand its temporal scope to include the first period after the fall of Milošević and speculation as to how similar or different the new regime was.

4. Koštunica's comment "I am not informed" (*nisam obavešten*) came to mark him for a long time thereafter, with detractors calling him, mildly, "Mister Uninformed" (*gospodin Neobavešteni*), or more baroquely "Saint Voja the Uninformed" (*Sveti Voja Neobavešteni*).

5. Unsigned, "Test za novu demokratsku vlast," *Danas*, 2 April 2001.

6. At that time the film had not been released in Serbia, and therefore if he was watching the film he had to have been watching a pirated copy. From the time sanctions were imposed on Serbia in 1992, the minor crime of copyright violation has been committed by probably every resident of the country, but Djindjić's remark was accorded symbolic importance because of the obvious contradiction with his stated goal of restoring a legal order.

7. State officials would regularly warn that the arrests of ICTY indictees might lead to mass protest or street violence, but no such response ever did in fact occur.

8. All the comments quoted in this paper can be found at http://www.b92.net. They will not be cited individually. The translations are mine. I make no claims for the representativeness of this sample. First of all, computer ownership and Internet access were not widespread in Serbia in 2001. Second, the listeners and readers of B92 represented a preselected (albeit large) group of urban culturophiles and opponents of the regime. Also, I do not know whether the writers whose messages I am quoting sent them from inside or outside the country, as nearly half the visitors to the B92 web pages visit from servers located in other countries. Finally, there is ample room for speculation as to whether online commenters on news stories constitute a unique group—often it appears they are more extreme in their positions (and more inclined to racism) than a random sample of the population. What cannot be doubted, however, is that online commenters give real-time commentary on contemporary events.

9. For a chronology of the events of the weekend, see Dokumentacioni centar Vremena, "Privodjenje za narodnu zabavu," *Vreme* 535, 4 April 2001.

10. The names of writers are the names or nicknames they provided on the comment form. I do not know whether these are the actual names of the people who wrote the messages. I have not changed these names to protect the identity of writers, since their comments do not take the form of responses made in interviews with me, but material which they published themselves.

11. Miloš Vasić, "Ko čuva Slobodana Miloševića: Objekti i lica," *Vreme* 522, 4 January 2001.

12. The line is spoken by Pavle Vujisić, a legend of Yugoslav theater and cinema, to Danilo Stojković, also a legend of Yugoslav theatre and cinema, in the 1982 film *Maratonci trče počasni krug* (*The marathon runners run the victory lap*). The comedy traces the misadventures of a family of dishonest interwar undertakers as they squabble over the family inheritance and enter into conflict with a coffinmaker-grave robber who was an early if unorthodox practitioner of recycling. While the film chronicles the descent of a family into criminality and brutality, Levi (2009: 96) identifies its importance as prophetic: "Because what *reasonable* person could predict in 1981 that reality could correspond to the madcap adventures of the Topalović family in an encyclopedic tragedy in which national pride would be measured by the number of coffins, and funeral rituals would be used for ethno-national purposes?"

13. Statements of support for Milošević were not frequent on the Radio B92 web site, since Milošević supporters were not generally part of B92's audience. An effort by Milošević supporters to collect signatures for a petition rejecting the charges, which can be found at the Srpska-Mreža web site, http://www.srpska-mreza.com/action/appeal.htm, garnered 1,341 signatures. Among the signers are some relatively well-known international figures, such as writer Michael Parenti, General Kostas Konstantinidis of Ex-NATO Generals for Peace and Disarmament, and Louis Wolf, publisher

of the political magazine *Covert Action Quarterly*. Several people signed as representatives of groups, among them the Ireland-Yugoslavia Friendship Society, Christians Against NATO Aggression, U.S. Friends of the Soviet People, Communist Party of Bohemia and Moravia, National-Bolshevik Section of the Parti Communautaire National-Européen, Israeli Communist Forum, and Workers World Party. One signatory signed the name Gertrude Stein, but Alice B. Toklas does not appear on the list.

14. The text of the initial indictment filed against Milošević on 2 April 2001 can be found at Free Serbia Dokumenti, http://www.xs4all.nl/~freeserb/facts/2001/02042001.html.

15. Unsigned, "Koštunica najavio za 'Dojče vele': Na redu sudjenja, *Glas javnosti*, 28 December 2000.

16. Scheveningen is best known as the site of the annual North Sea Jazz Festival.

17. At the time it would have been difficult to assess the charges for which Milošević could be tried by ICTY, since prosecutors had filed only a portion of the charges they intended to file.

18. Both Milošević's appeal and the findings of the freezer truck investigation would come to constitute important evidentiary moments in Milošević's trial before ICTY. See the description of events in Armatta (2010), Chapters 5 and 7.

19. The various debates around "national" positions developed by some writers, especially right-wing ones, in Serbia, have been explored in detail by Wachtel (1998) and many others. The figure of Dobrica Ćosić in particular has been the subject of extensive research by Budding (1997) and Miller (1999).

20. Tudjman (1981, 1989) sought to break the association of Croats with the crimes of the World War II-era Ustaša regime by contesting the official figures as to the number of victims of that regime. This portion of his work was largely responsible for his arrests and prosecutions in the 1970s and 1980s, and also for the widespread fear of his regime among Serbs after he was elected president of Croatia in 1990. In those two regards, Tudjman's efforts to liberate Croatia from the burden of historical responsibility through the politics of denial can be regarded as having had precisely the opposite effect.

21. A methodological note here: I make no ambitious claims for literary works that they are constitutive of national identities, as Wachtel (1998) argues, or that they represent untapped or secretly mystic populist reserves, as Anzulović (1999) argues. In fact, I do not know either how widely read either "patriotic" literature or the literature I am discussing is (statistics of this type in Serbia are notoriously unreliable), or how widely shared the ideas presented in these books (or any books) are. Of the writers whose work I discuss in this section, none are of the "best-selling" range with the exception of Arsenijević. Prodanović is well recognized and widely respected as a visual artist and cultural commentator, while Marković is a film director of solid reputation. But here I think it is sufficient to observe that this genre of literature makes available a set of perspectives which developed around the events discussed, and represents one of the ways that some writers tried to intervene in popular understanding.

22. Prodanović (2000: 10).

23. Prodanović (2000: 11).

24. Arsenijević (2000: 94–95, 96). The passage is in English in the original.

25. Various theses about the origins of all world civilizations with Serbs were promoted during the war period. For examples, see Luković-Pjanović (1990) and Šćekić (1994).

26. As Marković himself points out (2000: 159), the charlatan discussed in this passage is one Jovan I. Deretić, and is not to be confused with the Jovan Deretić with no middle initial, a distinguished literary historian whose *Istorija srpske književnosti* (1983) is the standard work in Serbian literary history. While the professor of literature died in 2002, the other fellow is still available to entertain television audiences.

27. Marković (2000: 157, 158–59).

28. Arsenijević (2000: 62–63).

29. Prodanović (2000: 26–27).

30. Unsurprisingly, no writer had anything positive to say about the propaganda leaflets NATO airplanes delivered together with explosives in 1999. Arsenijević and Rakezić both reproduce them in their books, certain that the foolishness of the propaganda speaks for itself. Marković (2000: 45) comments: "The content of those leaflets was one of the big surprises of this war for me. I have not seen anything so stupid and illiterate for a long time. Like somebody is joking. Aside from the grammatical and stylistic errors, the whole concept of this propaganda material was based on Serbian nationalism!!! Someone who is sending the message, and NATO is in the signature, is whining because of the loss of Serb territory in Croatia, in Bosnia, because of the loss of Sarajevo!? Milošević is responsible for everything and if it were not for him, Serbia would stretch all the way to Tokyo, says this clever propagandist. Either the propagandist is stupid, or he has complete contempt for the readers of the leaflets. Or maybe both are true: that it was thought up by an idiot and that his strategy is perfect for the public here."

31. Marković (2000: 151).

Chapter 4. Approaches to Guilt

Some passages presented in this chapter appeared in different form in Gordy and Dragović-Soso, in Djokić and Ker-Lindsay (eds.) (2010).

1. A selection of in-depth studies of media presentation of identities and memory is provided in Djerić (ed.) (2008).

2. See Boris Rašeta, "Umjesto u pritvoru, General Norac u bijegu," *Alternativna Informativna Mreža* (*AIM*), 9 February 2001.

3. Ante Gotovina became a major cause celebre in Croatia in the period between his indictment and his arrest in 2005.

4. Unsigned (SRNA), "Pismo Ivaniševića i još 10 sportista protiv izručenja Hagu," B92 vesti, 12 July 2001. On 14 July, Ivanišević's father declared the letter to be falsified, while Goran Ivanišević told reporters more equivocally that he "did not remember"

signing the letter, though he said the opinions expressed in it were largely ones he shared. The Independent Union of Sciences and Higher Education of Croatia issued a response telling "the gentlemen athletes" that "they will not feel the effect of any eventual sanctions against Croatia in their yachts and Ferraris." See "Ivanišević se 'ne seća' da je potpisao pismo osude vlade," B92 vesti, 14 July 2001.

5. Of course public opinion in Croatia is not unanimous, just as it is not anywhere else. See Vjeran Pavlaković, "Crvena zvezde, crne košulje: Simboli, komemoracije i sukobljene istorije Drugog svetskog rata u Hrvatskoj," in Djerić (ed.) (2009).

6. A discussion of the calls and messages received by B92 on the broadcast is provided by B92 director Veran Matić, "Rejecting the Truth: Viewer Reaction to the Television Documentary *A Cry from the Grave*" (2001). The film itself could be described as mixed: while on the one hand it contains footage documenting the behavior of a number of actors including Ratko Mladić and the forces in his command, its presentation of Naser Orić (convicted and acquitted on appeal by ICTY, then convicted of ordinary crimes on his return to Bosnia) in a heroic role was bound to be received controversially.

7. "Skupština Srbije o filmu o Srebrenici," B92 vesti, 12 July 2001.

8. President Koštunica had been conditioning cooperation with ICTY on the adoption of a law regulating that cooperation, which he began promising in January 2001. Within the course of a week in July 2001, the draft law was presented, offered to the parliament by the federal government, withdrawn from the parliament by the federal government, adopted by the federal government in the form of a decree, and suspended by the Federal Constitutional Court. Losing patience, prime minister Zoran Djindjić took the matter away from the federal government and ordered the Serbian police to deliver Milošević to ICTY. Even people who praised Djindjić's abrupt action acknowledged that many legal problems were involved.

9. Milošević was delivered to ICTY on 28 June 2001, one day before a conference of donor countries to arrange the timing and amount of financial assistance SRJ would receive was scheduled to begin. Unsurprisingly, this led to the widespread perception that Milošević was "exchanged" for international financial aid.

10. Zoran M. Marković, "Milošević deli DOS," *NIN*, 12 July 2001.

11. The declaration was published in the army journal *Narodna armija* on 19 October 1991, and is reproduced in Vasiljević (1995: 118–19).

12. Vasiljević (1995: 120–21).

13. Vasiljević (1995: 116).

14. As Armatta (2010) documents, however, the declarations were used by the defendants as evidence that they complied with international law. International law requires that violations actually be prevented and punished, though, not merely that a stated intention to do so appears in a document.

15. In their decision in the genocide suit brought by Bosnia-Herzegovina against Serbia, the majority of judges on the International Court of Justice (ICJ) found that specific and direct of evidence of a criminal policy was required (70, para. 188) and

explicitly denied the claim that there could be a "'pattern of acts' that 'speaks for itself'" (76, para. 207).

16. Several of these trials are discussed in Vasiljević (1995: 122–30).

17. Unsigned, "Yellow wasps—Local Thieves or War Criminals?" Sense news agency, 17 August 2010. The members of the "Yellow Wasps" (Žute ose) led by Vojin Vučković were retried in 2008 on more extensive charges.

18. See Unsigned, "Vidovdanski masakr," *NIN* 2637, 12 July 2001, 20.

19. In Stojanović (ed.) (2000: 170).

20. Wladimiroff had also been appointed by ICTY as one of the standby counsel in the Milošević case, but was removed from this role in 2003 after what were regarded as injudicious statements to the press.

21. In Stojanović (ed.) (2000: 214–15). The arguments offered by Ellis and Wladimiroff were offered before there were serious efforts at domestic prosecution anywhere in the former Yugoslavia. In the period following, ICTY did continue to insist on its primacy, and implemented the policy of referring cases to national courts conservatively and slowly.

22. Momčilo Krajišnik was speaker of the assembly of Republika Srpska and a member of the presidency of Bosnia-Herzegovina from 1996 to 1998. He was found guilty of crimes against humanity by ICTY in December 2006.

23. Biljana Plavšić was a vice president of Republika Srpska under Radovan Karadžić and succeeded him in the office. She pled guilty to charges of crimes against humanity in 2002.

24. On the political uses of prosecutions against Croatian Serbs, see Drago Hedl, "Regional Report: Croatian Serb Scapegoats," *IWPR Tribunal Report* 229, 9–14 July 2001.

25. Previously ICTY overstepped its bounds in exercising "primacy," as in the cases of Aleksa Krsmanović and Djordje Djukić, arrested on suspicion of war crimes by Bosnian police in 1996. Although no indictment against them existed, ICTY demanded and received their extradition. Krsmanović was released without charges, and while Djukić was indicted, he was never tried as he died of cancer soon afterward. The incident raised concern regarding the competence of ICTY, which while it could not arrest the suspects it had indicted, imprisoned people it had not charged. See Bass (2001: 250–51).

26. The initiatives discussed here are not, of course, the first transitional justice initiatives. Analysts like Elster (2004) argue that transitional justice has a long history, but this may well be an overinterpretation of incidents of victors' justice. Bass (2001) traces efforts to try former state leaders to the early nineteenth century, though it may be noted that few legal efforts had a meaningful domestic component and that until the International Military Tribunal at Nuremberg most efforts were abandoned. The major transitional justice initiatives that invite comparison would be (1) post-World War II prosecutions of Nazis and fascist collaborators, (2) the array of trials and commissions established following the removals of military regimes from power in Central

and South America, and (3) the post-civil war and postapartheid initiatives engaged since 1990 in Africa. The Yugoslav cases are distinct from the first category in their temporal closeness to the events and the lack of a clear military victory, from the second category in the degree of international involvement, and from the third in the absence of a meaningful movement to consider culturally based alternatives or complements to judicial processes.

27. In December 2010 the UN Security Council adopted Resolution 1966 (2010), which established a "residual mechanism" that would allow trials of people already indicted by the Yugoslavia and Rwanda tribunals to be carried out under international auspices. There was speculation that the establishment of the residual mechanism indicated continuing lack of trust in domestic courts to carry out major prosecutions. See Denis Džidić, "Hague Tribunal Successor Casts Doubts on Region's Courts," *BIRN Justice Report*, 14 February 2011.

28. For several examples, see Dimitrijević (ed.) (2000: 77–91, 207–15).

29. Institut društvenih nauka, *Jugoslovensko javno mnjenje 1996*, cited in Ognjen Pribićević, "Da li je minimalistički koncept demokratije još uvek validan? Slučaj Srbije" (1998).

30. Stjepan Gredelj, "Vrednosno utemeljenje blokirane transformacije srpskog društva," in Lazić (ed.) (2000: 228).

31. For several examples, see Humanitarian Law Center, "Trials of Kosovo Albanians," a selection of HLC press releases in relation to ongoing cases.

32. Goran Petronijević would later appear at ICTY as the coordinator of the defense for Radovan Karadžić. He had prominent roles earlier in defending one of the accused at the trial for the murder of Zoran Djindjić, and represented the turbo-folk singer Ceca in a case related to corruption in sports. In 2003 ICTY refused a request by Veselin Šljivančanin, indicted in the Ovčara massacre, to be represented by Petronijević. The chamber justified its decision by reference both to the Djakovica case and to the requirement that "counsel speak at least one of the Tribunal's working languages." See "The Prosecutor vs. Veselin Šljivančanin: Decision on Assignment of Defence Counsel," ICTY case IT-95–13/1-PT, 13 August 2003.

33. See Zoran Kosanović, "Sudjenje djakovičkim Albancima u Nišu: Za 143 Albanca kazna 1632 godine," AIM, 29 May 2001.

34. Z.M., "Sa Gordanom Mihajlović, predsednicom II opštinskog suda," *Republika* 263, 16–30 June 2001.

35. "Kraj agonije pravosudja: Rec Leposave Karamarković, predsednice Vrhovnog suda Srbije, na skupštini Društva sudija Srbije, održanoj 7. aprila u Palati pravde u Beogradu," *Republika* 262, 1–15 June 2001. Leposava Karamarković herself resigned from the court in 2003 under circumstances that were widely interpreted as representing political pressure. See Vera Didanović, "Pravosude u vanrednom stanju: Čistka ili bajpas," *Vreme* 638, 27 March 2003.

36. "Tapušković: Nema kadrova za pravosudje," B92 vesti, 13 June 2001. Tapušković would also appear at ICTY as defense counsel in several cases and as a standby counsel to Slobodan Milošević.

37. The text of the law, as it was adopted by the federal government in the form of a decree on 23 June 2001, is reproduced in "Uredba o saradnji sa haškim tribunalom: Sudska procedura kao u krivičnom postupku," *Danas*, 25 June 2001.

38. The legal foundation for the decision was in Article 16 of the 1992 federal constitution, which declared all international conventions and agreements to be a part of domestic law, and Article 135 of the 1990 Serbian constitution, which granted Serbia the right to ignore decisions of the federal government which it regards as being contrary to the national interest. Both articles were part of constitutions still in effect which had been imposed by governments under Milošević's control. Article 135 was most likely intended as ammunition in the conflict going on in 1990 between Milošević's Serbian regime and the federal government of the last prime minister, Ante Marković. See Miloš Vasić, "Slobodan Milošević pred Haškim sudom: Pritvorenik broj 039," *Vreme* 548, 5 July 2001.

39. A transcription of the exchange is presented in "Pravedno tranzitorno pravo," *Danas*, 14–15 July 2001.

40. "Pravedno tranzitorno pravo," *Danas*, 14–15 July 2001. The reasons to which Samardžić refers for a new federal constitution not being created were the conflicts between Serbian and Montenegrin political leaders over the continued existence of the federal state.

41. Zastupnički dom Hrvatskoga državnog Sabora, "Deklaracija o domovinskom ratu," 17 October 2000.

42. Organisation for Security and Cooperation in Europe (OSCE) Mission to Croatia, *Background Report: Domestic War Crime Trials, 2005*, 13 September 2006; also Cruvellier and Valiñas (2006); Lamont (2007).

43. OSCE Mission to Croatia, *Background Report: Domestic War Crimes Proceedings, 2006* (Zagreb, 3 August 2007).

44. A redacted U.S. intelligence report on Merčep's activities can be found at http://www.foia.cia.gov/browse_docs.asp?doc_no=0001063835. See also D. Hedl, "Croatia: Impunity Prevails," *Transitions Online*, 10 December 2005.

45. OSCE, "War Crimes Cases Started in January 2004–April 2009" (Sarajevo, April 2009).

46. OSCE Mission to Bosnia and Hercegovina, *Moving Towards a Harmonized Application of the Law Applicable in War Crimes Cases Before Courts in Bosnia and Herzegovina* (Sarajevo, August 2008).

47. C. Off, "Massacre at Podujevo, Kosovo," CBC News, 29 March 2004; V. Perić Zimonjić, "Serb 'Scorpions' Guilty of Srebrenica Massacre," *The Independent*, 11 April 2007.

48. ICTY case no. IT-95–13/1-PT, *The prosecutor of the Tribunal against Mile Mrkšić, Miroslav Radić and Veselin Šljivančanin*. Radić was acquitted of the charges, while the other two were convicted. Another indictee, Slavko Dokmanović, committed suicide in ICTY custody in 1998.

49. B. Vukičević, "La cocaina cambia la geopolitica," *Rinascita balcanica*, 8 May 2009, and "Sulla morta di Pukanić c'è ancora molto da dire," *Rinascita balcanica*, 12 May 2009.

50. There remains uncertainty as to whether Bosnian law permits the extradition of individuals convicted of crimes in another state, which at the time of writing (May 2009) seems likely to be the principal issue of contention in extradition hearings.

51. OSCE Mission to Croatia, *Background Report: Domestic War Crimes Proceedings, 2006* (Zagreb, 3 August 2007: 15–18).

52. "Bureaucracy," in Weber (1978: 956–1002).

53. Former chief of staff, Yugoslav army.

54. Former chief of staff, Yugoslav army and minister of defense of Yugoslavia.

55. Former chief of staff, Yugoslav army.

56. Former commander, army of Bosnia and Herzegovina.

57. Former chief of staff, Croatian army.

58. For a narrative of efforts to bring heads of state to account see Bass (2001) For a discussion of recent erosion of the doctrine of sovereign immunity, see Kelly (2005).

59. The point is extensively argued in Hartmann (2007).

60. Richard Goldstone, "Comment: The Tribunal's Progress," *IWPR Tribunal Update* 220, 7–12 May 2001.

61. Bass (2001: 207).

62. Bass (2001: 223).

63. Subsequently the former Liberian president Charles Taylor was tried by an international tribunal, and before that a former Iraqi president was tried and executed by an ad hoc court under rather less impressive circumstances.

64. Peskin and Boduszynski (2003); Delpla (2007); Nettelfield (2010).

65. One important instrument in this operation was a defense witness for Milošević, retired general Božidar Delić. Delić appeared so many times bringing documents that prosecutors had been told the military did not have that it quickly became clear that he kept a large private archive. Over time he came to be engaged by prosecutors as an unofficial source of evidence, and was recruited (unsuccessfully) to give evidence for the prosecution in other cases. M. Ivanović, Z. Jevtić, and V. Z. Cvijić, "General Delić dostavljao vojna dokumenta Tribunalu," *Blic*, 9 May 2008.

66. The Haradinaj case was received with little seriousness. In December 2008 he became the first ICTY indictee to be profiled in the entertainment magazine *Vanity Fair*. W. Langewiesche, "House of War," *Vanity Fair*, December 2008. In the same month, Astrit Haraqija and Bajrush Morina (IT-04–84-R77.4) were convicted of intimidating witnesses in the prosecution of Haradinaj. A former ICTY judge has written a reflection on the failure of witness protection. See Wald (2002).

67. Quoted in D. Bisenić, "Prvo pojavljivanje Slobodana Miloševića pred Haškim tribunalom: Smatram ovaj sud lažnim," *Danas*, 4 July 2001.

68. "Batićevo pismo Karli del Ponte," B92 vesti, 5 April 2001.

69. See the discussion in Hartmann (2007), and in Del Ponte (2008).

70. Čedomir Jovanović bears no relation to the politician of the same name who was a leader of the 1996–1997 student demonstrations, subsequently a vice president of the Democratic Party (DS), and leader of the DOS deputies' group in the Serbian parliament, and later leader of the Liberal Democratic Party (LDP).

71. B92 vesti, 15 June 2001.

72. In Africa as well the politics of referral to ICC have been controversial. See Peskin (2009a, 2009b).

73. A further difficulty facing ICC has been the refusal of the United States to support its work (Bill Clinton reversed U.S. policy toward ICC immediately before leaving office, but his successor George W. Bush reverted to the earlier policy, and Bush's successor Barack Obama has maintained Bush's policy). The primary objection of the United States to the ICC is that it would subject U.S. citizens to international jurisdiction, a case laid out by U.S. ambassador-at-large for war crimes David Scheffer in his address before the American Society for International Law, "International Criminal Court: The Challenge of Jurisdiction," 26 March 1999.

74. In her comprehensive overview of "truth commissions" since 1974, Priscilla Hayner outlines five basic aims of such commissions: "to discover, clarify, and formally acknowledge past abuses; to respond to specific needs of victims; to contribute to justice and accountability; to outline institutional responsibility and recommend reforms; and to promote reconciliation and reduce conflict over the past" Hayner (2001: 24).

75. This dilemma is explored in detail, especially with reference to South Africa, in Rotberg and Thompson (eds.) (2000), and in a more literary vein in Krog (1998).

76. Gordy and Dragović-Soso, in Djokić and Ker-Lindsay (eds.) (2010). The article was coauthored but the text cited above was principally composed by Jasna Dragović-Soso.

77. The Coalition for REKOM maintains a web site at http://www.zarekom.org/. It contains news, basic documents, and dispatches from the various public consultations that have been held as a part of the campaign. Conscious of the potential for controversy and the recent experience of failed initiatives of this type, the REKOM campaign has studiously avoided using the label "truth" for the proposed commission.

78. "Side Letters included with the Dayton Peace Agreement Documents Initialed in Dayton, Ohio on November 21, 1995," U.S. Department of State Geographic Bureaus, http://dosfan.lib.uic.edu/ERC/bureaus/eur/dayton/16SideLetters.html.

79. Gordy and Dragović-Soso, in Djokić and Ker-Lindsay (eds.) (2010), and Delpla (2007).

80. Mallinder (2009).

81. Vlada Republike Srpske, Komisija za istraživanje dogadjaja u i oko Srebrenice od 10. do 19. jula 1995, "Dogadjaji u i oko Srebrenice od 10. do 19. jula 1995" (2004), http://www.omeragic.se/internet/dokumenti/srebrenica.pdf.

82. The full text of the resolution is available at B92 vesti, "Vlada RS: Žaljenje zbog Srebrenice," 10 November 2004. The recognition and apology did not include a qualification of the crimes as genocide, which remains an issue of contention. Victims' organizations and internationals contend that the character of the Srebrenica killings as genocide has been established by ICTY and ICJ decisions, while a series of Serbian governments has resisted the label.

83. The commission was created by executive order, which was not preceded by debate. It was published in the official register *Službeni glasnik* on 30 March 2001 as Odluka o osnivanju Komisije za istinu i pomirenje, no. 1/2-03-0004/2001-1.

84. A brief history of the commission is outlined by Ilić (2005).

85. A third member, Tibor Varady, also resigned, but without publicly criticizing the commission.

Chapter 5. Moment II: The Djindjić Murder, from Outrage to Confusion

1. N. M. J., "Djindjić je potvrdio da je od Administracije SAD dobio negativnu poruku: Moramo znati status Srbije," *Blic*, 7 February 2003. About the charges that he was a foreign agent, he joked: "Vuk Karadžić was the first person to be called a German spy in Serbia because he knew German, while the people who called him that did not even know Serbian." *Reporter*, 31 January 2001.

2. The conspiracy is described in Vasić (2005: 148–54).

3. Miloš Vasić and Sonja Seizova, "Slučaj Dejana Milenkovića Bagzija: Hapšenje trgovačkog putinika," *Vreme* 707, 22 July 2004.

4. "Automobil u kom se nalazio Djindić izbegao sudar," B92 vesti, 21 February 2003.

5. Milorad Ulemek is sometimes identified as Milorad Luković. The family name he used from birth was Ulemek. The surname Luković is adopted from his former wife Maja Luković, from whom he has been estranged since 1998. Ulemek first used the surname for himself in an application for a diplomatic passport in 1994. See Isabel Vincent, "Serb Strongman 'Abandoned Me': Alleged Assassin's Canadian Bride living in West Toronto," *National Post*, 14 May 2004. In another version of the same narrative the diplomatic passport was issued on 19 November 1996, and Ulemek also held a Croatian passport issued under the name Vlado Vukomanović. See L. Z. N., "'Ekspert' medju diplomatama," *Večernje novosti*, 2 April 2003.

6. Ulemek was a former commander of JSO, while Spasojević maintained financial and other connections between JSO and the "Zemun clan." Buha was not engaged with state-sponsored paramilitary groups during the wars but did participate in theft and smuggling operations associated with them. See Dejan Anastasijević, "Veliko asfaltiranje," *Vreme* 964, 25 June 2009.

7. "Dulović: Pokušaj ubistva premijera," B92 vesti, 22 February 2003.

8. The quotation has been variously attributed to *Glas javnosti* on 24 February and to *Politika* on 21 February.

9. The contribution of JSO to regime change in October 2000 consisted in not obeying orders to attack demonstrators. In refusing these orders they were joined by the (much larger) police and military. It is a matter of debate how much this constituted a contribution: and armed attack on the approximately 500,000 demonstrators present in Belgrade on 5 October 2000 could well have produced many victims but would not necessarily have altered the course of events. The narrative in which Legija and JSO play a meaningful role is advanced in Bujošević and Radovanović (2001).

10. A public display of power by the members of JSO in November 2001 had as its immediate pretext the use of the unit to assist in the arrest of ICTY indictees. While this position was justified with patriotic rhetoric, it may also have been founded in the fear that JSO members could well become indictees themselves.

11. "Čume: Posle atentata se sklonili u kasarnu," *Blic*, 28 January 2003.

12. "Jadna je zemlja kad Čume rešava tajne," *Blic*, 28 January 2003. The reference to "dead commanders" probably refers to Željko Ražnatović, who had been murdered by organized crime associates in Belgrade in 2000.

13. Predrag Banović offered a guilty plea in the Keraterm case at ICTY, in which he admitted beating twenty-seven camp prisoners, causing the deaths of five of them. A sentence of eight years was agreed with the prosecution in 2003. The indictment against Nenad Banović was withdrawn and he was released in April 2002.

14. In fact, aside from JSO founder Franko Simatović, ICTY has not charged members of JSO.

15. Koštunica defended the use of uniforms and weapons in the rebellion and declared that it "had not, except maybe in the functioning of road traffic, threatened the security of the country." J. M., "Vojislav Koštunica o slučaju Crvene beretke: Vlast odgovorna za protest JSO," *Glas javnosti*, 16 November 2001.

16. The first major measure was the passage of a law on special enforcement against organized crime by Parliament on 18 July 2002. A narrative of "Operation Witness" and conflicts around it is offered by Vasić (2005), chap. 7.

17. The line appears in *Nacional*, 1 February 2003. I have not succeeded in finding the original edition of the publication where it first appeared, but it is quoted in several places, including in Popović and Nikolić (2006: 217), and in JUKOM (2005). These two publications do not give the title of the article in question. On 23 July 2009 the Supreme Court of Serbia banned the latter book after a lawsuit by Tijanić. The court did not find that the quotation was inaccurately reproduced, however, but rather that Tijanić's copyright had been violated. See JUKOM, "Vrhovni sud zabranio knjigu YUCOMa 'Slučaj službenika Aleksandra Tijanića zbog povredjenih moralnih prava Aleksandra Tijanića,'" 15 September 2009.

18. Tito's left leg was amputated in January 1980 due to a constricted artery, and he died in hospital in Ljubljana on 4 May. With his dour manner and cruel sense of humor, Tomislav Nikolić is known informally as "Toma the gravedigger." He was once manager of a cemetery in Kragujevac, but was never actually a gravedigger.

19. It is widely believed that as a result of the findings of "Operation Witness," the government intended to commence arrests and prosecutions against members of the "Zemun clan" and JSO on 13 or 15 March.

20. Some of the material used in the following section is quoted from government publications that were consulted in 2003 and are no longer available, most likely having been removed from the Internet with the disppearance of the ".yu" domain and the introduction of the ".rs" domain. The principal statement had been available at http://www.srbija.sr.gov.yu/vesti/2003–04/29/335683.html. The references that follow will be to an earlier publication by the author that cites the older statement. The full text of the original indictment is available at Wikisource, http://sr.wikisource.org/sr/ Optu%C5%BEnica_za_ubistvo_premijera_%C4%90in%C4%91i%C4%87a.

21. After a lengthy and complicated trial, twelve people were convicted on 23 May 2007. Clearly a smaller number of people was convicted than was charged in the original indictment. Part of the reason for this may be that some elements of the original indictment were presented in error. Another was that some suspects were inaccessible, either because they died in the meantime or were in the custody of ICTY. The principal reason, however, is that prosecutors decided to try people who carried out the plan, passing over the politicians and state security officials who participated in the development of the plan. This remains an issue of considerable controversy in Serbia.

22. Quoted in Gordy (2004).

23. Gordy (2004).

24. Gordy (2004).

25. E. H., "Scenario haosa," *Politika*, 8 April 2003.

26. Ibid. See also E. B., "'Haško bratstvo' planiralo ubistvo," *Blic*, 8 April 2003.

27. Anna Lindh, the foreign minister of Sweden who Djindjić was to meet at 3:30, was herself murdered in September the same year.

28. A recommendation to form a "concentration government" that would include "all parliamentary parties" was offered by Vojislav Koštunica on 17 March. See "Koštunica: Koncentraciona vlada je najmanje loše rešenje," B92 vesti, 17 March 2003. A government including "all parliamentary parties" would have returned Koštunica's party DSS to the government it left in 2002, and would also have brought in parties of the former regime, including SPS, SRS and SSJ.

29. Two efforts were made to elect a president following the end of Milan Milutinović's term in 2002 (Milutinović went to face trial before ICTY and was acquitted in 2009), both of which failed due to voter turnout below the required level of 50 percent. As the presiding officer of Parliament, Nataša Mićić took on the role of acting president, a position she occupied until February 2004. Serbia would have two more acting presidents, Dragan Maršićanin and Predrag Marković, before an elected president, Boris Tadić, took office in July 2004.

30. The full text of the declaration is at "Vanredna sednica Vlade Srbije," B92 vesti, 12 March 2003. The principal utility of the state of emergency was that it allowed

law enforcement to hold suspects in custody longer than forty-eight hours before charging them with a crime.

31. There does exist speculation that the killing was carried out intentionally, or that it had been carried out earlier and the confrontation staged. However no persuasive evidence has been offered to support this speculation, while there is ample reason to believe that two armed, experienced criminals could well enter into a fatal confrontation with police.

32. Ivan Stambolić disappeared while jogging in a Belgrade park in August 2000. Šare described his kidnapping and led police to the site where Stambolić was murdered and buried. Later another participant, Leonid Milivojević, corroborated Šare's testimony. See Dušan Stojanović, "Gruesome details emerge in murder of Milošević opponent," Associated Press, 23 February 2004. Vuk Drašković was attacked with firearms in a failed assassination attempt in 2000. Šare received protected witness status, and in July 2005 convictions were delivered in court against Milorad Ulemek, former head of state security Radomir Marković, and JSO members Branislav Berček, Dušan Maričić, Nenad Bujošević, Nenad Ilić, and Milorad Bracanović. Bracanović was made deputy director of the State Security service following the JSO rebellion in 2001. Slobodan Milošević and former army commander Nebojša Pavković were also charged in the case for having ordered the murder, but were not tried, as their presence was made impossible by their concurrent trials before ICTY. See Ivana Pejčić, "Ličnost dana: Milorad Bracanović, uslovna sloboda," *Danas*, 5 March 2011, and Tatjana Tagirov, "Izrečene presude za ubistvo Ivana Stambolića i atentat u Budvi: U službi gospodina predsednika," *Vreme* 759, 21 July 2005.

33. Unsigned, "Zavera 'patriotskih snaga,'" *Politika*, 1 April 2003.

34. Unsigned, "Zavera 'patriotskih snaga.'"

35. Unsigned (FoNet), "C-48: SDB ubacivala heroin u Hrvatsku," *Danas*, 29 April 2003.

36. Vesna Savić, "'Sablja' i u zakonima," *Novosadski nedeljnik* 299–300, April 2003.

37. Unsigned (Beta), "Nataša Mićić pozvala gradjane na jedinstvo," B92 vesti, 19 March 2003.

38. At trial he sought to recant his confession. He was not able to recant the video footage showing him leading police to the place where he practiced with the murder weapon and identifying shells from the weapon that were found to match the ones used in the murder.

39. E. B., "'Haško bratstvo' planiralo ubistvo," *Blic*, 8 April 2003.

40. Quoted in Lj. Milosavljević and J. Cerovina, "Gangsteri bi hteli državu," *Politika*, 15 March 2003.

41. Unsigned, "Milanović želeo RTS," *Blic*, 8 April 2003. Milanović, widely reviled as a propagandist, was beaten by demonstrators on 5 October 2000. In 2002 he was sentenced to ten years in prison for deliberately exposing employees of RTS to attacks by NATO bombs while protecting himself and other high ranking television officials.

In September 2010 a small group of people, among them the Austrian writer Peter Handke, launched a petition for the release of Milanović, claiming that he had escaped the bombing not by the implementation of his own order but rather "by some odd chance." The petition can be found at http://www.free-slobo.de/petmilan/petit-en.pdf.

42. Unsigned (editorial), "Taoci mračnih sila," *Vreme* 636, 13 March 2003.

43. T. Nježić and Z. Jovanović, "Ljubomir Simović: Nezamisliv zločin," *Blic*, 13 March 2003.

44. Milorad Pavić, "Živeo za svakog od nas," *Politika*, 16 March 2003.

45. Ivan Torov, "Snajperski izazov," *Politika*, 16 March 2003.

46. Miloš Minić, "Vreme za obračun sa masovnim ubicama," *Danas*, 20 March 2003.

47. The former prime minister of "Republika Srpske Krajine," Borislav Mikelić, was arrested as a part of Operation Sabre. See Rade Matijaš, "Sve odlučila 'mama,'" *Večernje novosti*, 6 April 2003.

48. Unsigned, "Grupe i BIA svadjale DOS," *Večernje novosti*, 29 March 2003.

49. E. H., "Scenario haosa," *Politika*, 8 April 2003.

50. Unsigned (Tanjug), "Proglas Socijalističke partije Srbije," *Borba*, 30 June 2001.

51. Unsigned (Tanjug), "Atak na čast, ponos i državu srpskog naroda," *Borba*, 29 June 2001 (quoting statement of Serbian Radical Party).

52. "Nino," in comments to the article "Koštunica: Koncentraciona vlada je najmanje loše rešenje," B92 vesti, 17 March 2003.

53. "Nino."

54. Jelena Kosanić, interview with Nebojša Čović, Radio B92, 13 March 2003.

55. SMMRI, "Istraživanje javnog mnenja," March 2003, 3.

56. Unsigned, "Ukinuto vanredno stanje u Srbiji," Center for Free Elections and Democracy, 22 April 2003.

57. R. D., "Uzeo 150 hiljada za adresu zaštićenog svedoka," *Danas*, 21 March 2003. The prosecutor in question was Milan Sarajlić.

58. An outstanding analysis of the rhetoric at the time of the funeral is offered by Greenberg (2006).

59. Not to be confused with the popular science fiction writer of the same name.

60. Usually a provider of comic material, the popular radio host Dragan Ilić commented in his weekly magazine column: "We saw the pictures, heard the names, and more importantly the nicknames of the most important criminals in Serbia. Aside from Legija (the Legionnaire), there are Šiptar (the Albanian), Budala (the Fool), Pacov (the Rat), Kum (the Godfather), Prevara (the Scam), Fuksa (the Whore), Ranac (the Rucksack), Jumba (a popular nickname for the Mercedes Benz 200 model). I admit that this assortment of physiognomies and nicknames frightened me. If that was their intention, they succeeded." Dragan Ilić, "TV manijak: Proizvodnja mita," *Vreme* 637, 20 March 2003.

61. Unsigned, "Zoran Živković: Srbija bez Prevara, Pacova i Budala," *Danas*, 16 March 2003.

62. He assumed the name Amfilohije on entering a monastic order in Greece in the 1960s.

63. Momir Turudić, "Portret savremenika—Amfilohije Radović: Ratnik u mantiji," *Vreme* 881, 22 November 2007.

64. Because of his long and close association with extremist politics, Radović is sometimes known by the malicious nickname "Risto Antihristo" (Risto the Antichrist).

65. Mirjana Kuburović, "Biblija za Miloševića," *Politika*, 25 June 2001.

66. Unsigned, "Narodu stid i sramota," *Večernje novosti*, 1 July 2001.

67. Unsigned, "Rana posred srca naroda," *Večernje novosti*, 15 March 2003.

68. Stojan Cerović, "Posle Djindjića," *Vreme* 637, 20 March 2003.

69. D. Vujanović, "Kajanje u senci haga," *Večernje novosti*, 17 March 2003.

70. Željko Cvijanović, "Srbija pred odgovorom: Šta je bilo 5. oktobar," *BlicNews*, 19 March 2003. The thesis is interesting particularly because the author, Željko Cvijanović, had been director of SRNA, the news agency of the "Republika Srpska" parastate in Bosnia-Herzegovina, during the Bosnian war and maintained very close ties with Radovan Karadžić and his party. He is currently editor of a little-read far-right magazine, *Novi Standard*.

71. Unsigned, "Koncentraciona vlada bez vanrednog stanja," *Večernje novosti*, 13 March 2003.

72. D. Miljković, "Kažnjena TV Leskovac," *Večernje novosti*, 3 April 2003. The verb "to Satanize" has been popular among apologists for violent nationalist movements since the middle 1990s. The Ukrainian politician Boris Olijnik advanced the term in his (1995) book, and a variant was introduced by the Bosnian politician Emil Vlajki (2001). A later entrant into the Satan pageant was Umeljić (2010).

73. Unsigned (FoNet), "Dragan Jočić: Akcija 'Sablja' je imala pozitivne rezultate!" *Kurir*, 27 July 2004. The operation had in fact lasted 42 days.

74. Aleksandar Roknić and Vuk Z. Cvijić, "Mukotrpno dokazivanje krivice," *Danas*, 2–3 August 2003.

75. Amnesty International, *Document—Serbia and Montenegro: Alleged Torture During "Operation Sabre."* EUR 70/019/2003, 4 September 2003.

76. Hugh Poulton was for several years AI's senior researcher on the region. He will also be known to London readers as vocalist, lyricist, and guitarist for the band the Walking Wounded. Their most recent CD, *Waiting on the Outside*, was released in 2009.

77. N. D., "Moguće da se radi o sistematskom mučenju," *Danas*, 6 September 2003.

78. Lj. M., "Sablja posekla ljudska prava," *Borba*, 21 May 2005. See also O. N, "'Potvrdjena tortura, ali ne i mučenje strujom," *Glas javnosti*, 21 May 2005, and R. O., "Saopštenja Biroa bez dozvole MUP," *Večernje novosti*, 21 May 2005.

79. B. Tončić, "Maltretiranje zbog zamene identiteta," *Danas*, 10 November 2004.

80. Dušan Telesković, "Bulatoviću 669.700 dinara," *Politika*, 31 August 2004.

81. N. B., "Svaki dan pritvora po 10.000 dinara," *Večernje novosti*, 27 October 2005.

82. Amnesty International, *Document—Serbia and Montenegro*. Former deputy state prosecutor Milan Sarajlić, who admitted to reciving 150,000 euros from the "Zemun clan" to obstruct criminal investigations, made then withdrew claims of torture, and was sentenced to three years for abuse of public office in June 2006. See Unsigned (FoNet), "Sarajlić tvrdi da nije maltretiran, ali . . . ," B92 vesti, 14 November 2003; and Unsigned (Beta), "Sarajliću tri godine," B92 vesti, 21 June 2006.

83. N. B., "Plati pa beži," *Večernje novosti*, 29 March 2003.

84. Unsigned (Beta), "Đoinčević osloboden krivice," B92 vesti, 22 July 2005.

85. M. D., "Đoinčević traži 20 miliona," *Politika*, 28 October 2005.

86. Dragica Pušonjić-Veljković, "Skuplja dara od zatvora," *Večernje novosti*, 18 December 2005.

87. Unsigned (Beta), "Država mora da plati Đoinčeviću," B92 vesti, 10 October 2007.

88. Unsigned, "Hajka na DSS," *Večernje novosti*, 10 April 2003. The former intelligence official Rade Bulatović is not to be confused with the person of the same name who played bass in the Yugoslav rock group Jakarta.

89. M. L., "Beretke traže odštetu od 40 miliona dinara," *Balkan*, 29 July 2004.

90. E. V. N., " 'Sablja' pred tužiocem," *Večernje novosti*, 21 May 2005.

91. E. Radosavljević, " 'Sablja' se vuče po sudu," *Večernje novosti*, 16 January 2008.

92. Dušan Telesković, "Bulatoviću 669.700 dinara," *Politika*, 31 August 2004. Bulatović would be appointed by incoming prime minister Koštunica to head the Security Intelligence Agency after the December 2003 election.

93. Unsigned, "Aci Tomiću odšteta od šest miliona dinara," *Blic*, 11 January 2008.

94. Živković's national security advisor Zoran Janjušević and director of the Bank Recovery Agency Nemanja Kolesar were accused of laundering money from a privatization sale through a company registered in the Seychelles. Criminal charges were filed in 2006, and the pair were acquitted in 2010. See Unsigned (Beta), "Janjušević-Kolesar: Prijave," B92 vesti, 7 March 2006, and R. D., "Kolesar i Janjušević nisu krivi," *Danas*, 23 December 2010.

95. A vote had been registered as cast by DS deputy (and well-known actress) Neda Arnerić on a day when she was not present but on holiday in Turkey. In 2004 two DS deputies, Vojislav Janković and Alen Selimović, were indicted in the case and Selimović was found guilty in 2006. See Unsigned, "Uslovna kazna zbog Bodruma," B92 vesti, 26 June 2006.

96. Unsigned, "Haški tribunal krši dogovor!," SENSE news agency, 21 October 2003.

97. Republička izborna komisija Republike Srbije, "Izveštaj o rezultatima izbora za narodne poslanike u Narodnoj skupštini Republike Srbije održanih 28. decembra 2003. godine." Serbian Parliament web site, http://www.rik.parlament.gov.rs/latinica/Sednice2/Izvestaj28Lat.htm.

Chapter 6. Denial, Avoidance, Shifts of Context: From Denial to Responsibility in Eleven Steps

1. As the lawyer representing the Djindjić family, Srđa Popović, noted in a later discussion of the need for engagement with the "political background" of the killing, "Legija once said about the JSO that we are just a bullet. Somebody else pulls the trigger, we fly to the place where we are aimed." Vesna Mališić, "Legija je samo metak" (interview with Srđa Popović), *NIN* 3141, 10 March 2011.

2. In 2005 Momčilo Perišić was charged with war crimes and crimes against humanity by ICTY. His was convicted in 2011.

3. The ICTY found that Pavković "had direct access to FRY President Milošević, who supported and adopted his proposals, despite protestations from others in the VJ." The importance of this is that beyond simply knowing about and failing to prevent or punish major violations of human rights (as was the case with his colleague Vladimir Lazarević), Pavković actively participated in political decisions to commit the crimes.

4. "DB uništio preko 35.000 stranica," B92 vesti, 17 November 2004. Marković was removed from office as one of the first acts of the Djindjić government, and was subsequently convicted as a part of the conspiracy to attempt the assassination of Vuk Drašković.

5. Vojislav Žanetić, "Hagalnica," *NIN* 2633, 14 June 2001.

6. The posters were placed by Obraz (Honor) a far-right group linked to the Serbian Orthodox Church. Unsigned (FENA), "Provokacija Otačestvenog pokreta 'Obraz': Ratko Mladić na plakatima u Beogradu," *Oslobodjenje*, 11 April 2006. City authorities responded by removing the posters, and within a few days the remaining ones had additional text placed on them by a pair of Danish artists: Pia Bertelsen and Jan Egesborg attached the slogans "we know you have weak nerves" and "we know you are a coward" to the posters. Unsigned (attributed to Beta), "Danski umetnici protiv Mladića," B92 vesti, 14 April 2006. Because of his high (in)visibility as a fugitive, Mladić was at the center of a number of publicity campaigns. There have been periodic campaigns (in 2007 and 2010) to cover over the street signs on Zoran Djindjić Boulevard to temporarily rename it Ratko Mladić Boulevard. In 2010 another far-right group, Naši 1389, responded to a campaign advertising a reward for information leading to the arrest of Mladić with one offering a reward for the exposure of "traitors." See Ognjen Zorić, "Odgovor desničara na nagradu za Mladića," Radio Slobodna Evropa, 3 November 2010.

7. In many years of travel through the region I have seen these shirts sold but have never seen a person wearing one.

8. As far as I am aware, the lyrics to this song are not published anywhere. I transcribed them from a recording. A recording of the song with strategically selected images is available as an online video at http://wn.com/Noz_zica_Srebrenica__ Serbian_Hip-Hop. The title of the site should not encourage anybody in the mistaken

belief that this sort of work is typical of Serbian hip-hop music. A quick check of the selections available indicates some similar examples, but most songs in praise of criminal acts are in the folk rather than rap (not even "gangsta") idiom.

9. Unsigned, "Srebrenica i Milica," *Večernje novosti*, 5 July 2005; A. Milošević and A. Kalaba, "Divljanje po zločinu," *Glas javnosti*, 7 July 2005. See also the description of the billboards incident in Obradović-Wochnik (2009: 66).

10. The activism of far-right groups began to receive extensive media attention in 2002 and has been a persistent theme of interest since then, usually when publicity stunts like the ones described above occur or when there is street violence. For early examples of coverage, see Vladimir Djukanović, "Šamari pljušte, 'Obraz' uzvrača," *Revija 92*, 21 July 2002, and Dragoslav Grujić, "Srpski talibani," *Vreme* 590, 25 April 2002. An extended interview with an unnamed neo-Nazi is available at V. B., "Pokret ćelavih mozgova," *Večernje novosti*, 15 November 2005.

11. The provocative use of such slogans by football fans was dramatized in Stefan Flipović's 2010 film *Šišanje* (The Skinning), which follows a confused teenager's path into neo-Nazi circles.

12. The operation "Krivaja" was commanded by the Army of the Serb Republic (VRS) but there is clear evidence that there was (1) command, control, and material support from the Yugoslav military, and (2) operational support from paramilitary formations under the command of the Serbian Ministry of the Interior.

13. Quoted in Zoran Tmušić, "Tresla se Bosna, Alija u Srebrenici," *Blic*, 13 July 2000.

14. Unsigned (attributed to Tanjug), "Novi podaci o masakru kod Srebrenice," *Politika*, 13 February 2000. The argument that the Srebrenica murders were the work of French intelligence would be revived by Radovan Karadžić at his trial in 2010. The "Spider" group was a group of Serbian mercenaries accused of espionage for France in 1999.

15. V. Mitrić, "Na mestu svojih zločina," *Večernje novosti*, 7 July 2000.

16. For example, B.S.P., "Hiljadu dodatnih žrtava?" and Radoje Andrić, "Dezertirali u svet," both in *Večernje novosti*, 9 July 2005. Also Borjan Popović, "I živi na spisku ubijenih" (interview with Milivoje Ivanišević), *Večernje novosti*, 13 July 2005.

17. V. Mitrić, "Nepravde do neba," *Večernje novosti*, 21 April 2000. In this instance what is at stake is a factual claim that the killings did not occur. There has been a separate recurring debate on the question of whether the killings constituted genocide or another type of crime, although for most observers the debate has been largely settled by the separate findings of ICTY and the International Court of Justice (ICJ).

18. Obradović-Wochnik (2009: 69).

19. Željko Vuković, "Srebrenizacija Srba i Srbije," *Večernje novosti*, 9 June 2005.

20. Petar Luković, "Vojislav Fernandel," *Feral Tribune* 787, 14 October 2000.

21. Ivana Dimić, "Pro doma sua" (open letter), *Danas*, 10 October 2000.

22. Unsigned, "Kruševački Otpor: Velika podela vazelina," B92 vesti, 14 October 2000. As it would turn out, most of the people who changed party in the wake of the events of October 2000 did not go all the way to "the other side" but rather to DSS.

23. Boris Tadić and Ivica Dačić, "Deklaracija o političkom pomirenju i zajedničkoj odgovornosti za ostvarivanje vizije Srbije kao demokratske, slobodne, celovite, ekonomski i kulturno razvijene i socijalno pravedne zemlje," 18 October 2008. The full text of the declaration was published in *Politika*, 21 and 22 October 2008.

24. In the television broadcast *Insajder* hosted by Jugoslav Ćosić, 14 March 2011.

25. Tamara Nikčević, "Intervju za *Dane*: Slavica Djukić Dejanović, SPS udarnica—Milošević i Djindjić su imali istog protivnika," interview for the magazine *BH Dani*, republished by *E-novine*, 10 March 2011.

26. Among the perspectives to which many in Serbia strenuously object are the suggestions at the time of the NATO bombing campaign in 1999 that Serbia required a "denazification" campaign. Hstorian Daniel Goldhagen, who famously argued in his (1996) book that the Holocaust could be traced to tendencies in German culture (see the response and debate with Christopher Browning in U.S. Holocaust Memorial Museum, *The "Willing Executioners"/"Ordinary Men" Debate*, 1996), made the analogy most directly in his essay in an American political magazine during the NATO military action of 1999, "A New Serbia," *New Republic*, 17 May 1999. In that article he argued for a corrective occupation of the country.

27. N. Dimitrijević (2000: 10).

28. Steve Crawshaw and Vesna Perić Zimonjić, "Yugoslavia's President-Elect Says Nothing Can Halt the Process of Change," *The Independent*, 5 October 2000.

29. Rade Vukosav, "Ko je kriv što ne znamo istinu," *Helsinška povelja* 27 (2000: 11).

30. Djordje Balašević, "Neću da pevam dok tuku klince" (interview with S. Vasović-Mekina), *Vreme* 495, 1 July 2000, 16.

31. Quoted in an interview with Antonela Riha and Jasna Janković, "Katarza," Radio B-92, 26 May 2001. I have not been able to confirm conclusively whether Djindjić was the first politician to cite Gottfried Wilhelm von Leibniz in a press interview. But I do feel comfortable in predicting that future politicians are not likely to continue this art of combinations.

32. Djordje Balašević, "Krivi smo mi," *Jedan od onih života* (album), Belgrade: UFA Media, 1993.

33. A general overview of the history of official apologies, types of apologies and motivations for and consequences of apologies is offered by Wyeneth (2001). See also the articles collected in Barkan and Karn (eds.) (2006). For a legal analysis see Bilder (2005–2006).

34. Borneman (2005).

35. Several of the complexities arising from this arrangement are narrated in Krog (1998).

36. If the sample is not restricted to domestic actors, first in the apology race would be Kofi Annan, who in 1999 apologized for the failures of the UN in Bosnia-Herzegovina. Aleksandar Dragićević, "UN Chief Apologizes for UN Failures in Bosnia," AP, 11 October 1999.

37. Vesna Perić Zimonjić, "Apology to Croats Earns Wrath of Serbia," Inter Press, 3 July 2000.

38. Amra Hadžiosmanović, "Belgrade, Zagreb Face Demand for Apology Before Post-War Summit," Agence France-Presse, 15 July 2002.

39. Aleksandar Mitić, "Belgrade, Zagreb Apologize for War But Problems Remain," Agence France-Presse, 10 September 2003.

40. Gabriel Partos, "Belgrade's Cautious Apology," BBC News, 13 November 2003.

41. Theoretically an apology from Tadić could carry more weight than an apology from Marović, as the federal president represented the smaller unit of the federation which was less involved in the wars. Unsigned, "Serbian President Apologizes to Bosnia over Balkans War," Agence France-Presse, 6 December 2004.

42. The full text of the RS government declaration is available at Unsigned, "Vlada RS: Žaljenje zbog Srebrenice," B92 vesti, 10 November 2004.

43. Unsigned, "Tadić: Svi dugujemo izvinjenje," B92 vesti, 6 December 2004.

44. See M. Nikić, "Minut ćutanja bez radikala," Politika, 12 July 2005; Unsigned, "Pokajanje u ime Srbije," Borba, 24 June 2005. A collection of excerpts from the various proposed and rejected texts is available at Unsigned, "Sve propale deklaracije o Srebrenici," Novinar.de, 21 March 2007. The full text of the government's 2005 declaration is published at Unsigned, "Zločini moraju biti kažnjeni," Borba, 16 June 2005.

45. Unsigned (quoting Boris Tadić), "Ispravno je otići," Večernje novosti, 9 July 2005.

46. Unsigned, "Serbian MPs Offer Apology for Srebrenica Massacre," BBC News, 31 March 2010.

47. Unsigned, "Croatian President Apologizes to Bosnia over War," CBC News, 14 April 2010.

48. Quoted in Dejan Vukelić and Nikola M. Jovanović, "Tadić bezbedan u Srebrenici," Blic, 21 June 2005. See also Bojan Tončić, "Tadić ide u Potočare iako nije poželjan," Danas, 21 June 2005. Radovan Karadžić would be arrested and extradited in 2008, and Ratko Mladić in 2011.

49. Quoted in Dejan Vukelić and Nikola M. Jovanović, "Tadić bezbedan u Srebrenici," Blic, 21 June 2005.

50. Unsigned, "Tadić u Srebrenici," Nacional, 11 July 2005; Vuk Stanić, "Lično ubio Srbina," Nacional, 11 July 2005. Another report claimed Tadić was subjected to anti-Serb chants at the memorial ceremony, including one that labeled him "the leader of the Četnici": Zoran Šaponjić, "Od zločina predstava," Glas javnosti, 12 July 2005. One other newspaper reported abusive chants (S. R. Mrkonjić and D. Vukelić,

"Zločinci bez vere i nacije," *Blic*, 12 July 2005, in passing rather than a major theme); no other paper made claims regarding the "Četnik" remark.

51. Gojković (2000: 18).

52. Apologies are also cheap: they cost nothing to give and do not necessarily do anything for the person to whom they are offered. On the day I wrote these lines I offered apologies to no fewer than four people. The first was to a neighbor after my dog barked at him. The second was to a person in the train on the way to work whom I wanted to pass to enter the train. The third was to another person on the same train who wanted to pass me to exit. The fourth was to the counterperson in the supermarket when I asked for an extra bag. Only on the first of these four occasions could my apology be said to have represented a sincere expression of regret.

53. There is nonetheless intense attention paid to research that establishes numbers of victims, particularly if these numbers turn out to be lower than the ones that had been in general use (without meaning to become an entrant in the competition over numbers, two quick observations here would be first, that for various reasons they often do, and second, that the number of victims is generally not known with certainty for acts of large-scale violence). Consequently, when the Sarajevo-based Research and Documentation Centre reported that on the basis of documentary evidence there were about 100,000 fatalities in the Bosnian War, centre director Mirsad Tokača became an object of disqualification in Bosnia and a cause celebre in Serbia. This is not because of any delight at the count of 100,000 victims, but because the number was smaller than the estimate of 250,000 based on informal sources and widely used during the war.

54. The refusal of ICTY prosecutors to bring charges against NATO for the use of cluster bombs and the destruction of civilian objects remains controversial. It was a theme in two memoirs released by former Tribunal officials: see Del Ponte (2008) and Hartmann (2007).

55. In April 2011 ICTY delivered its verdict in the case (IT-06–90) against Croatian generals Ante Gotovina, Ivan Čermak, and Mladen Markač for charges including killing, persecutions, and deportation. Gotovina and Markač were each found guilty on eight of nine counts and sentenced to twenty-four and eighteen years respectively, while Čermak was acquitted. The late Franjo Tudjman was found to be a party to the "joint criminal enterprise." However much of public opinion in Serbia appears to be unaware of the case or to ignore it. The initial indictments were filed in 2001 and 2004.

56. Proceedings for a retrial have commenced in the ICTY case (IT-04–84) against Ramush Haradinaj, Idriz Balaj, and Lahi Brahimaj for war crimes and crimes against humanity. Brahimaj was convicted while Haradinaj and Balaj were acquitted in 2008; in 2010 a retrial was ordered on the grounds that the initial trial had been impeded by evidence having been made unavailable.

57. Carla Del Ponte raised the organ trafficking charges in her 2007 book, claiming that she had begun an investigation but that ICTY had determined that events

after 1999 lay outside its jurisdiction. The charges were later revived by Council of Europe rapporteur Dick Marty (Council of Europe Parliamentary Assembly Document 12462, *Inhuman Treatment of People and Illicit Trafficking in Human Organs in Kosovo*, 2011). The report did not present evidence to support the claims of organ trafficking, however; rather it argued that grounds existed to call for additional investigation.

58. In its 2000 decision in the case against Zoran Kupreškić, Mirjan Kupreškić, Vlatko Kupreškić, Drago Josipović, Dragan Papić, and Vladimir Antić (IT-95–16-Z), the ICTY Trial Chamber explicitly addressed the *tu quoque* defense, arguing that while the defense had claimed that "the attacks committed against the Muslim population of the Lašva Valley were somehow justifiable because, in the Defence's allegation, similar attacks were allegedly being perpetrated by the Muslims against the Croat population. The Trial Chamber wishes to stress, in this regard, the irrelevance of reciprocity, particularly in relation to obligations found within international humanitarian law which have an absolute and non-derogable character. It thus follows that the *tu quoque* defence has no place in contemporary international humanitarian law. The defining characteristic of modern international humanitarian law is instead the obligation to uphold key tenets of this body of law regardless of the conduct of enemy combatants."

59. Trial transcript of 3 July 2001, p. 4. There are some unusual grammatical constructions in the trial transcripts, probably the result of transcribing a large volume of material without extensive editing, which I have left unaltered.

60. Trial transcript of 31 August 2004, pp. 32173–74.

61. Trial transcript of 31 August 2004, pp. 32174–75.

62. Trial transcript of 1 September 2004, pp. 32296–97.

63. The line came in his televised address to the country after his defeat. The full text is available at Unsigned, "Milošević napada lidere DOS," B92 vesti, 2 October 2000.

64. Željko Vuković, "Srebrenizacija Srba i Srbije," *Večernje novosti*, 9 June 2005.

65. Mila Alečković Nikolić, "Dodirljivi i nedodirljivi," *Politika*, 20 June 2005.

66. Between 2002 and 2005 repeated raids from the enclave of Srebrenica on surrounding villages principally populated by Serbs resulted in a number of civilian casualties. The number itself is uncertain: estimates range from a low of 119, the number documented by the Research and Documentation Centre based in Sarajevo, to about 600, the number claimed by RS authorities, to a high of about 1,200, the number claimed but not documented by Ivanišević (1994).

67. R. Kovačević, "Politička zloupotreba komemoracije," *Politika*, 15 July 2000.

68. A troubling element in the discussion of victimhood is that the national identity of victims is often taken as a given, as in unproblematic referral to "Serbian victims," "Albanian victims," and so on. The approach appears to elide the degree to which identity is structured by feeling and choice, an insight in sociology that dates back at least as far as Max Weber. Nobody asks victims how strongly they were tied to

one identity or another. In the case of victims of fatal crimes, if anybody did ask them they would of course not be able to answer.

69. See the analysis by Dulić (2009).

70. This quotation and the ones that follow in this paragraph and the next are from texts reproduced in Unsigned, "Sve propale deklaracije o Srebrenici," *Novinar*, 21 March 2007.

71. Jokić (2004: 255).

72. This is the number reached by Brunborg and Udal (2000). As of 11 January 2008, 4010 victims had been positively identified through remains. See Tabeau and Hetland (2008).

73. Srdjan Bogosavljević, "The Unresolved Genocide," in Popov (ed.) (1996). Bogosavljević did not estimate a precise number of victims but used existing research and a variety of other documents to produce minimum and maximum estimates. The figures offered here is his range for the number of probable Serb and Montenegrin victims. To this could plausibly be added Jews (minimum 60,000; maximum 70,000) and Roma (minimum 20,000; maximum 35,000), with the proviso in all cases that not all victims would have been victims of NDH. For an explanation of all available estimates of the number of victims and the reasons these vary widely, see Tomasevich (2001), especially chap. 17. Tomasevich draws attention to debate over the number of victims as "a macabre numbers game, with reality being subordinated to the overriding political and propaganda objectives of all parties concerned" (718). In making his case, Jokić opts for the high estimates rejected by both Bogosavljević and Tomasevich.

74. Republic of Rwanda (2002). Like all genocide numbers, these numbers are subject to dispute. For an explanation see Fujii (2009).

75. "The Ultimate Repression: The Genocide of the Armenians, 1915–1917," in Wallimann and Dobkowski, (eds.) (2000). Here, too, there is dispute regarding the number of victims, with the lowest estimate (favored by a series of governments of the Republic of Turkey) being around 300,000.

76. In one of the basic Srebrenica denial texts, precisely this argument is offered: "viewed in the context of the massive violence which is routinely practiced in the world today, even assuming that 8,000 were executed in Srebrenica, compared to the casualties resulting from the attacks on Iraq and Afghanistan, putting aside other examples of mass depopulation such as Guatemala or East Timor, that would still be a crime of modest proportions." Stefan Karganović, "Srebrenica: A Critical Overview," in Karganović (ed.) (2011: 18 n. 6).

77. M. T., "Marković preduhitrio radikale," *Danas*, 12 July 2005. The representatives of the Serbian Radical Party left the chamber complaining that parties had not agreed beforehand on a minute of silence. The attack in London was the bombing attack on public transportation facilities on 7 July 2005, in which 56 people were killed and around 700 injured.

78. Skupština grada Beograda—Sekretarijat za kulturu, Društvo arhitekata Beograda, Društvo urbanista Beograda, "Konkurs za idejno, likovno i arhitektonsko-urbanističko rešenje Savskog trga u Beogradu sa spomen obeležjem žrtvama rata i

braniocima otadžbine 1990–1999. godine," December 2005. Available at E-Kapija web site, http://www.ekapija.com/website/sr/page/35527.

79. Igor Lasić, "Jasenovac 2001: Nisu stradale brojke, već ljudi," *BH Dani* 236, 14 December 2001. See also Viktor Ivančić, "United Colors of Jasenovac," *Feral Tribune* 561, 17 June 1996.

80. Lea David, "Sećam se, dakle, postojim: Identitet Srba kao refleksija kulture sećanja," in Djerić (ed.) (2009: 164, 165).

81. Among the most prolific of these international allies of the historical revisionists are Edward Herman, a retired professor of finance who is best known as a onetime collaborator of Noam Chomsky (see his "The Politics of the Srebrenica Massacre," *Z Magazine*, 7 July 2005), and Diana Johnstone, an American journalist (see her "Using War as an Excuse for More War: Srebrenica Revisited," *Global Research*, 18 October 2005). The role of such international participants in the campaign is peripheral: none of them has expertise in the matters around which they are engaged, and it might be possible to surmise that their interest in Serbia and Srebrenica is subordinate to their larger concern with combatting what they perceive to be global imperialism. Hence they will not be considered in any great detail in this work.

82. Karganović (ed.) (2011: 189).

83. Karganović (ed.) (2011: 189).

84. Karganović (ed.) (2011: 144).

85. Karganović (ed.) (2011: 144 n. 4).

86. In Karganović: "It remains to be seen to what extent they are also a 'game changer' in terms of the overall assessment of what happened in Srebrenica" (2011: 131); "A brief but relevant digression will assist us in understanding better the Tribunal's game" (149). The authors may be thinking specifically of a card game, as at another point they refer to the existing evidence as a "colossal bluff" (18). Or perhaps it is a psychosocial parlor game as they suggest in calling it "a big Rorschach drawing" (18). In any case there is little rhetorical space left for readers who might interpret organized mass violence as something other than a game.

87. According to evidence presented by the members of the Srebrenica Historical Project themselves, the number of active combatants in the Srebrenica area was smaller than the documented number of victims, meaning that even if every single Bosnian soldier had been killed in combat or captured and executed, this would still not account for all victims.

88. That is the thesis offered by Karganović in chapter 4 of the text, "Genocide or Blowback?" (2011: 51–71). The implicit conclusion is that if the murders were "blowback" then there is support for a *tu quoque* argument, as well as for the general dismissive theme that bad things happen in the context of war. "Holistic" comes from (2011: 202).

89. Karganović (2011: 18).

90. Obradović-Wochnik (2009: 72 n. 14).

91. Karganović (ed.) (2011: 23) (Stefan Karganović quoting personal correspondence from George Pumphrey, who also contributed a chapter to the volume).

92. Karganović (ed.) (2011: 75).

93. Karganović (ed.) (2011: 30–31).

94. Karganović (ed.) (2011: 135).

95. Karganović (ed.) (2011: 11). To be sure, it is not a discussion of methodology used in their study or any other study but rather a discussion of methodology in principle.

96. Perhaps if it did offer a genuine analysis of data it could be called a reanalysis of data?

97. Indeed the authors introduce the text with a (not quite accurate) claim that "Our purpose is not to argue with the cult of Srebrenica, or for that matter to dispute or deny anything." Karganović (ed.) (2011: 17).

98. In the Rodney King case, defense attorneys succeeded in challenging what appeared to be unassailable evidence—a videotape showing a group of officers beating and kicking an unarmed man at a traffic stop—by reconstructing the videotape at slow speed and adding a voiceover, asking jurors to evaluate each blow and kick individually and to conclude that if the beating victim was moving then the use of force was justified. See Feldman (1994).

99. One of the most prominent Holocaust denial organizations goes by the name of the Institute for Historical Review. The choice of name is strategic: desecrating the memory of victims is bad manners at the least, but what reasonable person could be opposed to reviewing history? A reader does not see what sort of review the institute undertakes without seeing the materials produced by the group.

100. Karganović (ed.) (2011: 18).

101. For a characteristic example of critique in the domestic literature in Serbia, see Nakarada (2008), especially part 2, "Putevi suočavanja." In addition to scholarly works there exists a large number of polemical works, of which probably the best known is Čavoški (2007).

102. V. Dimitrijević (2003).

103. Unsurprisingly, issues of gender play a meaningful role in the attack discourse. See Daša Duhaček, "The Making of Political Responsibility: Hannah Arendt and/in the Case of Serbia, in Lukić, Regulska, and Zaviršek (eds.) (2006), and the essays in Giles et al. (eds.) (2004). For a sustained version of the critique of these figures in an academic key, see Radojičić (2008, 2009).

104. I do not know what a centrist position between advocacy and condemnation of crime could possibly resemble.

105. Marijana Milosavljević, "U kandžama politikanata," *NIN*, 7 July 2005.

106. Željko Vuković, "Srebrenizacija Srba i Srbije," *Večernje novosti*, 9 June 2005.

107. Unsigned, "Odbor za istinu o Srebrenici," *Borba*, 25 June 2005.

108. The text by Antonić in *Vreme* and his replies to his critics (but not the texts by the critics themselves) are reproduced in Slobodan Antonić, "Misionarska

inteligencija u današnjoj Srbiji," in Antonić (ed.) (2003: 293–312). The identification of the group occurs on page 294.

109. Antonić (2003: 293).

110. Antonić (2003: 293–94).

111. Antonić (2003: 296).

112. Antonić (2003: 294).

113. Not that I have anything against Brigitte Bardot. Or Jane Birkin.

114. The point is made explicitly on page 295, and implicitly in several instances in the long passage (296–99), in which Antonić sets out what he regards as the fundamental assumptions of the "missionaries."

115. Antonić (2003: 299, 301).

116. Antonić (2003: 301). The donkey and mosquito apposition works more felicitously in the original language, where the animals (magarac and komarac) rhyme.

117. In his book, Antonić republished his original article and his responses to his critics, but not the essays by his critics. Those are available in "Polemika u listu 'Vreme' povodom teksta Slobodana Antonića," Nova srpska politička misao (online edition), http://starisajt.nspm.rs/PrenetiTekstovi/antonic_polemika_vreme2.htm.

118. The term "denazification" is more impressive than the actual record of the short-lived denazification program in occupied Germany after 1945, which saw a very small number of major offenders pursued and in all occupation zones a majority of cases ending in exoneration, suspension of the proceedings, or amnesty. See Volker Berghahn and Uta Poiger, "Analysis of Denazification Categories in the Western Occupation Zones," in Occupation and the Emergence of Two States, 1945–1961, German History in Documents and Images; Germany (Territory Allied occupation, 1945–1955: U.S. Zone), Office of Military Government, Civil Administration Division, Denazification, Cumulative Review. Report, 1 April 1947–30 April 1948. Lithographed by the Adjutant General (Berlin: OMGUS, 1948); and Vogt (2000).

119. Several responses to the use of the term are collected in an appendix to Ristić and Leposavić (2000).

120. See his interview with Gordana Jocić, Nezavisna svetlost, 8–15 July 2000. For an overview of the activity of Sava Janjić see Little (2007: 123–50).

121. Unsigned, "Uhapšena devetorica policajaca zbog zločina nad 48 Albanaca iz Suve Reke: Pobili žene i decu, osramotili naciju," Blic, 27 October 2005.

122. Dorotea Čarnić, "Osudjeni na 231 godina," Politika, 13 December 2005. The citation from Marko Miljanov is from his book published in 1901 (all his publications were posthumous), Primjeri čojstva i junaštva, which has been republished in several versions since.

123. The text comes from a public address at a conference held in Potočari in 2005. It was published as Nataša Mićić, "Pravo na kaznu," Danas, 15 July 2005.

124. The issue of whether Serbia can be said to have a democratic tradition is one of the objects of contention among politically engaged intellectuals in Serbia, as it has

implications for the issue of whether in a process of democratization there exists a tradition to be restored or not, and also for the question of whether opposition to modernity is a negative constant in Serbian political history. See Perović, Obradović, and Stojanović (eds.) (1994); and Dimić (ed.) (2005).

125. Obviously, authoritarian political structures both under Communist and under nationalist rule used rhetorics of collective destiny and collective goals to mobilize citizens, but in the process imposed collective concepts which were not a part of popular culture (the false collectives of the proletariat and the people), and offered means of collective participation which were wholly ritualized while they marginalized genuine public participation.

126. Jaspers's *Die Schuldfrage* was published in Germany in 1946 and first translated into English in 1948. The edition I have used for this discussion is the translation by Savić (1999).

127. Gojković (2000: 19).

128. Unsigned, "Otpor: Katastrofalan poraz Miloševića," Free B92 vesti, 26 September 2000.

129. Arendt (1966: 333)

130. "Generally" so considered, but not universally! The forced migration of most of the Serb population of Croatia has its advocates as well. And in 2011 organ harvesting came back into fashion.

131. The use of the term "massacre" here is not meant to indicate a position on the debate over whether the events constituted genocide. Although there are judicial rulings on this point that would seem to settle the matter, it remains an object of debate in Serbia, some of which will be considered in the next chapter.

Chapter 7. Moment III: The "Scorpions" and the Refinement of Denial

1. Other events have led to the filing of genocide charges, particularly in the Milošević, Karadžić, and Mladić cases. However, there have been no verdicts in these: the Milošević trial ended without a verdict, the Karadžić trial is still ongoing, and the Mladić trial began in May 2012.

2. Milošević trial (IT-02–54) testimony of 1 June 2005, 40274. See the description by Armatta (2010: 420–24).

3. The paramilitaries wore red berets, associated with the Unit for Special Operations (Jedinica za specijalne operacije, JSO) of the Serbian Interior Ministry. The film begins with scenes filmed at the paramilitaries' base in Djeletovci in Croatia, which testimony in another trial (Tolimir trial transcript [IT-05–88/2-PT], 25 November 2010, 8127) established was under the control of Serbian State Security. Eventually the judges would reject use of the videotape as evidence, on the grounds that it did not bear directly on Milošević's individual involvement. Consequently, its main significance would be as an object of public discussion and interpretation rather than a court exhibit.

4. The taking of Srebrenica was not treated as a major news event in Serbia in July 1995. There were reports that the city had been captured but it was not given prominence and it was not a subject of commentary. Discussion of Srebrenica increased after charges were leveled, and then largely took the form of denial. See Nezavisno udruženje novinara Srbije, "Politička propaganda i projekt 'Svi Srbi u jednoj državi,'" *Dosije* 31 (November 2009–January 2010). An overview of domestic press coverage of Srebrenica from 1995 to 2001 is offered by Tamara Skrozza, "Laži i obmane," *Vreme* 550, 19 July 2001.

5. UN Security Council, Fiftieth Year, 3564th Meeting, 10 August 1995, S-PV.3564, 3.

6. Ibid., 6.

7. S/RES/1010 (1995).

8. As is well known, no verdict was rendered in the Milošević trial, owing to the death of the indictee in 2006. Among the most important points linking Milošević to the crimes were (1) the financial and logistical links between the Yugoslav army and the Army of Republika Srpska, and (2) the engagement of forces commanded by the Interior Ministry of Serbia in the crimes. The first of these points was largely confirmed in a verdict by the International Court of Justice (ICJ), but that verdict determined that financial and logistical engagement did not constitute complicity in genocide. International Court of Justice, *Case Concerning the Application of the Convention on the Prevention and Punishment of the Crime of Genocide (Bosnia and Herzegovina vs Serbia and Montenegro)*, 26 February 2007.

9. Petar Ignja, "Slike iz Srebrenice," *NIN*, 19 July 2001. I am not certain whether the reference to the author's surroundings as a "less civilized world" was intended ironically.

10. Velimir Ćurguz Kazimir, "Zavera stida," *Vreme* 550, 19 July 2001.

11. Unsigned, "Duga lista izvora," *Politika*, 5 September 2002; Unsigned, "U Srebrenici ubijeno 2000 Muslimana," 3 September 2002.

12. Unsigned (Tanjug and Srna), "Izveštaj ekspertskog tima Biroa vlade RS za odnose sa Haškim tribunalom: U Srebrenici 2000 žrtava, uglavnom vojnika," *Blic*, 3 September 2002.

13. Unsigned, "Duga lista izvora"; Unsigned, "U Srebrenici ubijeno 2000 Muslimana."

14. The report appears to have been produced by a single person, Darko Trifunović, who is listed in the front matter under the heading "prepared by." Documentation Center of Republic of Srpska Bureau of Government of RS for Relation with ICTY (2002).

15. The Srebrenica commission in Republika Srpska is in fact the only "truth commission" in the region to have actually produced a report.

16. *Prosecutor v. Miroslav Deronjić: Sentencing Judgement*, ICTY Case IT-02–61-S, 30 March 2004, pp. 68–70.

17. B. Tončić, "Šest hiljada srebreničkih žrtava," *Danas*, 12 June 2002. The NIOD report itself was published as feuilleton in the daily paper *Danas* from 26 April to 30 May 2002.

18. D. Stojaković, "Nisu žrtve svi poginuli," *Večernje novosti*, 10 November 2004.

19. Unsigned, "Svi bi istinu o Srebrenici," *Glas javnosti*, 31 August 2003.

20. Among the victims were both young children and elderly men, neither likely to have been in active military service.

21. See the transcript of Omer Karabeg's radio broadcast "Most" published as "Smrt u zaštićenoj zoni," *Danas*, 30–31 August 2003 (discussion with Jasmin Odobašić and Milan Bulajić).

22. Naser Orić was charged by ICTY for two counts of war crimes (IT-03–68), convicted in 2006, then acquitted on appeal in 2008. In 2008, after his return from ICTY, he was charged by Bosnian authorities with extortion and illegal possession of weapons in a set of events not related to the wars.

23. As noted in the previous chapter, there is dispute over the number of victims of these attacks.

24. Mladić's statement came shortly after the conquest of Srebrenica and was originally reported in *Večernje novosti* on 13 July 1995. Tamara Skrozza, "Laži i obmane," *Vreme* 550, 19 July 2001.

25. Dušan Marić, "Srpska glava vredela pola džaka brašna," *Revija 92*, 12 December 2004.

26. Tamara Skrozza traces the story to an article in *Večernje novosti* on 17 July 1995. See her article "Laži i obmane." In 2005 a person named Kemal Mehmedović testified in the trial of Vidoje Blagojević and Dragan Jokić before ICTY. Mehmedović had been a prisoner of war in 1995. There is no indication that this may be the person described in the article, but it is equally likely that the Mehmedović in the article is a fictional character. See Emir Šuljagić, "Serb Executions Recounted," Institute for War and Peace Reporting, 30 April 2005.

27. J. Slatinac, "Povampiren srebrenički šehit pobegao iz zatvora," *Politika ekspres*, 26 December 2003. See also P. Vasović and D. P. Veljković, "Odbegli robijaš medu nestalima," *Večernje novosti*, 20 December 2003.

28. S. Pešević and M. Labus, "Dalja potraga za 'nestalima,'" *Večernje novosti*, 11 November 2004. The name in parentheses is the name of the person's father in the genitive case.

29. Unsigned (Fond za humanitarno pravo), "Istina pobedjuje zločin," *Politika*, 4 June 2003.

30. Gordana Tomljenović, "Srebrenica—Osam godina agonije," *Borba*, 20–21 September 2003.

31. Branka Branković, "Početak kraja agonije za Republiku Srpsku zbog Srebrenice," *Danas*, 10 November 2004. *Danas* published the commission's report as a feuilleton beginning on 16 June 2004.

32. Unsigned (Tanjug), "Korak ka otrežnjenju," *Politika*, 24 June 2004; Unsigned, "Vlada RS: Žaljenje zbog Srebrenice," B92 vesti, 10 November 2004.

33. Unsigned (Beta), "Istina o Srebrenici skida anatemu s naroda," *Glas javnosti*, 16 June 2004.

34. Mira Beham, "Iznudjena katarza," *NIN*, 15 July 2004. The article followed on a wave of earlier claims that the RS government had been forced or blackmailed to produce the report. See Unsigned, "Vlada RS bila ucenjivana," *Večernje novosti*, 11 September 2003; Unsigned (Tanjug), "Izveštaj RS o Srebrenici pod pritiskom," *Večernje novosti*, 10 September 2003. Those claims were denied by RS president Dragan Čavić, see Dubravka Vujanović, "Vlada RS nije ucenjivana," *Večernje novosti*, 12 September 2003.

35. Milenko Marić, "Ešdaunovo postkuvajtsko otkrivanje istine," *Borba*, 26–27 April 2004.

36. S. Pešević, "Ešdaun zakopava istinu," *Večernje novosti*, 21 April 2004. See also E. B., "Marko Arsović: Povući saglasnost na spisak nastradalih," *Blic*, 10 April 2010.

37. V. Kadić, "Zacrnili Srebrenicu!" *Večernje novosti*, 11 November 2004. The article cites the testimony of former prisoner Spaso Samouković. The same quotations from the same person were used in an earlier article by the same author: V. Kadić, "Al Kaida tri godine ubijala u Srebrenici," *Revija 92*, 10 August 2004.

38. The name of the group refers to collections of ecclesiastical and civic law in the Byzantine church, the earliest version of which dates to the early sixth century and is attributed to St. John Scholasticus. The Nomokanon of St. Sava dates to 1219 and is considered the highest legal code of the Serbian Orthodox Church. The use of the name by a student group probably represents a rhetorical attempt to unify ecclesiastical traditions with legal ones and invoke national religious authorities as a source of law.

39. Some news stories report that the law faculty declined to approve a request to hold the meeting in April because of the provocative subtitle. In an official statement the law faculty management rejects this suggestion, declaring instead that in April they had requested that Nomokanon receive approval from the student parliament, and that Nomokanon returned with that approval. See Uprava Pravnog fakulteta, "Saopštenje Uprave Pravnog fakulteta u Beogradu o održavanju tribine 'Istina o Srebrenici' na Pravnom fakultetu," 21 May 2005. The document is available at the Faculty of Law website, http://www.ius.bg.ac.rs/informacije/stavPF.htm.

40. Unsigned (B92), "Srebrenica u Beogradu," B92 vesti, 17 May 2005.

41. Radinović had previously taught strategy at a military college. Although not well known to the public, he gave testimony for the defense in some ICTY cases.

42. Ognjanović had been engaged to represent Milošević on his arrest on domestic charges in 2001. ICTY appointed him and another lawyer to serve as counsel, creating an unusual relationship between the Tribunal, appointed defense counsel, and a defendant who declined legal representation. See Milanka Šaponja-Hadžić, "Regional

Report: Milošević's 'Curious' Legal Advisors," Institute of War and Peace Reporting, 22 February 2005.

43. Probably Serbia's leading postconflict hagiographer, Ljiljana Bulatović's best-known works (1996, 2002, 2010) are celebratory biographies of Karadžić and Mladić.

44. Unsigned, "Beograd u atmosferi poricanja zločina," Radio Slobodna Evropa, 17 May 2005.

45. The law faculty defended the holding of the meeting on the ground of free speech, lamented that the event would damage the faculty's already poor reputation, and promised an "energetic investigation" and the "appropriate disciplinary procedure" against "all who abused academic freedom for inappropriate political activity, who physically attacked people who disagreed with them," and who caused the autonomy of the university to be violated by calling in police officers to restore order. No investigation or disciplinary procedure, if these ever occurred, was ever announced. See Uprava Pravnog fakulteta, "Saopštenje" (2005).

46. The confrontations that occurred at the meeting are described in Unsigned (B92), "Srebrenica u Beogradu," B92 vesti, 17 May 2005; Unsigned, "Osporavanje zločina u Srebrenici," B92 vesti, 18 May 2005; Inicijativa mladih za ljudska prava, "Izveštaj sa tribune 'Istina o Srebrenici'," May 2005.

47. Uprava Pravnog fakulteta, "Saopštenje" (2005).

48. Unsigned, "Nomokanon: Nemamo veze sa Obrazom," B92 vesti, 23 May 2005.

49. Unsigned, "Tribina o Srebrenici bila naučni skup," Politika, 19 May 2005.

50. For a sample of the opinions catalyzed by the panel, see (endorsing) P. Stojković, "Druga strana medalje," Večernje novosti, 18 May 2005, and (condemning) Bojan Tončić, "Užasni zadah srpske sramote," Danas, 19 May 2005.

51. Prosecutor Geoffrey Nice used only a few minutes of the footage in his questioning, asking whether Obrad Stevanović could recognize the faces of any of the perpetrators. A segment of the film lasting just over thirty minutes was shown in various places around Serbia in June and July 2005. The full footage lasts over two hours. Various versions of the film, including edited ones, have been posted at various places on the Internet. Although there does exist some published speculation based on the fact that an edited version of the film was broadcast, the unused material does not contain any major revelations or secrets. The remainder of the filmed material dates from before the taking of Srebrenica and is also not likely to be of interest for any other reason (except to devotees of films that document corpulent men standing around in mountain landscapes and occasionally frolicking, a niche market that may well exist).

52. The summary of the film is my own. Another summary is presented in Unsigned, "Streljali u šetnji," Večernje novosti, 11 June 2005.

53. The film also points to another institutional association. In the initial scene the members of the "Scorpions" receive a benediction from a local monk, Father Gavrilo (Vidosav Marić), who chants to them that they should "destroy the enemy which rises up against the Serbian Orthodox people" and asks God to "grant that your

faithful army should subdue the enemy people." See N. Nikšić, "Otac Gavrilo blagosiljao paravojsku," *Politika*, 7 June 2005.

54. The film was not completely unknown before its introduction into the trial record. It had been available for rental at a video club called Laser in the town of Šid, and came into the hands of the Belgrade-based Fund for Humanitarian Law, which forwarded it to the ICTY prosecutor. Dorotea Čarnić, "Kaseta prodata Hagu zbog osvete," *Politika*, 12 April 2006.

55. A. Roknić, "Zločincima da se sudi po pravdi, ako je ima," *Danas*, 27 January 2006; E. Radosavljević, "Pucali u glavu," *Večernje novosti*, 27 January 2006; Dorotea Čarnić, "Snimak jedini trag," *Politika*, 27 January 2006.

56. Unsigned (Beta), "Više od dve trećine gradana smatra da Srbija treba da saradjuje," Centar za razvoj neprofitnog sektora Arhiva vesti za mesec Maj 2005.

57. O. P., "Škorpioni pred poslanicima," *Politika*, 6 June 2005.

58. Dubravka Vujanović, "Srebrenica naš najveći autogol," *Večernje novosti*, 20 June 2005.

59. Although Ivona Živković identifies herself as a film director in the article, I am not aware of any film she has directed. She does maintain a web site in which she identifies herself as a journalist. The content is a combination of opinion pieces, conspiracy theory, and alternative medicine. At one time she worked in RTS, as described in Zora Latinović, "Preko suspenzije do TV zvezda," *NIN* 2685, 13 June 2002.

60. Ivona Živković, "Srebrenica, laži i video trake," *Ogledalo*, 8 June 2005.

61. E. R., "Montaža u političke svrhe," *Večernje novosti*, 15 September 2005.

62. An electronic copy of the film can be dowloaded at http://istina.srpskinacionalisti.com/. The quotations that follow, both from the speeches at the presentation and from the film, are from my transcription of the electronic copy of the film, which includes the introductory addresses by SRS leaders Tomislav Nikolić and Aleksandar Vučić.

63. I was in the audience as well, having come with two friends to observe the event.

64. It is the custom for priests to take on a new name upon joining a monastic order, after which point their family and given names are referred to as their "earthly" names.

65. Smilja Avramov's testimony opened Milošević's defense before ICTY.

66. A major proponent of the Praxis school in the 1960s, by the 1980s Mihailo Marković had developed into one of the authors of the Memorandum of the Serbian Academy of Sciences and Arts and would take on a leading role in Milošević's party before hardliners were expelled following the Dayton peace agreement in 1995. Mihailo Marković died in 2010.

67. One of the best-loved authors of anecdotes and aphorisms in an earlier period, Branislav Crnčević was intensively active in the interests of the Serb parastates in

Bosnia-Herzegovina and Croatia in the 1990s. A longtime supporter and friend of Milošević, he joined SRS in 2003. He died in 2011.

68. Tomislav Nikolić and Aleksandar Vučić split from SRS in 2008, forming the Serbian Progressive Party (Srpska napredna stranka, SNS) and taking most of the leadership and membership of SRS along with them.

69. The executed prisoner was identified as Rade Rogić and two members of his family were present for the introductory speeches. Another scene is presented as "the torture of Milan Nedimović," though from the footage one can see an old man shouted at and a poster of Radovan Karadžić burned in front of him, but no torture. The fighters are also shown desecrating a church. It is unclear from the narration whether the fighters shown are genuinely mujahedeen or Bosnian soldiers—in one scene they are shown listening to an address and singing a song in Serbo-Croatian, which would suggest that they were not mujahedeen. There was indeed a military presence of international volunteers in the Bosnian war, but it was small and not universally welcomed by political and military authorities.

70. Unsigned (B92 and Beta), "Nikolić: Film je odgovor," B92 vesti, 7 July 2005.

71. Gradjani za istinu o Srebrenici, "Appeal to President Boris Tadić and the Serbian Parliament: Do Not Gamble with Your Country's Future! No to the Srebrenica Resolution!" 8 February 2010.

72. The date corresponds to the commemoration of the Srebrenica killings, but not to incidents in which there were large numbers of Serb civilian victims. The largest crime alleged in the area against Serb civilians was in Kravica in January 1993, with 49 victims. In the Orić case (IT-03-68-T, pp. 230–36) ICTY was unpersuaded that the attack on Kravica constituted a legal violation.

73. Dragan Banjac, "Prebrojavanje mrtvih"; Glas javnosti, 16 July 2005.

74. Unsigned, "U Bratuncu pomen srpskim žrtvama," and "Srebrenica: 10 godina od zločina," B92 vesti, 11 July 2005.

75. Kristina Ćirković, "Spomenik Srbima stradalim u Kravici," Glas srpske, 12 June 2009.

76. V. Č., "Bratunac: Otkriven i osveštan spomen krst za 3.267 poginulih Srba," SRNA news, 14 July 2009.

77. Z. Šaponjić, "Ne ponovilo se ni Srbima, ni nikome," Glas javnosti, 11 July 2005.

78. A. N. B., "A duša boli," Borba, 14 July 2005.

79. S. Vojinović, "Opozicija tvrdi da Tadić mora da ode i u Bratunac," Press, 14 July 2010. The first quotation is attributed to politician Aleksandar Vučić, the second to politician Velimir Ilić, and the third appears to come directly from the journalist who wrote the article.

80. A brief history of the formation is given by Dejan Anastasijević, "Ubod Škorpiona," Vreme 677, 25 December 2003.

81. Unsigned, "Cvjetanu ponovo 20 godina," B92 vesti, 17 June 2005. The original conviction was handed down in March 2004 and confirmed in June 2005. Another

"Scorpion," Dejan Demirović, was also charged in the crime but had not yet been extradited from Canada. In 2009 three more "Scorpions" were convicted of the massacre in Podujevo: Željko Djukić, Dragan Medić, and Dragan Borojević. See N. Jovanović, "'Škorpioni' osudeni na po 20 godina zatvora," *Blic*, 19 June 2009.

82. The unit was founded in 1991 as a regular unit of the Yugoslav Army. In 1992 they came under the command of Republika Srpska Krajina, the Serb parastate that existed in Croatia until 1995. There is a dispute as to the date on which it passed to the command of the Serbian Interior Ministry, but it was likely at some point in 1995. In the Kosovo conflict of 1998–1999, they operated as members of the Special Antiterrorism Unit (Specijalna antiteroristička jedinica, SAJ).

83. *The Prosecutor v. Jovica Stanišić and Franko Simatović* (IT-03–69-PT), third amended indictment, 10 July 2008.

84. Marko Albunović, "Preko Ledenog do države," *Politika*, 18 January 2006.

85. Dejan Anastasijević, "Ubod Škorpiona," *Vreme* 677, 25 December 2003.

86. Quoted in Aleksandar Roknić, "Komandant negirao optužnicu," *Danas*, 21 December 2005; Dorotea Čarnić, "Streljanje umesto razmene," *Politika*, 21 December 2005. See also D. Ć., "Boca: Nek laje, ja sam Obilić," *Glas javnosti*, 23 February 2006.

87. O. P., "Škorpioni pred poslanicima," *Politika*, 6 June 2005.

88. O. P., "Škorpioni pred poslanicima."

89. Unsigned, "Ne obesmisliti sećanje na žrtve," *Danas*, 12 July 2005.

90. See, for example, A. Roknić, "Komandant Slobodan Medić ne priznaje zločin," *Danas*, 16 February 2006.

91. It is a poor defense: the accused are judged on what they did, not on what documents said they said they might do. And among the duties of a commander is to prevent and punish violations. This issue was the basis of the decisions in the Bosnian genocide case before ICJ, as well as in the convictions of Gotovina and Markač before ICTY.

92. Croatia filed a similar suit and Serbia filed a countersuit. These have yet to be heard and the two states are negotiating to mutually withdraw their cases. Neither the suit nor the countersuit has any prospect of success, as none of the crimes committed in the conflict involving Serbia and Croatia has been characterized as genocide by any judicial body.

93. I. Lovrić and B. Popović, "Udaraju nam žig genocida," *Večernje novosti*, 24 June 2005.

94. J. J., "Kandić: Istraga brza, kvalifikacija zločina je sporna," *Danas*, 8–9 October 2005.

95. V. Lalić, "Masakr ili genocid?" *Večernje novosti*, 5 July 2005. The "stuff happens in a war" thesis depends for its force on the contention (discussed above) that victims were active members of warring organizations.

96. S. Pešević, "Genocida nije bilo," *Večernje novosti*, 6 July 2005. Nazis were not tried for genocide, as both the passage (1948) and the coming into force (1951) of the Genocide Convention occurred after 1945.

97. After a chequered record commanding peacekeeping forces in Somalia, Lewis MacKenzie went on to command peacekeepers in the first period of the siege of Sarajevo in 1992. He was removed from the position in October 1992 and retired from the Canadian military in March 1993. Since then he has been known for taking contrarian stands in the media.

98. Lewis MacKenzie, "Nije bilo masakra nad 8,000," *Večernje novosti*, 16 July 2005. The contention that genocide requires the destruction of a group in its entirety rather than a part of a group conflicts with Article II of the Genocide Convention, which defines genocide as "acts committed with intent to destroy, in whole or in part" several types of groups.

99. V. Lalić, "Masakr ili genocid?" *Večernje novosti*, 5 July 2005. The text to which she refers is a 1970 self-published manuscript by Alija Izetbegović, who was later to become the first president of Bosnia-Herzegovina; the first actual publication of the manuscript was in English language translation as Unsigned, "The Trial of Muslim Intellectuals in Sarajevo (The Islamic Declaration)," *South Slav Journal* 6, 1 (Spring 1983): 55–89. The one sentence most frequently quoted by detractors of Izetbegović is "there can be no peaceful coexistence between the Islamic faith and non-Islamic social and political institutions" (22). While not an appealing formulation it hardly demonstrates genocidal intent. In other sections of the book, as in the ones on "the equality of people" (25), "freedom of consciousness" (31), "relations with other communities" (37), and "Christianity and Judaism" (52–54), there are gestures in the opposite direction. Nowhere in the text does Izetbegović propose an Islamic state in Bosnia-Herzegovina or indeed mention Bosnia-Herzegovina.

100. R. O. and D. M. S., "Presuda mimo suda," *Večernje novosti*, 29 June 2005; also T. S. and M. T., "Aligrudić: Ni dobra, ni tačna," *Danas*, 29 June 2005.

101. Unsigned (Tanjug), "Na Kosovu nije bilo genocida," *Večernje novosti*, 7 September 2001; also B. Radomirović, "Nije bilo genocida," *Politika*, 8 September 2001.

102. Branko Dragaš, "Zločin i kazna," *Svedok*, 21 June 2005. The term *genocidal people* appears frequently in the discourse on war crimes. It was raised during the reaction to the Gotovina and Markač verdicts in Croatia as well. As law it is utter nonsense: no such category exists, and no process exists for putting "peoples" in such a category, and no consequences exist for being put in this nonexistent category.

103. Dragoslav Rančić, "Srebrenica u Vašingtonu," *Politika*, 30 June 2005. The killings in Srebrenica were committed in July 1995, and Republika Srpska became an "international creation" in December 1995.

104. These were discussed in Chapter 6: Nataša Kandić of the Fund for Humanitarian Law, Biljana Kovačević-Vučo of the Lawyers' Committee for Human Rights, and Sonja Biserko of the Serbian Helsinki Committee. Also sometimes included in the attacks were Staša Zajović of the Women in Black and Borka Pavićević of the Center for Cultural Decontamination.

105. Quoted in Ljubiša Obradović, "Ratni radovi Tomislava Nikolića: (Ne)običan dobrovoljac," *Nezavisna svetlost*, 23 June 2005. See also Unsigned (Fonet and Beta),

"Šta je Toma Nikolić radio u Antinu," B92 vesti, 23 June 2005. Antin is a town in Slavonia in which there were armed clashes toward the end of 1991.

106. Unsigned, "Koliko su blizu Antin i Srebrenica," B92 vesti, 19 June 2005. The evidence suggests that the crime occurred toward the end of September or in early November 1991.

107. Ljubiša Obradović, "Ratni radovi Tomislava Nikolića: (Ne)običan dobrovoljac," *Nezavisna svetlost*, 23 June 2005.

108. Unsigned, "Ko je ubijao u Antinu?" B92 vesti, 17 June 2005.

109. Unsigned, "Krivična prijava protiv Nataše Kandić," B92 vesti, 23 June 2005.

110. Unsigned, "Nataša Kandić: Dokaze tražiti u KOS-u," B92 vesti, 19 June 2005.

111. Unsigned, "Lažljivica!" *Kurir*, 6 February 2009.

Chapter 8. Nonmoments: Milošević, Karadžić, Šešelj, and Mladić

1. Armatta (2010: 459–70) provides a chronology of events in the Milošević trial.

2. Milošević had an undergraduate degree in law but had never qualified as a practitioner of law nor engaged in the profession. Consistent with his declared refusal to acknowledge the authority of the Tribunal, he paid little attention to procedure or to rules of evidence, frequently preferring to use the courtroom as a television studio from which he could offer domestic audiences a set of arguments that were more rhetorical than legal.

3. Svetozar Vujačić would gain publicity again by representing Radovan Karadžić in his extradition hearing in 2008.

4. S. V., "CIA snajka," *Kurir*, 18 March 2006.

5. Both in *Večernje novosti*, 12 March 2006.

6. *Večernje novosti*, 12 March 2006, passim.

7. Milovan Brkić, "Kad slavuj utihne, vrane zagrakću," *Tabloid*, 16 March 2006.

8. Both letters are published in *Svedok*, 21 March 2006.

9. Armatta offers a summary of the investigation and findings (2010: 424–29); the results were duly reported in domestic media, e.g., unsigned (Beta), "Milošević nije otrovan," *Politika*, 18 March 2006.

10. V. Jokanović, "Merenje pulsa nacionalizma," *Politika*, 13 March 2006.

11. Srboljub Bogdanović, "Šunjanje oko Aleja," *NIN*, 16 March 2006.

12. Front page of *Blic*, 13 March 2006.

13. Responding to the obituary notice, psychologist and popular radio host Žikica Simić referred directly to the signers: "An obituary notice like this shows just how much we were pawns in a game which certain people occupying certain positions of power with certain psychological characteristics played among themselves, while we ordinary citizens were here to pay the price, often with our own lives. While Mladen Naletelić-Tuta and Ante Gotovina and Slobodan Milošević and Vojislav Šešelj played their games, many people's lives were played out into nothingness." Quoted in Dragoslav Grujić, "Posmrtne epistole," *Vreme* 793, 16 March 2006.

14. The notice was reproduced in D. Perić, "Čitulje i kontračitulje," *NIN*, 23 March 2006.

15. The obituary notice appeared in *Politika*, 17 March 2006.

16. The series, directed by Radivoje Andrić, was intended to use satire as a means of helping citizens to understand and overcome the discomfort associated with entering a new cultural and political milieu. As is often the case in such efforts (like the American series *All in the Family* in the 1970s, intended to combat bigotry by ridiculing it), the character of Mile became more a cultural hero than a figure of fun.

17. The editor of *Politika*, Ljiljana Smajlović, apologized for the notice and its "inappropriate, offensive tone which demonstrates oversight on our part and a lack of good taste." Lj. Smajlović, "Lažna čitulja," *Politika*, 18 March 2006; S. S. Rovčanin, "Obračun u čituljama," *Večernje novosti*, 18 March 2006.

18. Vesna Perović, "Krivica ne umire," *Danas*, 15 March 2006.

19. Željka Jevtić, "Rasturio i zemlju i porodicu," *Blic*, 19 March 2006.

20. Vl. J., "Gnev i uzdržanost," *Politika*, 12 March 2006.

21. Unsigned, "Milošević nije žrtva," *Svedok*, 14 March 2006.

22. Quoted in D. Spalović, "Bogdanović: Nije zaslužni gradjanin," *Politika*, 14 March 2006.

23. Dragan Jovanović, "Moskva suzama ne veruje," *NIN*, 23 March 2006; Biljana Baković, "Poslednji miting za Miloševića," *Politika*, 19 March 2006; unsigned, "Milošević buried in his home town," BBC News, 18 March 2006.

24. Jelena (9), Dragiša (10), and Stefan (11) Tmušić were in the custody of their mother Ana Tmušić at the time of the rally. Their father Zoran Tmušić did not have the mother's consent to bring them to the site or to put them on costumed display. Jelena Grujić, "Deca u stroju," *Vreme* 794, 23 March 2006.

25. Miloš Vasić, "Generali atamani," *Vreme* 794, 23 March 2006.

26. Unsigned, "Ministarstvo odbrane: Može samo u civilu," *Blic*, 19 March 2006.

27. N. D., "Pamtiće ga zahvalna Srbija," *Danas*, 20 March 2006.

28. Unsigned, "Šešelj: Danas, dragi Slobo, ne postoji niko tužniji od mene," *Kurir*, 19 March 2006.

29. Unsigned, "Nisu uspeli da ga slome, zato su ga ubili," *Svedok*, 21 March 2006. The referential universe in Marković's speech is telling. Saying no to a superpower was a legendary quality of Tito, establishing his reputation for independence in 1948. And there is a conscious effort to keep alive the myth that Milošević was accused of causing wars rather than committing crimes.

30. N. D., "Pamtiće ga zahvalna Srbija," *Danas*, 20 March 2006.

31. Quoted in Unsigned, "Miloševićevim žrtvama," *Borba*, 20 March 2006.

32. Unsigned, "Počast Miloševićevim žrtvama."

33. Kenarov (2006).

34. SPS deputy leader Ivica Dačić, quoted in B. Baković, "Dačić: Milošević ubijen," *Politika*, 12 March 2006.

35. Rade Stanić, "Uvod u drugi život Slobodana Miloševića," *Europa*, 16 March 2006.

36. Dragoljub Žarković. "148 sati sahrana," *Vreme* 793, 17 March 2006.

37. Unsigned, "Man drives stake in grave of Slobodan Milošević," dalje.com, http://dalje.com/en-world/man-drives-stake-in-grave-of-slobodan-milosevic/24459. Novelist and literary theorist Tomislav Longinović (1995) draws a clear association between the emergence of the vampire legend into global consciousness and the rise of national states. Bram Stoker's iconic vampire was a local powerholder, and his novel that popularized the previously local cultural figure was simultaneous with the establishment of national states in the region. Like national states, vampires are representative of people, emerging from them, and parasitic upon them, exercising power over them and surviving off their resources.

38. I am not certain precisely when the use of this rhetorical figure begins, but can affirm that it is a standard device used for describing the post-2000 governments by far-right parties like the Serbian Radical Party (SRS) and in commentary journals like *Nova Srpska Politička Misao* and *Novi Standard*, which support similar political actors and share authors.

39. In the reports of some international journalists much is made of the fact that T-shirts can be found on sale with images of Karadžić and Mladić. While this is the case, it is also the case that T-shirts are offered for sale with a wide variety of other images, most of which are not interpreted as constitutive of the character of the buyer, seller, or wearer.

40. Luka Karadžić had his own legal history: after a trial that stretched out for years due to the consistent efforts of his attorneys to delay proceedings, he was finally convicted, in 2011, of causing the death of a pedestrian while driving his Mercedes Benz in an intoxicated state.

41. V. Z. C., "Karadžić uzeo identitet poginulog rezerviste," *Blic*, 24 July 2008.

42. Unsigned (attributed to B92 and Beta), "Karadžić general bioenergetike," B92 vesti, 24 July 2008.

43. H. A. and Ig. M., "Karadžićevi savjeti: Kod problema sa seksom najbolja je terapija u paru," Index.hr (a Croatian web portal), 22 July 2008.

44. Index.hr reproduced Karadžić's articles for *Zdrav život*.

45. The ethnomusicologists Milman Parry and Albert Lord had extensively researched ancient oral forms of music and storytelling in the Balkans, with the research summarized in Lord's enormously influential (1960) book. The form is considered in the region to be a repository of folk and national legend, and to have been vital in the construction and maintenance of regional and national traditions. The more recent uses of the genre to celebrate and magnify contemporary political events and figures have been documented by a number of researchers, including Čolović (2000, 2011) and Halili (2010).

46. Tamara Marković-Subota, "Guslao u 'Ludoj kući' ispod svoje slike," *Blic*, 23 July 2008.

47. Unsigned (attributed to B92), "Karadžićeva potreba za pažnjom," B92 vesti, 23 July 2008. The distance diagnosis is attributed to the psychiatrist and criminologist Leposava Kron.

48. Dejan Kožul, "Gospodar života i smrti: Velika Karadžićeva prevara," *e-Novine*, 24 July 2008.

49. Unsigned (attributed to B92, Fonet, Beta, and Tanjug), "Miting završen, nema šetnje," B92 vesti, 29 July 2008.

50. Željka Jevtić, "Gubitnici izbora koriste Karadžića kako bi opstali," *Blic*, 30 July 2008.

51. Unsigned (attributed to B92), "Podnete krivične prijave protiv 45 lica," B92 vesti, 29 April 2003.

52. The distinction was established in the verdict of the Čelebići case (IT-96–21) in 2001, and as a contribution to the doctrine of command responsibility has proved to be useful subsequently, particularly considering that in conflicts with a high degree of participation by informal and paramilitary groups legal chains of command might not always apply.

53. *The Prosecutor of the Tribunal Against Vojislav Šešelj, Third Amended Indictment* (IT-02–67-T), 7 December 2007, paragraph 5.

54. The argument was made by Šešelj himself; see Unsigned, "Šešelj: Sude mi za verbalni delikt," *Danas*, 11 July 2007.

55. Although presented as traditional, the interpretation of the practice of self-representation as a right is relatively new. It was established by the U.S. Supreme Court in the 1975 *Faretta v. California* decision, adopted as the basis for extending the privilege to Slobodan Milošević in his trial. Prior to 1975, the general direction of law had been moving in the opposite direction, toward ensuring that all criminal defendants be represented by counsel. In the common law tradition the practice of clients representing themselves was either a result of necessity—trained attorneys were rare and expensive—or adopted as a punitive measure to restrict defendants' ability to contest evidence and increase the probability of obtaining a conviction. Since the *Faretta* decision, most predictions of its critics have been borne out in practice: courts have faced insurmountable procedural difficulties, defendants have suffered from their lack of understanding of law and procedure, the legitimacy of legal processes has been undermined, courtrooms have been used as fora for abuse and intimidation, and insane defendants have been permitted to damage themselves. See Cerruti (2009).

56. Although Vojislav Šešelj did have himself appointed a professor of the Faculty of Law of the University of Belgrade in 2000, this was a display of political power that did not magically transform him into either a lawyer or an academic.

57. Quoted in Adrienne N, "Šešelj revels in court theatrics," *Institute for War and Peace Reporting*, 4 November 2005.

58. Milošević trial transcript, 6 September 2005, pp. 43798–99.

59. The demand that Šešelj made at his arraignment to receive translations only in Serbian, which he justified by the claim that he could not understand Croatian or Bosnian, was quickly declined by the trial chamber. See "Prosecutor v. Vojislav Šešelj: Order on the Translation of Documents," 6 March 2003, available at the ICTY web site, http://www.icty.org/x/cases/seselj/tord/en/030306.htm.

60. Šešelj trial transcript, 17 February 2004, 210–11.

61. Vasić (2005) traced the source of leaked information that Šešelj frequently produced with great fanfare in the media and which comprise most of the content of his published books directly to connections in the security services.

62. The number of publications authored by Šešelj is constantly increasing. These books are generally not available in bookstores and are distributed by the Serbian Radical Party. The content of the books rarely corresponds to the titles.

63. Šešelj was briefly employed in two instances at the Faculty of Political Sciences of the University of Sarajevo between 1979 and 1982, and later moved to the Institute for Social Research, but the only time he held the rank of professor was in his brief appointment to the Faculty of Law in Belgrade in 2000, an appointment that cannot be attributed to his academic credentials.

64. D. Dž, "ICTY Approves Funding for Vojislav Šešelj Defense," *Balkan Investigative Reporting Network Justice Report*, 18 May 2011.

65. Although rule 98 bis allows for the possibility of a summary acquittal, this has not been the outcome in any case so far. However, in a number of cases the trial chamber has used the 98 bis ruling to eliminate some charges from the indictment prior to the presentation of the defense.

66. Viktor Marković, "Haški tribunal osudio sebe na Šešelja," Njuz.net, http://www.njuz.net/haski-tribunal-osudio-sebe-na-seselja/, 4 May 2011.

67. For some reason there was no shortage of internationals willing to praise Mladić publicly, whether sincerely meant or done for strategic reasons. If the praise was delivered for strategic reasons, the strategy succeeded on the *New York Times* correspondent David Binder, who in a polemic on Mladić (in late 1995!) described him as "a superb professional." David Binder, "The Madness of General Mladić" (letter), *New York Review of Books*, 21 December 1995.

68. Unsigned (attributed to *Danas*), "Mladića penzionisao Koštunica," B92 vesti, 8 June 2011. The members of the Supreme Defense Council were the presidents of the federal state and of its two constituent republics, the federal prime minister and defense minister, and the head of the military staff. Without entering into the question whether it was unusual for a council of this type to make basic personnel decisions, in order to issue an order for Mladić to retire the council members would have to have known there was a need for such an order to be issued.

69. Unsigned, "Mladića ispitati o slučaju Topčider," B92 vesti, 27 May 2011.

70. Unsigned, "Transkripti Wikileaksa: Vlasti u Srbiji su sve do 2009. znale gdje su Mladić i Hadžić!" *Jutarnji list*, 28 May 2001; Drago Hedl, "Zoran Mijatović: Ja sam

uhapsio Miloševića. Mladića smo mogli imati isti dan. Točno smo znali tko ga i gdje štiti!," *Jutarnji list*, 29 May 2011.

71. Ana Lalić, "Mladić se krio i u ženskom manastiru u Zrenjaninu," *Blic*, 29 May 2011.

72. Unsigned (attributed to B92), "Mladićevo psihičko stanje gore," B92 vesti, 29 May 2011.

73. A representative example from the final day of his domestic custody can be seen in Unsigned, "Mladić u Hagu—uručena mu optužnica," *Večernje novosti*, 31 May 2011; and Emina Radosavlević and Milena Marković, "Mladić: Neću se živ vratiti," *Večernje novosti*, 31 May 2011.

74. Unsigned (attributed to Tanjug), "Vekarić: Mladić loše, ali veoma komunikativan," *Kurir*, 26 May 2011.

75. Branislav Jelić, O jagodama i tudjoj krvi," *e-Novine*, 30 May 2011.

76. The occasional tabloid story appears, suggesting that the death of Ana Mladić was not a suicide. The source of such stories appears to be Mladić's biographer Ljiljana Bulatović.

77. Miloš Vasić, "Mladićevo hapšenje i šta dalje," *Vreme* 1064, 26 May 2011.

78. Unsigned, "Sneki, samo ovako pročitaj!" *e-Novine*, 3 June 2011. The slip of paper with the phonetic statement written on it might be falsified, but its text and the rendering of the minister's pronunciation are faithful to the filmed records of her announcement.

79. Alan Pejković, "Ratkojada," *Peščanik*, 27 May 2011.

80. D. Petrović and Lj. Bukvić, "Meštani ogorčeni, Lazarevo postaje Mladićevo," *Danas*, 26 May 2011.

81. Violence at political events that attracted crowds from the nationalist right had become a regular occurrence following a large public meeting to protest the declaration of independence by Kosovo in February 2008, and a riot to intimidate the participants in a gay pride rally in October 2010.

82. The head of the party formed by people who had deserted SRS, Tomislav Nikolić, gave a statement supporting the arrest and extradition as a legal obligation of Serbia. Unsigned (attributed to Tanjug), "Nikolić: Hapšenje Mladića bila obaveza Srbije," *Blic*, 29 May 2011. The reading of the letter, which was inflammatory in tone, by a minor led to (rhetorical but not legal) accusations of child abuse. Much of the text of the letter is reproduced in Unsigned (attributed to Beta), "Šešelj: Tadić će odgovarati," B92 vesti, 29 May 2011.

83. Unsigned (attributed to B92 and Beta), "Miting SRS završen u neredima," B92 vesti, 29 May 2011.

84. Marija Maleš, "Privedeno 179 demonstranata, povredjeno 11 gradjana i 32 policajca," *Blic*, 30 May 2011.

85. Unsigned (attributed to Beta), "SRS: Vlast treba da saopšti ko je organizovao nerede," *Blic*, 30 May 2011.

86. As of the time of writing, no request has been made and consequently no decision has been taken on the joinder of the trials.

87. Unsigned, "Mladić će probati da opovrgne sve," B92 vesti, 5 June 2011.

88. As observed in Chapter 4, ICJ did not find in its decision that Serbia was not implicated in the Srebrenica genocide, but rather that a strict interpretation of the Genocide Convention requires demonstrating a more extensive level of command and control than the plaintiffs were able to establish.

89. The interview was republished by the electronic magazine *e-Novine* as Tamara Nikčević, "Mladić je morao izvršiti samoubistvo," *e-Novine*, 23 June 2011.

90. Unsigned (attributed to Press), "Mladić odigrao partiju šaha sa Šešeljem a Gotovina mu pravi škampe?" *Nezavisne novine*, 14 June 2011.

91. Alternatively, D. Stojanović (2010) has argued that a pattern exists in the political history of Serbia by which society and culture develop more quickly than the state, which responds by taking measures to weaken them.

92. Durkheim (1982).

93. Osiel (2009); Naomi Roht-Arriaza, "The Need for Moral Reconstruction in the Wake of Past Human Rights Violations: An Interview with José Zalaquett," in Hesse and Post (eds.) (1999).

94. Durkheim (1951).

Chapter 9. Politics and Culture in Approaching the Past

1. The special prosecutor for organized crime announced a reopening of the investigation in December 2010. See Zoran Glavonjić, "Počela istraga političke pozadine ubistva Djindjića," Radio Slobodna Evropa, 7 December 2010.

2. A minor political scuffle followed the special prosecutor's announcement that former prime minister Vojislav Koštunica would be called upon to make a statement, and Koštunica's announcement that he would refuse a call to make one. Unsigned (attributed to Beta), "Koštunica negirao povezanost sa pozadinom ubistva Djindjića," *Politika*, 12 March 2011.

3. For details, see unsigned, "Jocić negira krivicu," Radio-televizija Srbije, 20 April 2010.

4. Council of Europe Parliamentary Assembly (2011).

5. The Trial Chamber judgment in case IT-06–90 (Operation Storm) was handed down on 15 April 2011.

6. Merčep was indicted for killings of civilians in June 2011. See Unsigned (attributed to Hina), "Mučni detalji optužnice: Merčep optužen i za ubojstvo porodice Zec," *Nacional*, 10 June 2011.

7. Indrit Krasniqi, Iliyas Khalid, and Quam Ogumbiyi received life sentences in the February 2011 attack (although each was already serving a sentence for murder). The presiding judge, Richard Henriques, declared in handing down the sentence that he had "no doubt what you intended was an act of revenge for those crimes." Unsigned, "Radislav Krstić Wakefield Jail Attackers Get Life Terms," BBC News, 21

February 2011; Martin Wainwright, "Srebrenica General's Attackers Get Life for Revenge Stabbing in Prison," *The Guardian*, 21 February 2011.

8. Unsigned, "Bosnia, Serbia and Europe: Dragging Up the Past," *The Economist*, 2 March 2010; Marija Antunović, "Divjak Arrest Exposes Balkan Prosecutors' Failings," *Institute for War and Peace Reporting* 683, 15 March 2011.

9. On 15 May 1992 an attack was staged on the Fifteenth Motorized Brigade of JNA as it was withdrawing from Tuzla. The incident probably resulted in about 50 deaths and 44 injuries, though the precise number of victims has not been established. One Bosnian officer, Ilija Jurišić, was charged with involvement in the attack by Serbian prosecutors. He was convicted in 2009 and his conviction was reversed on appeal in 2010.

10. Probably the best publicized of these initiatives was the Truth and Reconciliation Commission (TRC), formed after the departure from power of the apartheid regime in South Africa. Priscilla Hayner (2001, 2010) compares forty such initiatives.

11. See the discussion in Bass (2001), especially chap. 5. A suggestion as to the lack of interest in pursuing such cases might be given by the story of the arrest of Adolf Eichmann, who would later be regarded as a symbol for organized state violence. Information about his location arrived from private investigators to Fritz Bauer, attorney general of the state of Hesse in West Germany. Sensing that prosecution in German courts would probably encounter disinterest and obstruction, Bauer slipped information to the Israeli Foreign Ministry—which was also not interested. The operation to kidnap the fugitive went into action only after Bauer felt compelled to threaten Israeli services with embarrassment for failing to act (Cesarini 2004: 222–36).

12. Ernst Renan, "What Is a Nation?" The text is from a lecture delivered in Paris in 1882 and has been republished widely since, including in Eley and Suny (eds.) (1996: 41–55).

13. Stuart Hall, "The Question of Cultural Identity," in Hall et al. (eds.) (1996: 616).

14. Quoted in Rodriguez Molas (1984: 13). The translation from the Spanish is mine.

15. For an especially provocative account, see Stannard (1992).

16. See Hirsch (2002). The commission report and recommendations are available at http://www.tulsareparations.org/.

17. Under international pressure, Turkish prosecutors abandoned a case against the celebrated novelist Orhan Pamuk for violating article 301 of the Turkish penal code, which forbids insults to state institutions or national identity. However, similar charges were not withdrawn in cases brought against less well known people. Ian Traynor, "Turkey Draws Back from Prosecuting Outspoken Novelist," *The Guardian*, 23 January 2006; Unsigned, "Court Drops Turkish Writer's Case," BBC News, 23 January 2006.

18. The much-cited and much-maligned phrase "new world order" was first introduced in its contemporary context by George H. W. Bush in an address before

the U.S. Congress on 11 September 1990. Although it was offered without a clear set of specific referents, it has been widely understood to refer to a (never explicitly proposed) set of new foundations for global order in the aftermath of the Cold War. While some observers saw in it a reference to the rising prominence of the rule of law as a basis for order, others regard it more dismissively as a pretext for the assertion of global power by the United States.

19. A similar argument in relation to the war in Vietnam was proposed by Hallin (1989), though this argument referred specifically to the effect of television news coverage on the American public. Hallin argued that over time, particularly in the last phases of the war when public support had already largely weakened, regular exposure to nonmythologized and discouraging details such as casualties accelerated the collapse of official narratives justifying involvement in the war.

20. A detailed presentation of the argument that commitment to human rights remains largely on the level of rhetoric is offered by Mertus (2004).

21. As of the date of writing, the most recent indictment filed by ICC is against Libyan leader Muammar Khadafy, against whom NATO forces had been operating a military campaign for three months.

22. These questions have been treated extensively in Lamont (2010); Nettelfield (2010); Peskin (2008); and Subotić (2009).

23. I described the contours of this conflict in greater detail in Gordy (2004).

24. One of the influential works of social research during the period carried the title *The Destruction of Society* (Lazić et al. 1994). Some later theorists used a more dramatic term, "sociocide" (Turza 2003; Radenović 2008).

25. The center was founded in January 1995 "as a gathering site for the antiwar campaign and for intellectual and artistic platforms opposed to the politics of terror on the territory of the former Yugoslavia" and remains in continuous operation.

26. For example, according to the Helsinki Committee for Human Rights in Bosnia-Herzegovina, in 2008 there were still 15,000 people unaccounted for from the conflict. Helsinki Committee for Human Rights in Bosnia-Herzegovina, *NGO Progress Report on the Follow-Up of the Concluding Observations*, CCPR/C/BH/CO/1, 5 October 2008.

27. This need is of course not shared by perpetrators or people associated with them, unless the argument is applied to crimes committed by people whose activity was commanded by an opposing side.

28. There is of course always an implicit conflict between the need for guilty parties to be punished and the need for stories to be told. In a criminal trial, the accused has little motivation to reveal more than is absolutely necessary, while victims are encouraged to share not their entire stories but only those elements that have a direct bearing on establishing guilt or innocence. Narrative testimony is potentially much fuller, but for perpetrators in particular there is not much reason for them to tell their stories unless they are offered something—like protection from revenge or immunity from prosecution—in return.

29. An ambitious effort to resolve the dilemma of translation between the inter-personal and social levels of analysis is offered by Petrović (2010). In this case, how-ever, the empirical discussion moves quickly toward factors that can be measured, such as collective perceptions and social stereotypes. Direct application of therapeutic concepts to abstractions like the health of the collective remain, as they must, on the level of analogy.

30. I have been peripherally involved in the REKOM campaign as an academic consultant at some of their events. Full disclosure: for my participation, I received a canvas tote bag for shopping, which is purple and very handy.

31. The basic documents for the REKOM initiative, including the proposed stat-ute of the commission, are available at http://www.zarekom.org/documents/index .en.html.

32. The most eclectic attack on REKOM I have seen described it as a "British-Serbian espionage scam." Tomislav Jelić, "REKOM: Još jedna britansko-srpska špijunska podvala," *Lika Online*, 28 June 2011.

33. Nenad Jovanović, "Podrška REKOM-u najmanja u Hrvatskoj," *Novosti*, 24 June 2011.

34. For example, F. Vele, "Branko Todorović o podvali Nataše Kandić: REKOM je nanio veliku štetu pomirenju u regionu," *Dvevni avaz*, 29 June 2011.

35. The transcripts are published in Koalicija za REKOM (2011).

36. The film was released in 2010. I have in fact not seen it; just reading about it horrifies me.

37. Geoffrey MacNab, "Serbian Film: Is This the Nastiest Film Ever Made?" *The Independent*, 19 November 2010. It may be worth noting that the review was not negative, but praised the boldness and importance of the artists' vision. A more unqualified condemnation is offered by David Cox, "Serbian Film: When Allegory Gets Nasty," *The Guardian*, 13 December 2010.

38. Unsigned, "'Srpski film' pred zabranom?" B92 vesti, 30 September 2010.

39. Unsigned "Španija: Zabrana za 'Srpski film'" B92 vesti, 5 November 2010.

40. The film was also excluded from the Bournemouth film festival on the ground that it was "vile and disgusting." Fiona Pendlebury, "Bournemouth film festival pulls 'vile' movie," *Bournemouth Echo*, 26 October 2010.

41. Fiona Bailey, "A Serbian film Is 'Most Cut' Movie in 16 Years," BBC News, 26 November 2010.

42. Srdjan Spasojević, "Director's Statement," on the UK promotional web site for *A Serbian Film*, http://www.aserbianfilm.co.uk/statement.html.

43. Spasojević, "Director's Statement."

44. Bailey, "A Serbian Film Is 'Most Cut' Movie in 16 Years."

45. Damir Pilić, "Srpski Film: Bebu je silovao Slobo," *Slobodna Dalmacija*, 12 December 2010.

46. Štiks (2006). In 2010 the novel was adapted to a theatre performance by the Yugoslav Drama Theatre (JDP) in Belgrade in collaboration with the MESS Theater Festival in Sarajevo.

47. The film was released in 2006, and received wide international distribution and several awards.

48. The film was released in 2003, with a screenplay adapted from Pavičić's (1997) novel.

49. The film was released in 2001, and received an Academy Award.

50. The film was released in 2004, with a screenplay by Filip David.

51. The term is used to refer to the institutions of the European Union, an elite-led project with uncertain popular support and weak structures of accountability. Similarly in Serbia, the point is made that democratic institutions, while they exist formally, do not function as important decisions are made informally in the leaderships of political parties rather than formally in representative institutions. See Ivana Masti-lović Jasnić, "Srbija je poslednja partijska država u Evropi" (interview with Ognjen Pribićević), *Blic*, 2 July 2011.

Bibliography

Print and Electronic Periodicals

Much of the research conducted for this study involved simply following the daily news and then seeking more information about particular topics as they emerged. The Internet made it relatively easy to follow a particular number of periodicals. Other periodicals that are not available online I was able to follow more intermittently, or when I was in places where they were sold. Some of the periodicals cited in the text are ones that do not maintain an online presence, or were published for a period and then ceased. The material cited from those was found during a period spent in the archive of the newspaper *Večernje novosti* in 2006.

Alternative Information Network	www.aimpress.ch (no longer available)
Blic	www.blic.rs
B92	www.b92.net
Borba	(published until 2009)
Danas	www.danas.rs
Dnevnik	www.dnevnik.rs
e-Novine	www.e-novine.com
Glas javnosti	www.glas-javnosti.rs/
Helsinška povelja	www.helsinki.org.rs
Index	www.index.hr
Institute for War and Peace Reporting	www.iwpr.net
NIN	www.nin.co.rs/
Nova srpska politička misao	www.nspm.rs
Politika	www.politika.rs
Radio Slobodna Evropa	www.slobodnaevropa.org
Republika	www.republika.co.rs/
Sense News Agency	www.sense-agency.com
Večernje novosti	www.novosti.rs
Vreme	www.vreme.com

Articles

Bantekas, Ilias. 1999. "The Contemporary Law of Superior Responsibility." *American Journal of International Law* 93, 3.

Bilder, Richard. 2005–2006. "The Role of Apology in International Law and Diplomacy." *Virginia Journal of International Law* 46.

Borneman, John. 2005. "Public Apologies as Performative Redress." *SAIS Review* 25, 2.

Budding, Audrey Helfant. 1997. "Yugoslavs into Serbs: Serbian National Identity, 1961–1971." *Nationalities Papers* 25, 3.

Cerruti, Eugene. 2009. "Self-Representation in the International Arena: Removing a False Right of Spectacle." *Georgetown Journal of International Law* 40.

Delpla, Isabelle. 2007. "In the Midst of Injustice: The ICTY from the Perspective of Some Victims' Associations." In Bougarel, Helms, and Duijzings (eds.), (2007).

Dimitrijević, Nenad. 2000. "Prošlost, odgovornost, budućnost." *Reč* 57, 3.

Dimitrijević, Vojin. 2003. "Two Assumptions of the Rejection of Responsibility: Denial of the Act and Denial of the Rule." *Columbia International Affairs Online*.

Dulić, Tomislav. 2009. "Mapping Out the 'Wasteland': Testimonies from the Serbian Commissariat for Refugees in the Service of Tudjman's Revisionism." *Holocaust and Genocide Studies* 23, 2.

Elster, Jon. 2006. "Redemption for Wrongdoing: The Fate of Collaborators After 1945." *Journal of Conflict Resolution* 50, 3.

Fein, Helen. 2005. "Defining Genocide as a Sociological Concept." In Simone Gigliotti and Berel Lang, eds., *The Holocaust: A Reader*. Contemporary Debates in Philosophy. Oxford: Blackwell.

Feldman, Allen. 1994. "On Cultural Anasthaesia: From Desert Storm to Rodney King." *American Ethnologist* 21, 2.

Gojković, Drinka. 2000. "Budućnost u trouglu." *Reč* 57, 2.

Gordy, Eric. 2003. "Accounting for a Violent Past, by Means Other Than Legal." *Journal of Southeast European and Black Sea Studies* 3, 1.

———. 2004. "Serbia After Djindjić: War Crimes, Organized Crime, and Trust in Public Institutions." *Problems of Post-Communism* 51, 3.

Greenberg, Jessica. 2006. "Goodbye Serbian Kennedy: Zoran Djindjić and the New Democratic Masculinity in Serbia." *East European Politics and Societies* 20, 1.

Harff, Barbara, and Ted Gurr. 1988. "Toward Empirical Theory of Genocides and Politicides: Identification and Measurement of Cases Since 1945." *International Studies Quarterly* 32.

Ilić, Dejan. 2005. "Jugoslavenska komisija za istinu i pomirenje, 2001–?" *Reč* 73, 19.

Jokić, Alekasandar. 2004. "Genocidalism." *Journal of Ethics* 8, 3.

Kenarov, Dimiter. 2006. "The Little Box That Contains the World: Serbia After the Death of Milošević." *Virginia Quarterly Review* 82, 3.

McMahon, Patrice, and David Forsythe. 2008. "The ICTY's Impact on Serbia: Judicial Romanticism Meets Network Politics." *Human Rights Quarterly* 30, 2.

Mertus, Julie. 2008. "When Adding Women Matters: Women's Participation in the ICTY." *Seton Hall Law Review* 38.

Miller, Nicholas. 1999. "The Nonconformists: Dobrica Ćosić and Mića Popović Envision Serbia." *Slavic Review* 58, 3.

Obradović-Wochnik, Jelena. 2009. "Knowledge, Acknowledgement, and Denial in Serbia's Responses to the Srebrenica Massacre." *Journal of Contemporary European Studies* 17, 1.

Peskin, Victor. 2005. "Beyond Victor's Justice? The Challenge of Prosecuting the Winners at the International Criminal Tribunals for the Former Yugoslavia and Rwanda." *Journal of Human Rights* 4, 2.

———. 2009a. "Caution and Confrontation in the International Criminal Court's Pursuit of Accountability in Uganda and Sudan." *Human Rights Quarterly* 31, 3.

———. 2009b. "The International Criminal Court, the Security Council, and the Politics of Impunity in Darfur." *Genocide Studies and Prevention* 4, 3.

Peskin, Victor, and Mieczyslaw Boduszynski. 2003. "International Justice and Domestic Politics: Post-Tudjman Croatia and the International Criminal Tribunal for the Former Yugoslavia." *Europe-Asia Studies* 55, 7.

Radojičić, Mirjana. 2008. "Ex-jugoslovenski slučaj i borba za njegovu interpretaciju—Primer nevladinih organizacija Srbije." *Sociološki pregled* 42, 2.

Radenović, Sandra. 2008. "Vrednosti i život." *Republika* 432–33.

Roht-Arriaza, Naomi, and Lauren Gibson. 1998. "The Developing Jurisprudence on Amnesty." *Human Rights Quarterly* 20, 4.

Subotić, Jelena. 2009. "The Paradox of International Justice Compliance." *International Journal of Transitional Justice* 3, 3.

Turza, Karel. 2003. "On Modernity in General and on the Main Obstacles to Modernity in Serbia in the 20th Century and Afterwards." *Sociologija* 45, 2.

Vukomanović, Milan. 2008. "The Serbian Orthodox Church as a Political Actor in the Aftermath of October 5, 2000." *Politics and Religion* 1.

Wald, Patricia M. 2002. "Note from the Field: Dealing with Witnesses in War Crime Trials: Lessons from the Yugoslav Tribunal." *Yale Human Rights and Development Law Journal* 5.

Wyeneth, Robert. 2001. "The Power of Apology and the Process of Historical Reconciliation." *Public Historian* 23, 3.

Books

Adamic, Louis. 1934. *The Native's Return.* New York: Harper and Brothers.

Andreopoulos, George, ed. 1997. *Genocide: Conceptual and Historical Dimensions.* Philadelphia: University of Pennsylvania Press.

Antonić, Slobodan, ed. 2003. *Nacija u strujama prošlosti: Ogledi o održivosti demokratije u Srbiji.* Belgrade: Čigoja štampa.

Anzulović, Branimir. 1999. *Heavenly Serbia: From Myth to Genocide.* New York: New York University Press.

Arendt, Hannah. 1963. *Eichmann in Jerusalem: A Report on the Banality of Evil.* New York: Viking.

———. 1966. *The Origins of Totalitarianism.* New York: Harcourt Brace.

Armatta, Judith. 2010. *Twilight of Impunity: The War Crimes Trial of Slobodan Milošević.* Durham, N.C.: Duke University Press.

Arsenijević, Vladimir. 2000. *Meksiko: Ratni dnevnik.* Beograd: Rende.

Baćević, Ljiljana, et al. 2003. *Promene vrednosti i tranzicija u Srbiji: Pogled u budućnost.* Beograd: Institut društvenih nauka.

Banac, Ivo. 1989. *With Stalin Against Tito: Cominformist Splits in Yugoslav Communism.* Ithaca, N.Y.: Cornell University Press.

Barkan, Elazar. 2000. *The Guilt of Nations: Restitution and Negotiating Historical Injustices.* New York: Norton.

Barkan, Elazar, and Alexander Karn, eds. 2006. *Taking Wrongs Seriously: Apologies and Reconciliation.* Stanford, Calif.: Stanford University Press.

Bass, Gary J. 2001. *Stay the Hand of Vengeance: The Politics of War Crimes Tribunals.* Princeton, N.J.: Princeton University Press.

Bieber, Florian, and Carsten Wieland, eds. 2005. *Facing the Past, Facing the Future: Confronting Ethnicity and Conflict in Bosnia and Former Yugoslavia.* Ravenna: Longo Editore.

Blom, J. C. H. et al. 2002. *Srebrenica: Reconstruction, Background, Consequences of the Fall of a Safe Area.* Amsterdam: Netherlands Institute for War Documentation.

Borejn, Aleks (Alex Boraine), and Dženet Levi (Janet Levy). 2000. *Zalečenje nacije?* Trans. Vanja Savić. Beograd: Samizdat FreeB92.

Borejn, Aleks (Alex Boraine), Dženet Levi (Janet Levy), and Ronel Šefer (Ronel Scheffer), eds. 2000. *Suočavanje s prošlošću: Istina i pomirenje u Južnoj Africi.* Trans. G. Dimitrijević. Beograd: Samizdat FreeB92.

Bosnia and Herzegovina, Republic of Srpska, the Republic of Srpska Government Commission for Investigation of the Events in and Around Srebrenica Between 10th and 19th July 1995. 2004a. *Report from the Commission for Investigation of the Events in and Around Srebrenica Between 10th and 19th July 1995.* Banja Luka.

———. 2004b. *Addendum to the Report of the 11th June 2004 on the Events in and Around Srebrenica Between 10th and 19th July 1995.* Banja Luka.

Bougarel, Xavier. 2004. *Bosna: Anatomija rata.* Trans. J. Stakić. Beograd: Fabrika knjiga.

Bougarel, Xavier, Elissa Helms, and Ger Duijzings, eds. 2007. *The New Bosnian Mosaic: Identities, Memories, and Moral Claims in a Post-War Society.* Farnham: Ashgate.

Browning, Christopher R. 1992. *Ordinary Men: Reserve Police Battalion 101 and the Final Solution in Poland.* New York: HarperPerennial.

Brunborg, Helge, and Henrik Udal. 2000. *Report on the Number of Missing and Dead from Srebrenica.* The Hague: ICTY.

Bujošević, Dragan, and Ivan Radovanović. 2001. *5. Oktobar: Dvadeset četiri sata prevrata.* Beograd: Medija Centar.

Bulatović, Ljiljana. 1996. *General Mladić.* Beograd: Nova Evropa.

———. 2002. *Radovan.* Beograd: Evro.

———. 2010. *Raport komandantu.* Beograd: Udruženje pisaca Poeta.

Byford, Jovan. 2005. *Potiskivanje i poricanje antisemitizma.* Beograd: Helsinški odbor za ljudska prava u Srbiji.

———. 2006. *Teorija zavere: Srbija protiv "novog svetskog poretka."* Beograd: Dosije.

Campbell, David. 1998. *National Deconstruction: Violence, Identity, and Justice in Bosnia.* Minneapolis: University of Minnesota Press.

Cesarini, David. 2004. *Becoming Eichmann: Rethinking the Life, Crimes and Trial of a "Desk Murderer".* London: DaCapo.

Čavoški, Kosta. 1995. *Na rubovima srpstva: Srpsko pitanje danas.* Beograd: Tersit.

———2002. *Presudivanje istoriji u Hagu.* Beograd: Hilandarski fond.

———. 2005. *Okupacija.* Novi Sad: Orpheus.

———. 2007. *Hag protiv pravde.* Beograd: Beoknjiga.

Charny, Israel W., ed. 1984. *Toward the Understanding and Prevention of Genocide: Proceedings of the International Conference on the Holocaust and Genocide.* Boulder, Colo.: Westview Press.

Chirot, Daniel, and Clark McCauley. 2006. *Why Not Kill Them All? The Logic and Prevention of Mass Political Murder.* Princeton, N.J.: Princeton University Press.

Cohen, Lenard, and Jasna Dragović-Soso, eds. 2008. *State Collapse in Southeastern Europe: New Perspectives on Yugoslavia's Disintegration.* West Lafayette, Ind.: Purdue University Press, 2008.

Cohen, Stanley. 2001. *States of Denial: Knowing About Atrocities and Suffering.* Cambridge: Polity Press.

Čolović, Ivan. 2000. *Divlja književnost: Etnolingvističko proučavanje paraliterature.* Beograd: XX vek, 2000.

———. 2011. *The Balkans: The Terror of Culture.* Trans. V. Arandjelović. Baden-Baden: Nomos.

Connerton, Paul. 1989. *How Societies Remember.* Cambridge: Cambridge University Press

Council of Europe Parliamentary Assembly. 2011. *Investigation of Allegations of Inhuman Treatment of People and Illicit Trafficking in Human Organs in Kosovo.* Resolution 1782.

Cruvellier, Thierry, and Marta Valiñas. 2006. *Croatia: Selected Developments in Transitional Justice.* New York: International Center for Transitional Justice Occasional Paper Series.

Čupić, Čedomir. 2001. *Politika i zlo.* Beograd: Čigoja štampa.

Cvetković, Vladimir, ed. 2002. *Rekonstrukcija institucija: Godina dana tranzicija u Srbiji.* Beograd: Institut za folozofiju i društvenu teoriju.

Deák, István, Jan T. Gross, and Tony Judt, eds. 2000. *The Politics of Retribution in Europe: World War II and Its Aftermath*. Princeton, N.J.: Princeton University Press.

Del Ponte, Carla. 2008. *La caccia: Io e i criminali di guerra*. Milano: Feltrinelli.

Deretić, Jovan. 1983. *Istorija srpske književnosti*. Beograd: Nolit.

Dimić, Ljubodrag, ed. 2005. *Srbija 1804–2004: Tri vidjenja ili poziv na dijalog*. Beograd: Udruženje za društvenu istoriju.

Dimitrijević, Nenad, ed. 2000. *Ljudska prava u Jugoslaviji 1999*. Beograd: Beogradski centar za ljudska prava.

———. 2001. *Slučaj Jugoslavija: Socializam, nacionalizam, posledice*. Beograd: Samizdat B92.

———. 2011. *Duty to Respond: Mass Crime, Denial and Collective Responsibility*. Budapest: Central European University Press.

Djerić, Gordana, ed. 2008. *Intima javnosti*. Beograd: Reč.

———, ed. 2009. *Pamćenje i nostalgija: Neki prostori, oblici, lica i naličja*. Beograd: Filip Višnjić.

Djokić, Dejan and James Ker-Lindsay, eds. 2010. *New Perspectives on Yugoslavia: Key Issues and Controversies*. London: Routledge.

Djuliman, Enver, ed. 2000. *Teško pomirenje*. Sarajevo: Norwegian Helsinki Committee.

Documentation Center of Republic of Srpska Bureau of Government of RS for Relation with ICTY. 2002. *Report About Case Srebrenica (The First Part)*. Banja Luka: Grafid.

Drakulić, Slavenka. 2004. *Oni ne bi ni mrava zgazili*. Beograd: Samizdat B92.

Dubil, Helmut. 2002. *Niko nije oslobodjen istorije: Nacionalsocijalistička vlast u debatama Bundestaga*. Trans. A. Bajazetov-Vučen. Beograd: Samizdat B92.

Durkheim, Emile. 1951. *Suicide: A Study in Sociology*. Trans. John A. Spaulding and George Simpson, ed. George Simpson. New York: Free Press. 1982.

———. 1982. *The Rules of Sociological Method*. Ed. Steven Lukes, trans. W. D. Halls. Glencoe, Ill.: Free Press.

Edwards, Paul, ed. 1967. *The Encyclopedia of Philosophy*. Vol. 3. New York: Macmillan and Free Press.

Eley, Geoff and Ronald Suny, eds. 1996. *Becoming National: A Reader*. Oxford: Oxford University Press.

Elster, Jon. 2004. *Closing the Books: Transitional Justice in Historical Perspective*. Cambridge: Cambridge University Press.

Encensberger, Hans Magnus. 1980. *Nemačka, Nemačka, izmedju ostalog*. Trans. D. Gojković Beograd: BIGZ.

Fondacija, Heinrich Boell. 2005. *Srebrenica: Sjećanje za budućnost*. Sarajevo: Fondacija Heinrich Boell.

Fujii, Lee Ann. 2009. *Killing Neighbors: Webs of Violence in Rwanda*. Ithaca, N.Y.: Cornell University Press.

Giles, Wenona, Malathi de Alwis, Edith Klein, Neluka Silva, and Maja Korać, eds. 2004. *Feminists Under Fire: Exchanges Across War Zones.* Toronto: Between the Lines.

Gojković, Drinka, Natalija Bašić and Valentina Delić. 2003. *Ljudi u ratu: Ratovanje I.* Beograd: Dokumentacioni centar Ratovi, 1991–99.

Goldhagen, Daniel. 1996. *Hitler's Willing Executioners: Ordinary Germans and the Holocaust.* New York: Knopf.

Golubović, Zagorka and Isidora Jarić. 2010. *Kultura i preobražaj Srbije: Vrednosna usmerenja gradana u promenama posle 2000. godine.* Beograd: Službeni glasnik.

Gordy, Eric. 1999. *The Culture of Power in Serbia: Nationalism and the Destruction of Alternatives.* College Park: Pennsylvania State University Press.

Hadžić, Miroslav, ed. 2004. *Nasilno rasturanje Jugoslavije: Uzroci, dinamika, posledice.* Beograd: Centar za civilno-vojne odnose.

Halili, Rigels. 2010. "Orality and Literacy: Oral Epic Poetry Among Serbs and Albanians." Ph.D. dissertation, University of Warsaw.

Hall, Stuart, David Held, Don Hubert, and Kenneth Thompson, eds. 1996. *Modernity: An Introduction to Modern Societies.* London: Blackwell.

Hallin, Daniel. 1989. *The Uncensored War: The Media and Vietnam.* Berkeley: University of California Press.

Halpern, Joel and David Kideckel, eds. 2000. *Neighbors at War: Anthropological Perspectives on Yugoslav Ethnicity, Culture and History.* University Park: Pennsylvania State University Press.

Hartmann, Florence. 2007. *Mir i kazna: Tajni ratovi medjunarodne politike i pravde.* Trans. Biljana Marojević. Beograd: Filip Višnjić.

Hastings, James, John A. Selbie, and Louis H. Gray, eds. 1980 [1905]. *Encyclopaedia of Religion and Ethics.* Edinburgh: T and T Clark.

Hayner, Priscilla. 2001. *Unspeakable Truths: Confronting State Terror and Atrocity.* London: Routledge.

———. 2010. *Unspeakable Truths: Transitional Justice and the Challenge of Truth Commissions.* London: Routledge.

Heller, Agnes. 1993. *A Philosophy of History in Fragments.* London: Blackwell.

Hesse, Carla, and Robert Post, eds. 1999. *Human Rights in Political Transitions: Gettysburg to Bosnia.* New York: Zone Books.

Hirsch, James. 2002. *Riot and Remembrance: The Tulsa Race War and Its Legacy.* Boston: Houghton Mifflin.

Ilić, Saša. 2010. *Pad Kolumbije.* Beograd: Fabrika knjiga.

Ishay, Micheline. 2004. *The History of Human Rights: From Ancient Times to the Globalization Era.* Berkeley: University of California Press.

Ivanišević, Milivoje. 1994. *Hronika naših groblja ili slovo o stradanju srpskog naroda Bratunca, Milića, Skelana i Srebrenice.* Beograd: Komitet za prikupljanje podataka o izvršenim zločinima protiv čovečnosti i medjunaraodnog prava.

Izetbegović, Alija. 1970. *Islamska deklaracija: Jedan program islamizacije muslimana i muslimanskih naroda.* Sarajevo: Self-published.

Jansen, Stef. 2005. *Antinacionalizam: Etnografija otpora u Beogradu i Zagrebu.* Beograd: XX Vek, 2005

Jaspers, Karl. 1999. *Pitanje krivice.* Trans. V. Savić. Beograd: Samizdat FreeB92.

Jokić, Aleksandar, ed. 2001. *War Crimes and Collective Wrongdoing: A Reader.* Oxford: Blackwell.

Jovanović, Nebojša. 2003. *Idemo na Zagreb.* Beograd: Vajat.

Jović, Dejan. 2009. *Yugoslavia: A State That Withered Away.* West Lafayette, Ind.: Purdue University Press.

JUKOM. 2005. *Slučaj službenika Aleksandra Tijanića.* Beograd: JUKOM.

Karganović, Stefan, ed. 2011. *Deconstruction of a Virtual Genocide: An Intelligent Person's Guide to Srebrenica.* The Hague: NGO Srebrenica Historical Project.

Kaufman, Stuart J. 2001. *Modern Hatreds: The Symbolic Politics of Ethnic War.* Ithaca, N.Y.: Cornell University Press.

Kelly, Michael. 2005. *Nowhere to Hide: Defeat of the Sovereign Immunity Defense for Crimes of Genocide and the Trials of Slobodan Milošević and Saddam Hussein.* New York: Peter Lang.

Kerr, Rachel. 2004. *The International Criminal Tribunal for the Former Yugoslavia: An Exercise in Law, Politics, and Diplomacy.* New York: Oxford University Press.

Koalicija za REKOM. 2011. *Konsultativni process o utvrdjivanju činjenica o ratnim zločinima i drugim teškim kršenjima ljudskih prava počinjenim na području nekadašnje SFRJ.* Beograd: Fond za humanitarno pravo.

Koonz, Claudia. 2003. *The Nazi Conscience.* Cambridge, Mass.: Harvard University Press.

Koštunica, Vojislav and Kosta Čavoški. 1990. *Stranački pluralizam ili monizam: Obnova i zatiranje posleratne opozicije.* Beograd: Privredno-pravni priručnik.

Kritz, Neil J., ed. 1995. *Transitional Justice: How Emerging Democracies Reckon with Former Regimes.* Vols. 1–3. Washington, D.C.: U.S. Institute of Peace.

Krog, Antjie. 1998. *Country of My Skull: Guilt, Sorrow, and the Limits of Forgiveness in the New South Africa.* New York: Three Rivers Press.

Kuljić, Todor. 2006. *Kultura sećanja: Teorijska objašnjenja upotrebe prošlosti.* Beograd: Čigoja štampa.

Lamont, Christopher. 2007. *State Compliance with International Criminal Tribunal for the former Yugoslavia Article 29 (d) and (e) Obligations: A Comparative Exploration of Croatia and Serbia.* Research paper 116. Athens: Research Institute for European and American Studies (RIEAS).

———. 2010. *International Criminal Justice and the Politics of Compliance.* Farnham: Ashgate.

Lazić, Mladen *et.al.*, ed. 1994. *Razaranje društva: Jugoslovensko društvo u krizi 90-ih.* Beograd: Filip Višnjić.

———, ed. 2000. *Rači hod: Srbija u transformacijskim procesima.* Beograd: Filip Višnjić.

———. 2005. *Promene i otpori: Srbija u transformacijskim procesima.* Beograd: Filip Višnjić.

Levi, Pavle. 2009. *Raspad Jugoslavije na filmu.* Beograd: XX Vek.

Linz, Juan J., and Alfred Stepan. 1996. *Problems of Democratic Transition and Consolidation: Southern Europe, South America and Post-Communist Europe.* Baltimore: Johns Hopkins University Press.

Lipstadt, Deborah E. 1993. *Denying the Holocaust: The Growing Assault on Truth and Memory.* New York: Free Press.

Little, David. 2007. *Peacemakers in Action: Profiles of Religion in Conflict Resolution.* Cambridge: Cambridge University Press.

Longinović, Tomislav. 1995. *Vampires like Us: Writing Down "The Serbs".* Belgrade: Belgrade Circle.

Lord, Albert. 1960. *The Singer of Tales.* Cambridge, Mass.: Harvard University Press.

Lukić, Jasmina, Joanna Regulska, and Darja Zaviršek, eds. 2006. *Women and Citizenship in Central and Eastern Europe.* Farnham: Ashgate.

Luković-Pjanović, Olga. 1990. *Srbi: narod najstariji.* Beograd: Dosije.

Magaš, Branka. 1993. *The Destruction of Yugoslavia: Tracking the Breakup, 1980–1992.* London: Verso.

Maier, Charles S. 1988. *The Unmasterable Past: History, Holocaust and German National Identity.* Cambridge, Mass.: Harvard University Press.

Mallinder, Louise. 2009. *Retribution, Restitution and Reconciliation: Limited Amnesty in Bosnia-Herzegovina.* Belfast: Institute of Criminology and Criminal Justice, Queens University.

Marković, Goran. 2000. *Godina dana.* Beograd: Forum Pisaca.

Mazower, Mark. 1998. *Dark Continent: Europe's Twentieth Century.* New York, Penguin.

Mertus, Julie. 2004. *Bait and Switch: Human Rights and U.S. Foreign Policy.* London: Routledge.

Mihailović, Srećko, ed. 2000. *Javno mnenje Srbije: Izmedu razočaranja i nade.* Beograd: Centar za proučavanje alternativa.

Milić, Andjelka, ed. 2004. *Društvena transformacija i strategije društvenih grupa: Svakodnevnica Srbije na početku trećeg milenijuma.* Beograd: Institut za sociološka istraživanja Filozofskog fakulteta u Beogradu.

Milić, Andjelka and Ljiljana Čičkarić. 1998. *Generacija u protestu: Sociološki portret učesnika Studentskog protesta 96/97 na Beogradskom univerzitetu.* Beograd: Institut za sociološka istraživanja Filozofskog fakulteta u Beogradu.

Minow, Martha. 1998. *Between Vengeance and Forgiveness: Facing History After Genocide and Mass Violence.* Boston: Beacon.

Naimark, Norman. 2001. *Fires of Hatred: Ethnic Cleansing in Twentieth-Century Europe.* Cambridge, Mass.: Harvard University Press.

Nakarada, Radmila. 2008. *Raspad Jugoslavije: Problemi tumačenja, suočavanja i tranzicije*. Beograd: Službeni glasnik.

Nemanjić, Miloš, and Slobodan Vuković, eds. 1996. *Jugoslovensko društvo krajem devedesetih*. Beograd: Sociološko društvo Srbije.

Nettelfield, Lara. 2010. *Courting Democracy in a Post-Conflict State: The Hague Tribunal's Impact in Bosnia-Herzegovina*. New York: Cambridge University Press.

O'Donnell, Guillermo, and Philippe Schmitter. 1986. *Transitions from Authoritarian Rule: Tentative Conclusions About Uncertain Democracies*. Baltimore: Johns Hopkins University Press.

Olijnik, Boris. 1995. *Satanizacija Srba: Kome ona treba?* Belgrade: Srpsko-ukrajinsko društvo.

Osiel, Mark. 1997. *Mass Atrocity, Collective Memory, and the Law*. New Brunswick, N.J.: Transaction Publishers.

———. 2009. *Making Sense of Mass Atrocity*. Cambridge: Cambridge University Press.

Paris, Erna. 2000. *Long Shadows: Truth, Lies and History*. Toronto: Knopf.

Pavičić, Jurica. 1997. *Ovce od gipsa*. Split: A.B. Gigantic.

Pavlowitch, Stevan. 2008. *Hitler's New Disorder: The Second World War in Yugoslavia*. London: Hurst.

Perović, Latinka, Marija Obradović and Dubravka Stojanović, eds. 1994. *Srbija u modernizacijskim procesima XX. veka*. Beograd: Institut za noviju istoriju.

Peskin, Victor. 2008. *International Justice in Rwanda and the Balkans: Virtual Trials and the Struggle for State Cooperation*. Cambridge: Cambridge University Press.

Petrović, Nebojša. 2010. *Psihološke osnove pomirenja izmedju Srba, Hrvata i Bošnjaka*. Beograd: Institut za psihologiju.

Popov, Nebojša, ed. 1996. *Srpska strana rata: Trauma i katarza u istorijskom pamćenju*. Beograd: Republika.

Popović, Nebojša, and Kosta Nikolić. 2006. *Vojislav Koštunica: Jedna karijera*. Beograd: JUKOM.

Power, Samantha. 2002. *A Problem from Hell: America and the Age of Genocide*. New York: HarperCollins.

Premec, Vladimir, ed. 1978. *Hrestomatija etičkih tekstova*. Sarajevo: Svjetlost.

Prodanović, Mileta. 2000. *Ovo bi mogao biti Vaš srećan dan*. Beograd: Stubovi culture.

Radenović, Sandra. 2008. *Oblici rasizma u Srbiji nakon petooktobarskih promena (2001–2006)*. Beograd: Akademska misao.

Radojčić, Mirjana. 2009. *Istorija u krivom ogledalu: Nevladine organizacije u Srbiji i politika interpretiranja skorije južnoslovenske prošlosti*. Beograd: Institut za političke studije.

Rakezić, Aleksandar (Zograf). 1999. *Bulletins from Serbia: E-mails and Cartoon Strips from Behind the Front Line*. Hove: Slab-o-Concrete Publications.

Ratner, Steven, and Jason Abrams. 2001. *Accountability for Human Rights Atrocities in International Law*. Oxford: Oxford University Press.

Rawls, John. 1971. *A Theory of Justice*. Cambridge, Mass.: Harvard University Press.

Republic of Rwanda, Ministry for Local Government; Department for Information and Social Affairs B.P. 3445 Kigali. 2002. *The Counting of the Genocide Victims: Final Report*. Kigali.

Rigby, Andrew. 2001. *Justice and Reconciliation After the Violence*. London: Lynne Reinner.

Ristić, Snežana and Radonja Leposavić. 2000. *Glasovi iz crne rupe: Šta ste radili u toku rata*. Beograd: Samizdat Free B92.

Rodríguez Molas, Ricardo. 1984. *Historia de la tortura y el orden represivo en la Argentina*. Buenos Aires: Editorial Universitaria.

Rotberg, Robert I., and Dennis Thompson, eds. 2000. *Truth v. Justice: The Morality of Truth Commissions*. Princeton, N.J.: Princeton University Press.

Sanford, Nevitt, and Craig Comstock, eds. 1971. *Sanctions for Evil: Origins of Social Destructiveness*. San Francisco: Jossey-Bass.

Šćekić, Drasko. 1994. *Sorabi: Istoropis*. Beograd: Sfairos, 1994.

Scheper-Hughes, Nancy, and Philippe Bourgois, eds. 2004. *Violence in War and Peace: An Anthology*. Oxford: Blackwell.

Sen, Armatya. 2006. *Identity and Violence: The Illusion of Destiny*. New York: Norton.

Simić Bodrožić, Ivana. 2010. *Hotel Zagorje*. Zagreb: Profil.

Singleton, Fred. 1976. *Twentieth-Century Yugoslavia*. New York: Columbia University Press.

Skopljanac Brunner, Neda, Alija Hodžić, and Branimir Kristofić, eds. 1999. *Mediji i rat*. Beograd: Argument.

Stan, Lavinia, ed. 2009. *Transitional Justice in Eastern Europe and the Former Soviet Union: Reckoning with the Communist Past*. New York: Routledge.

Stannard, David. 1992. *American Holocaust: The Conquest of the New World*. New York: Oxford University Press.

Staub, Ervin. 1989. *The Roots of Evil: The Origins of Genocide and Other Group Violence*. Cambridge: Cambridge University Press.

Štiks, Igor. 2006. *Elijahova stolica*. Zagreb: Fraktura.

Stojanović, Dubravka. 2010. *Ulje na vodi: Ogledi iz istorije sadašnjosti Srbije*. Beograd: Peščanik.

Stojanović, Lazar, ed. 2000. *Spotlight on War Crimes Trials*. Trans. Djurdja Stanimirović Belgrade: Humanitarian Law Center.

Stojanović, Svetozar. 1997. *The Fall of Yugoslavia: Why Communism Failed*. Buffalo, N.Y.: Prometheus.

Stover, Eric, and H. M. Weinstein. eds. 2005. *My Neighbor, My Enemy: Justice and Community in the Aftermath of Mass Atrocity*, Cambridge: Cambridge University Press.

Subotić, Jelena. 2009. *Hijacked Justice: Dealing with the Past in the Balkans*. Ithaca, N.Y.: Cornell University Press.

Suljagić, Emir. 2006. *Postcards from the Grave*. London: Saqi.

Tabeau, Ewa, and Arve Hetland. 2008. *Srebrenica Missing: The 2007 Progress Report on the DNA-Based Identification by ICMP*. The Hague: ICTY.

Teitel, Ruti. 2000. *Transitional Justice*. Oxford: Oxford University Press.

Thompson, Mark. 2005. *Forging War: The Media in Serbia, Croatia, and Bosnia and Herzegovina*. Luton: University of Luton Press.

Todorov, Tzvetan. 2003. *Hope and Memory: Lessons from the Twentieth Century*. Princeton, N.J.: Princeton University Press.

Todorović, Mirjana, ed. 2002. *Kultura ljudskih prava*. Beograd: Beogradski centar za ljudska prava.

Tomanović, Smiljka, ed. 2006. *Društvo u previranju: Sociološke studije nekih aspekata društvene transformacije u Srbiji*. Beograd: Institut za sociološka istraživanja Filozofskog fakulteta u Beogradu.

Tomasevich, Jozo. 1975. *The Chetniks: War and Revolution in Yugoslavia, 1941–1945*. Stanford, Calif.: Stanford University Press.

———. 2001. *War and Revolution in Yugoslavia: Occupation and Collaboration*. Stanford, Calif.: Stanford University Press.

Tudjman, Franjo. 1981. *Nationalism in Contemporary Europe*. New York: Columbia University Press.

———. 1989. *Bespuća povijesne zbiljnosti: Rasprava o povijesti i filozofiji zlosilja*. Zagreb: Matica Hrvatska.

Umeljić, Vladimir. 2010. *Teorija definicionizma i fenomen genocida: Etika i vlast nad definicijama*. Beograd: Magna Plus, 2010.

Valentino, Benjamin. 2004. *Final Solutions: Mass Killing and Genocide in the Twentieth Century*. Ithaca, N.Y.: Cornell University Press.

Vasić, Miloš. 2005. *Atentat na Zorana Djindjića*. Beograd: Narodna knjiga.

Vasiljević, Vladan. 1995. *Zločin i odgovornost: Ogled o krivičnom pravu i raspadu Jugoslavije*. Beograd: Prometej.

Vlajki, Emil. 2001. *Demonizacija Srba: Zapadni imperijalizam, njegovi zločini, sluge i laži*. Beograd: Knjižara Nikola Pašić.

Vogt, Timothy. 2000. *Denazification in Soviet-Occupied Germany: Brandenburg, 1945–1948*. Cambridge, Mass: Harvard University Press, 2000.

Vujović, Sreten, ed. 2008. *Društvo rizika: Promene, nejednakost i socijalni problemi u današnjoj Srbiji*. Beograd: Institut za sociološka istraživanja Filozofskog fakulteta u Beogradu.

Wachtel, Andrew Baruch. 1998. *Making a Nation, Breaking a Nation: Literature and Cultural Politics in Yugoslavia*. Stanford, Calif.: Stanford University Press.

Walker, David M., ed. 1980. *The Oxford Companion to Law*. Oxford: Oxford University Press.

Wallimann, Isidor, and Michael Dobkowski, eds. 2000. *Genocide and the Modern Age: Etiology and Case Studies of Mass Death*. Syracuse, N.Y.: Syracuse University Press.

Weber, Max. 1978. *Economy and Society: An Outline of Interpretive Sociology*. Ed. Guenther Roth and Claus Wittich. Berkeley: University of California Press.

Williams, Raymond. 1981. *The Sociology of Culture*. Chicago: University of Chicago Press.

Index